EXPLORING THE
BRITANNIC

EXPLORING THE
BRITANNIC

THE LIFE, LAST VOYAGE AND
WRECK OF *TITANIC*'S TRAGIC TWIN

SIMON MILLS

ADLARD
COLES

LONDON • OXFORD • NEW YORK • NEW DELHI • SYDNEY

ADLARD COLES
Bloomsbury Publishing Plc
50 Bedford Square, London, WC1B 3DP, UK

BLOOMSBURY, ADLARD COLES and the Adlard Coles logo are trademarks of
Bloomsbury Publishing Plc

First published in Great Britain 2019

A catalogue record for this book is available from the British Library

Library of Congress Cataloguing-in-Publication data has been applied for

ISBN: HB: 978-1-4729-5492-3;
          eBook: 978-1-4729-5493-0

2 4 6 8 10 9 7 5 3 1

Typeset in Bliss and Palatino
Designed by Nicola Liddiard, Nimbus Design
Printed and bound in China by C&C Offset Printing Co

Bloomsbury Publishing Plc makes every effort to ensure that the papers used in the
manufacture of our books are natural, recyclable products made from wood grown in
well-managed forests. Our manufacturing processes conform to the environmental
regulations of the country of origin

To find out more about our authors and books visit www.bloomsbury.com
and sign up for our newsletters

CONTENTS

INTRODUCTION

Whenever I am interviewed, the first question I am nearly always asked is: 'why did you buy the *Britannic*?'

Fair question, and even after all this time my answer today is exactly the same as it was over 20 years ago – I have not got the faintest idea! Perhaps I was just in the right place at the right time – though the only justification I could think of at the time was that I was single, had a well-paid job and had money to spare. Perhaps it also had something to do with the thrill and kudos of owning something unique? I suppose all of these reasons have some validity...

I have never forgotten the look of what can only be described as complete bewilderment on my father's face when I first told him that I had bought the wreck. Perhaps he could not believe what he was hearing, or maybe he just thought that his son and heir had finally lost his few remaining marbles, but even now I remember not only his next three words to me, but also the subdued manner in which he said them. 'You've done... what?' It was not exactly the ringing endorsement I had expected, his brief pause, which could only have lasted for barely a second, speaking volumes.

Even so, the fact remains that on 20 August 1996 I had signed a piece of paper that, had I but known it, would change the direction of my life for ever. The whirlwind of circumstances over the previous days had been so unexpected that I'd hardly had time to catch my breath before the deed was done. Suddenly I was no longer just a busy camera technician carving out a moderately successful living in the British film industry; I was now, in addition, the proud owner of the UK government's legal title to the 900-foot wreck of the sister ship of the *Titanic*, when up to that point researching shipwrecks had been just a hobby.

Another curious thing I remember is that although the *Britannic* was suddenly all mine, I really had no idea what I actually wanted to do with it. My first instinct had been to do nothing at all, but a host of maritime historians, marine biologists, engineers, scientists and technical divers appeared to have other ideas. They certainly gave me ample food for thought, and it didn't take me long to realise that in spite of what the legal paperwork stated, the reality was that I would never control the *Britannic*; rather, the *Britannic* now controlled me. Suddenly I was headed down a road to somewhere I would never previously have thought possible, turning round every now and then to make sure that no one was taking any pot shots at the target now fixed firmly to my back.

Over the years I've come to realise that no one can just 'own' something like the *Britannic*.

With rights come responsibilities, particularly when you have the legal title to something as remarkable as the sister ship of the *Titanic*, so in spite of my evident naivety at the outset, I suspect that deep down I always knew that I was not embarking on an ordinary voyage of discovery. Like bootlegging in America during Prohibition, working on the *Britannic* has not just been a job – it's been more of an adventure.

Inevitably, everything that has been achieved over the last 20 years has come at a cost, not just financial, but also personal and professional, so the time has come to put things into their proper context, while at the same time acknowledging the work of the many individuals and organisations who have helped to make it all possible.

Whether doing so will ever help me to understand how a simple hobby ultimately turned into a life-changing obsession is another matter.

PART 1

THE *BRITANNIC*
AND THE GREAT WAR

GENESIS

Everyone knows how magnificently extravagant the *Titanic* was designed to be. Even though she was one of a trio, all too often the history books write of a ship beyond comparison, and of the fantastic opulence of the floating palace that would ultimately be remembered for all the wrong reasons. The reality, however, is that in the early 20th century the ships built on such a huge scale were not just intended for millionaires.

Although the ships of the White Star Line were renowned for their steadiness, comfort and luxury, the Olympic-class vessels were only made possible by the huge scale of emigrant traffic that existed between Europe and America. In the late 19th century not all shipping companies had the best interests of their emigrant clientele at heart, with some providing wholly inadequate facilities for the thousands who chose to cross from the Old World to the New. By 1855 things were so bad that the United States Congress had passed an act designed to regulate the conditions under which emigrants should be transported to America. Essentially, it required moderately humane conditions on board, including ceilings at least 6 feet high, separate berths measuring at least 2 feet by 6 feet, single men and women to be quartered separately, adequate ventilation, three cooked meals a day, sidelights and an adequately supplied ship's hospital.

Even with the regulations in place, not all of the shipping companies observed the act in the spirit in which it was intended. However, with massive improvements taking place in shipbuilding technology and the advent of a new class of emigrant ship, in 1882 the American Immigration Act was revised to further tighten the regulations, setting in motion the chain of events that would culminate in the construction of the giant liners of the early 20th century.

It did not take long for the competition on the North Atlantic route to intensify, as the shipping lines vied with each other to operate the largest or fastest ships on their individual routes. During the 19th century that route had been plied mainly by British vessels, with

▶ An illustration from the 1877 White Star Line Official Guide, showing the hurricane deck of the first *Britannic*. (Titanic Historical Society)

▶ The steerage accommodation also received specific mention in the 1877 White Star Line guide. (Titanic Historical Society)

growing competition from the German Norddeutscher Lloyd (NDL) and Hamburg Amerika Lines (HAPAG) by the turn of the new century. For the purposes of this story, however, our focus needs to be on the White Star Line. Its founder, Thomas Ismay, entered the North Atlantic scene relatively late in the day, in 1871, by which time the Cunard, Inman, Guion and National Lines were already well established on the Liverpool to New York route. Ismay was effectively taking a huge gamble, but the unique relationship between his White Star Line and the Belfast shipbuilders Harland & Wolff meant that their vessels would be remembered as the finest on the North Atlantic. One cannot help but feel that the inauguration of the White Star Liverpool–New York service by the 3,707-ton SS *Oceanic* on 2 March 1871 was one of the giant technological leaps that would ultimately result in the American immigration laws being updated a little over ten years later. With the subsequent additions of the *Atlantic*, *Baltic* and *Adriatic*, followed by the even larger *Britannic* and *Germanic*, White Star was definitely in the ascendant.

It was not all good news, however. In 1898, the loss of the Blue Riband for the fastest crossing of the North Atlantic to NDL's *Kaiser Wilhelm der Grosse*, followed by the sale of the White Star Line in 1901 to the American financier J.P. Morgan's International Mercantile Marine combine (IMM), finally put pressure on the British government to make a loan to

the Cunard Line to finance the construction of the *Lusitania* and *Mauretania*. With a gross tonnage each of over 30,000 tons and a maximum speed of over 25 knots, the two Cunard sisters eclipsed anything that the White Star Line had to offer in terms of both size and speed. It was this combination of legislative, economic and technological factors that left the White Star Line with little option but to retaliate in equal measure. Bearing in mind the company's reputation for excellence, perhaps it is no surprise that its response, when it came, would be a bold one.

BIRTH OF A LEGEND

It all began early one summer evening in 1907, when Joseph Bruce Ismay, chairman of the White Star Line and president of IMM since 1904, dined at the Belgravia home of Lord William Pirrie, the chairman of Harland & Wolff. By the time their dinner was concluded these two men had set in motion plans for the *Olympic* and the *Titanic*, two huge ships the like of which had never been seen before. The men tasked with creating such vessels for the White Star Line, which would ultimately culminate in the *Britannic*, were Lord Pirrie and his brother-in-law, Alexander Montgomery Carlisle. Both were accomplished marine architects in their own right. Pirrie had joined Harland & Wolff as an apprentice in 1862,

◀ The first *Britannic* entered service in 1874. (Titanic Historical Society)

▲ Downshire House, London, Lord Pirrie's Belgravia home where the *Olympic* and *Titanic* were first conceived during the summer of 1907.

☆ WHITE STAR LINE R.M.S. "OLYMPIC" ☆
COMPARED WITH VARIOUS FAMOUS BUILDINGS.

eventually becoming a partner in 1874 and rising to the position of company chairman in 1895 on the death of Sir Edward Harland. Carlisle, on the other hand, had joined the company in 1870, and by 1889 had risen to the position of chief naval architect. These two men would go on to play a pivotal role in the design of some of the most famous White Star vessels, including the *Teutonic* and *Majestic*, the *Oceanic*, the 'Big Four' (*Celtic*, *Cedric*, *Baltic* and *Adriatic*) and the Olympic class.

The division of labour between Pirrie and Carlisle has not always been fully understood, but Carlisle's testimony at Lord Mersey's inquiry following the loss of the *Titanic* spelled it out. When questioned about his role in working out the designs of the Olympic class, he responded, 'Yes, they were entirely designed practically by Lord Pirrie. The details, the decorations, the equipments, and general arrangements all came under me.'

Carlisle's early retirement at the end of April 1910 came almost six months before the launch of the *Olympic*, by which time the specific designs had long been completed. However, as general manager of the company Carlisle had also overseen the complete reconstruction of the north-east part of the shipyard where the White Star leviathans would

▲ Promotional postcard from 1911, emphasising the huge size of the Olympic-class liners.

▌ Postcard from 1911 advertising the *Olympic* and *Titanic*'s steerage-class facilities.
(Titanic Historical Society)

▶ The Harland & Wolff builder's model, now on display at the Merseyside Maritime Museum.
Although supposedly restored as the *Titanic*, the promenade and B-deck window arrangements are undeniably *Britannic*.

be built. In fact, this was not the first time that Harland & Wolff had made alterations to accommodate the construction of White Star vessels. When Thomas Ismay ordered the first four ships for the company's Liverpool–New York service, the slipways had to be specially constructed, and then were further strengthened when the *Britannic* and *Germanic* were ordered three years later. Building the *Teutonic* and *Majestic* had obliged the shipyard to construct two completely new slips, not to mention the construction of the Alexandra Graving Dock to accommodate the new generation of liners; now, 20 years later, the White Star Line was once again pushing the established boundaries of construction.

The project presented Harland & Wolff with a number of logistical problems, as the construction of the two new slipways would not only temporarily reduce the capacity of the shipyard, but would also require an enormous investment of capital. The erection of a huge gantry above the slipways, complete with cranes and elevators, by the Arrol

Engineering Company would also cost the not inconsiderable sum of £100,000, and once the vessels had been launched, a new floating crane, built by the German Benrather Company, would be required in order to complete the fitting out, adding another £30,000 to the shipyard's costs.

From a financial point of view, however, the introduction of turbine technology was perhaps a step too far. The Olympic-class designs called for a novel combination of reciprocating engines and a low-pressure turbine, but up to this point Harland & Wolff had lacked the naval clientele to justify the huge expenditure that a properly equipped turbine works would have required. The problem was resolved in June 1907 following a merger with the shipbuilder John Brown & Company, at which point the order for the marine turbine for the White Star liner *Laurentic* – an essential experiment before deciding upon the final arrangement of the Olympic-class propelling machinery – was placed with the Glasgow company.

It was not just Harland & Wolff who needed to improve their facilities. The largest graving dock at Belfast was the Alexandra Dock, which could accommodate vessels of up to 825 feet in length and 80 feet wide; but as the Olympic class had an overall length of 850 feet between perpendiculars, and a massive beam of over 90 feet, the Belfast Harbour Commissioners were also obliged to undertake the construction of the Thompson Graving Dock in order to accommodate them. The port facilities at Southampton, 320 miles to the south-east, were also massively upgraded, with the construction of the new White Star Dock. All things considered, the Americans got off quite lightly; the New York harbour authorities were eventually persuaded to extend the White Star berth at Pier 59 by about 90 feet in order to better protect the sterns of the new ships, but even this was done reluctantly, and the work was carried out only after IMM had appealed to Washington.

By the autumn of 1908 construction at Belfast was finally ready to begin; on 16 December of that year the keel of Yard No. 400, the SS *Olympic*, was laid on Slipway No. 2, followed three months later, on 31 March 1909, by the laying of the keel of Yard No. 401, the SS *Titanic*, on Slipway No. 3.

Although the *Olympic* and the *Titanic* were built side by side, the White Star Line was putting everything into making sure that the *Olympic* was completed as quickly as possible, while work on the *Titanic* continued at a slower pace. This helped to ensure that the machine

◄ 20 October 1910: The SS *Olympic* is launched at Belfast from Slipway No. 2. (Harland & Wolff)

shops would not be overwhelmed, but it also had the added benefit of allowing the builders to modify and improve the building process in the second ship as any problems in the construction of the *Olympic* became apparent. As the lead ship of the class gradually took shape over the next 19 months, Carlisle's retirement had left the day-to-day management of the project in the hands of Lord Pirrie's nephew, Thomas Andrews, a managing director of Harland & Wolff and also head of the design department. Finally, on 20 October 1910, the *Olympic* was ready to be launched.

Although the launch of a ship of this calibre was a gala event, the established White Star policy was not to hold an actual launching ceremony. As a result, no bottle of champagne was broken over the ship's bow; instead, the yard foreman simply waited for the precise moment when the tide was judged to be at its maximum height before releasing the launching triggers. Slowly the 24,600-ton hull began to move down the 750-foot sliding ways, and 62 seconds later the *Olympic* was fully afloat, having reached a maximum speed of 12½ knots during the launching process.

As the crowds began to disperse, the ship was towed to the deep-water wharf, where the hugely expensive 200-ton Benrather crane would begin the exacting process of fitting

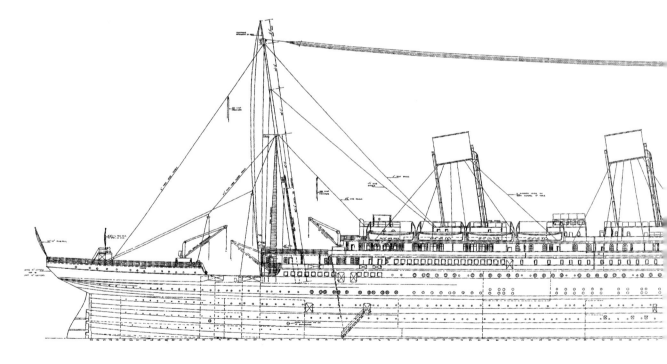

out. Over the next seven months the empty hull would gradually be transformed into a floating palace, until the time came on 2 May 1911 for the *Olympic* to begin her basin trials, when for the first time her engines were turned while still in port. On the morning of 29 May, having taken on 3,000 tons of best Welsh coal, the *Olympic* proceeded along Belfast Lough and into the Irish Sea to successfully complete two days of sea trials, notching up a maximum speed of 21¾ knots during the various speed tests.

The following day, with propitious timing, not only did Harland & Wolff hand over the *Olympic* to her new owner, but the *Titanic* was also successfully launched from Slipway No. 3. Finally the White Star Line was in a position to begin to compete with the *Lusitania* and the *Mauretania*. As the *Olympic* departed Belfast for Liverpool at 4.30pm, less than 30 months after the laying of her keel, the company's confidence in its latest generation of ocean liner could not have been greater.

▼ Original builder's rigging plan of Yard No. 401: SS *Titanic*. (Harland & Wolff)

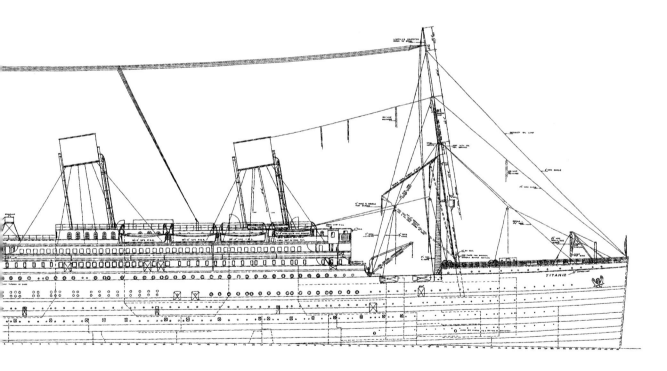

BACK TO THE DRAWING BOARD

When Joseph Bruce Ismay cabled his congratulations to Lord Pirrie following *Olympic*'s maiden arrival at New York, he described her as 'a marvel'. Ismay actually had every reason to feel such pride in the company's latest flagship, with a crossing time of 5 days, 16 hours and 42 minutes, made all the more impressive by the fact that this speed was achieved without the need to light any of the five single-ended boilers. The only mishap had been a minor collision with the 200-ton tug *O.L. Hallenbeck* as the vessel was being docked at Pier 59. At the time no one was greatly concerned by this brief encounter, but later events would show that a few lessons in the operation of such large ships should have been learned by Captain Edward Smith and his crew.

Ismay's cable also helped determine the company's decision regarding the ship's future running mates. Originally the *Olympic* and *Titanic* had been conceived to compete with Cunard's *Lusitania* and *Mauretania*, but that company was already building the *Aquitania*, its own version of an Olympic-class liner, and there was also German competition in the

form of Albert Ballin's HAPAG Line, which was building an even larger trio, the *Imperator*, the *Vaterland* and the *Bismarck*. Thus, in order to maintain a balanced White Star service, a third ship would be required. The decision had probably been made before the *Olympic* had even departed from Southampton, but although the contract for a third ship was not officially signed until 23 October 1911, the paperwork at Harland & Wolff confirms that on 28 June the shipyard and engine works had been ordered to proceed on the construction of Yard No. 433, the SS *Britannic*. With Slipways No. 2 and 3 occupied by other contracts, Harland & Wolff couldn't begin on this third ship until the Royal Mail steamer *Arlanza* was ready to be launched in the autumn, but with the *Olympic* now in service, they could at least focus on the completion of the *Titanic*.

As the *Olympic* settled into her established routine between Southampton and New York, there were already plans to improve the *Titanic* and the *Britannic*. The schedule, however, was not helped when on 20 September 1911, at the beginning of only her fifth crossing to New York, the *Olympic* collided with the armoured cruiser HMS *Hawke* while in the Solent. Somehow the 7,350-ton armoured cruiser was pulled into the *Olympic*'s starboard quarter by the hydrodynamic forces of the larger ship's propellers; the result was a 12-foot triangular hole just aft of *Olympic*'s O bulkhead, extending down from D deck, with the *Olympic*'s hull plating being driven some 8 feet into the ship. Below the waterline, *Hawke*'s ram bow had also smashed a pear-shaped hole some 7 feet wide in the hull, damaging the propeller shaft bossing, the shaft and all three blades of the starboard propeller. This accident did not affect the subsequent design of either the *Titanic* or the *Britannic*, but it did necessitate the return of the *Olympic* to Belfast for urgent repairs, during which time work was once again diverted from the *Titanic*.

The *Olympic* would not leave Belfast until 20 November, with Harland & Wolff paying close attention to the toll that four months of commercial service had taken on the ship's hull. It was probably inevitable that the construction of ships of such a previously unimagined scale would throw up a number of structural issues, but while Captain Smith and his crew still had a lot to learn in the operation of such a huge ship, the same was true for the builder. The first indication of problems had actually come at a relatively early stage, when it became evident that panting in the *Olympic*'s hull was leading to a number of unforeseen structural issues. As early as 17 October 1911, this resulted in a table of particulars being prepared for Lord Pirrie giving the projected beam of the *Britannic* as 93 feet

◁ *Olympic*'s damaged starboard quarter after the collision in the Solent with the armoured cruiser HMS *Hawke* on 20 September 1911.

According to legend, the *Britannic* was originally to have been called *Gigantic*, although the origin of this flyer remains obscure. (Titanic Historical Society)

and 6 inches – already one foot wider than that of the *Olympic* and the *Titanic*. In their 1996 paper 'The Sinking of S.S. Titanic Investigated by Modern Techniques', Harland & Wolff naval engineers Charles Hackett and John Bedford hypothesised that this increased size was possibly in order to bring *Britannic*'s lightship GM (also known as metacentric height) closer to that of the *Olympic*, rather than that of the *Titanic*, which differed somewhat following modifications to her B deck arrangement with additional cabins. At this time little consideration was given to the structural issues that, even at this early stage, had begun to manifest themselves in the *Olympic*, and it is not certain whether this alteration was actually a consequence of these problems. Even if any structural issues had been noted, certainly the options for further widening the ship were limited, as the entrance to the Thompson Graving Dock was only 96 feet wide, but it is clear that even before her keel had been laid, from a structural point of view the *Britannic* was going to be a very different ship.

The structural questions were further heightened in the early months of 1912. On 24 February, while on an eastbound crossing, the *Olympic* had dropped a propeller blade, necessitating another return to Belfast for the ship to be dry docked while a replacement was fitted. The propeller blade was not a major issue in itself, but at the same time Francis Carruthers, the Board of Trade's engineer and ship surveyor at Belfast, undertook an inspection of the *Olympic*'s hull, during which he noted that while there were no signs of stress in the sides of the ship above the waterline, a number of cracks had begun to appear in the deckhouses of the ship's superstructure between and in the region of the two expansion joints. Beneath the waterline, in way of Boiler Room 6, some 300 rivets were also in need of replacing or additional caulking, while at the other end of the ship, about 100 rivets on both sides of the turbine engine room needed to be drilled out and replaced. These observations would also lead to additional riveting in this area of the *Titanic*'s hull.

The discovery had not come a moment too soon, as by that time building work on the *Britannic* was already underway. The launch of the Royal Mail steamer *Arlanza* on 23 November 1911 had finally cleared the space needed for construction to begin on Slipway No. 2, and one week later, on 30 November, the keel of Yard No. 433, the SS *Britannic*, had been laid on the same slipway upon which the *Olympic* had been built. With the *Olympic* in service, *Titanic* being fitted out and work on the third vessel finally underway, it was only a matter of time before the *Britannic*, benefiting from all of the experience learned in the building and operation of her two siblings, would take her place as the new White Star flagship on the company's Southampton to New York express service.

But it was not to be. On 2 April 1912, after successfully completing her engine trials in the Irish Sea, the *Titanic* had departed from Belfast to assume her role alongside the *Olympic*. At midday on Wednesday 10 April the *Titanic* pulled away from Berth 44 in the White Star Dock, and after making scheduled calls at Cherbourg and Queenstown, at 1.30pm on 11 April the ship headed west into the North Atlantic, bound for New York. She would not be seen again for 73 years. At 11.40pm on the night of Sunday 14 April the *Titanic* had her appointment with destiny when she collided with an iceberg. Two hours and 20 minutes later the largest ship in the world was gone, sunk on her maiden voyage! It would be several months before the facts were made public, in the form of two official inquiries in both New York and London, but as far as the *Britannic* was concerned, from the marine engineering perspective the immediate fallout would be immense.

▲ One of the Harland & Wolff engineering records, confirming that the name *Britannic* was always intended for the ship. (Harland & Wolff)

MORE QUESTIONS THAN ANSWERS

In terms of what had gone wrong, the answer remains: pretty much everything. As the *Titanic* raced through the water at a speed in excess of 20 knots, the lookout's warning had come just too late to save the ship. Ordering 'Hard-a-starboard', First Officer William Murdoch had attempted to manoeuvre around the port side of the berg, but an invisible spur beneath the waterline had torn into the *Titanic*'s starboard side, resulting in extensive underwater damage along some 250 feet of the ship's hull. With the forward six watertight compartments open to the sea, the scale of the damage far exceeded the designed four-compartment margin of safety, and before long Captain Smith knew the worst, courtesy of Thomas Andrews, who had been on board to represent the builder and observe the ship on her maiden voyage. The rest is history. The *Titanic* sank at 2.20am on the morning of Monday 15 April 1912, taking with her Captain EJ Smith, Thomas Andrews and a total of 1,503 passengers and crew. Only 705 dazed survivors in 18 lifeboats were left to be rescued two hours later by the Cunard liner *Carpathia*.

The recriminations would come later, but in the meantime there was no doubting that a hitherto confident world, suddenly jolted out of its complacency, not only demanded answers but wanted them quickly. For the White Star Line and Harland & Wolff, their latest and most illustrious creations would also be subjected to the closest scrutiny. Thomas Andrews would undoubtedly have been the man to whom all attention would have turned, but tragically he had gone down with the ship, so the man on whom Harland & Wolff would rely to salvage the company's reputation would be Edward Wilding, who, on Andrews' death, had become the new head of the design department.

Throughout the spring of 1912 the designers pored over the *Olympic*'s plans, and it did not take long for Wilding to come to the same conclusions that had bedevilled Andrews that night. Put simply, although the *Titanic* was capable of floating with her four forward compartments flooded, the freak nature of the underwater damage had resulted in six compartments being opened to the sea. As the ship gradually sank by the head, the transverse bulkheads dividing the boiler rooms were overwhelmed by the rising water one by one, effectively sealing the ship's fate.

On paper, the maths seemed cruelly inescapable – but was it really that straightforward? On 9 October 1912 the *Olympic* arrived back at Belfast to be retrofitted throughout the winter

▷ Detail of the additional strengthening required in the area of B deck, confirming that the original Olympic-class design underwent considerable reinforcement in this area. (Harland & Wolff)

▷ Plan of the *Britannic*'s raised and strengthened forward transverse bulkheads. (Harland & Wolff)

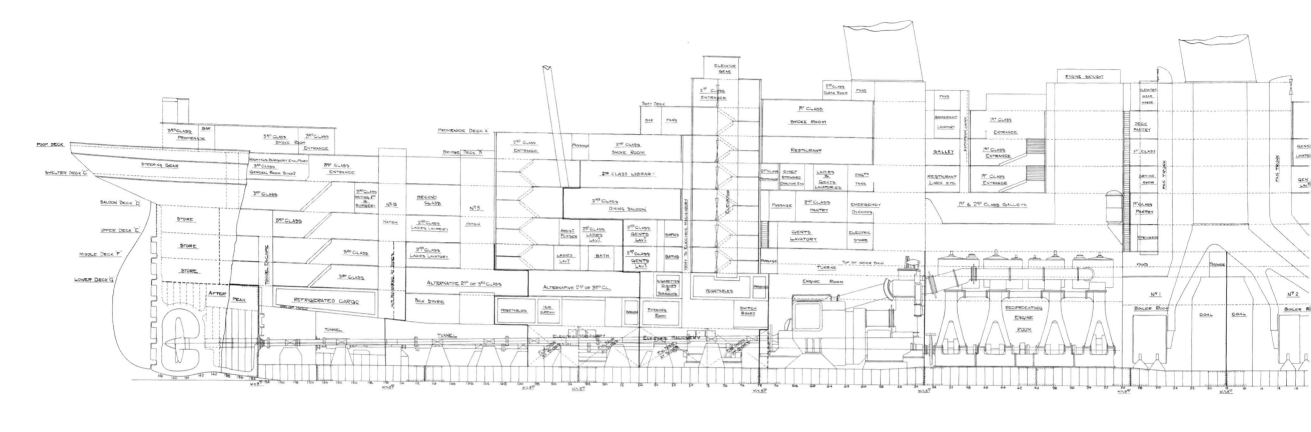
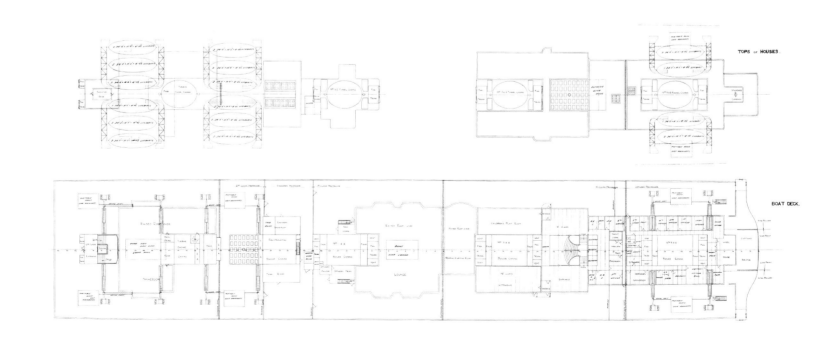

[Overleaf]

SS *Britannic*
Harland & Wolff Yard No. 433
(C)

[Overleaf]

SS *Britannic*
Harland & Wolff Yard No. 433
<u>**Dimensions: 850 ft x 93 ft 6″ x 64 ft 6″ to Shelter Deck (C)**</u>

The original elevation and general arrangement for
the SS *Britannic* show both subtle and distinct differences
when compared to those of the *Olympic* and *Titanic*. Having
undergone extensive cleaning and restoration, through these
plans it is now possible to compare the layout with the earlier
ships, to better understand how the White Star Line would
modify their third Olympic class liner, based on the
experience of operating the two earlier vessels.
All plans reproduced courtesy of Harland & Wolff Ltd.

Starboard Elevation
Tops of Houses
Boat Deck
Promenade Deck (A)
Bridge Deck (B)

of 1912–13. As would be expected, this included the installation of higher transverse bulk-heads, a watertight double skin extending along the boiler and engine room compartments, and increased lifeboat capacity extending to everyone on board. More interestingly, by the time the work was complete in April 1913, notes taken by Francis Carruthers, the Board of Trade surveyor at Belfast, suggest that the work extended beyond a matter of simply increasing the ship's watertight integrity. His list of the works carried out includes considerable

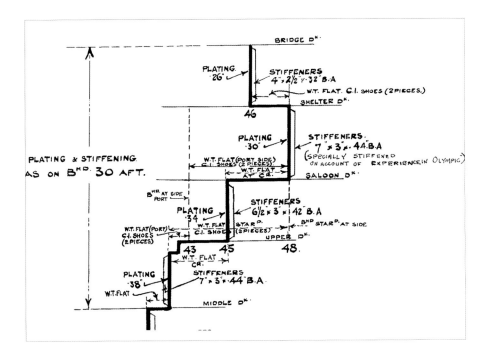

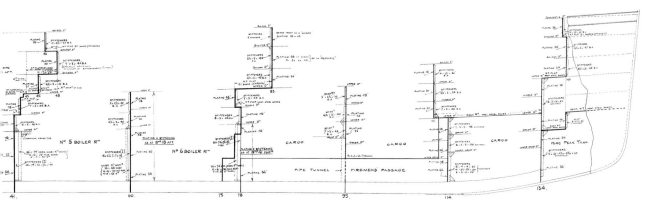

Nº 433.
PLAN OF INNER SKIN.
SCALE ¼ = ONE FOOT

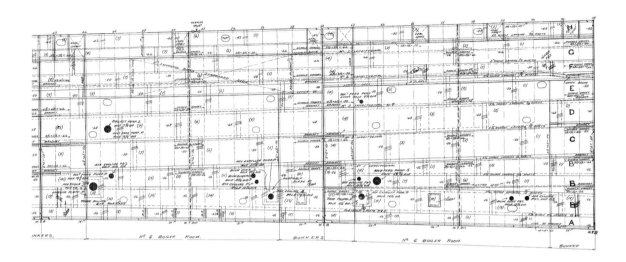

Nº 433.
FRAMING PLAN OF INNER SKIN.
SCALE ¼ = ONE FOOT VERTICAL.   SCALE ⅛ = 1 FOOT LONGITUDINAL.

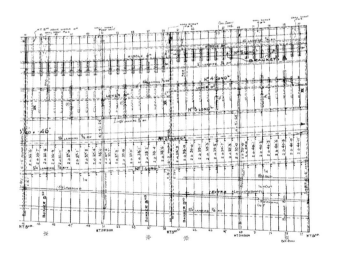

▲ Detail of the strengthened framing and double skin incorporated into the *Britannic* after the *Titanic* disaster. (Harland & Wolff)

additional stiffening to bulkheads 1, 4, 10 and 16, which had all been raised to the height of B deck, and it seems clear that while work was being carried out to increase the *Olympic*'s watertight subdivision, Harland & Wolff had also taken the opportunity to address a number of existing structural issues that had become apparent. As a direct result of this additional reinforcement, the rebuilt *Olympic* of April 1913 was a considerably stronger and stiffer ship than the *Olympic* of two years earlier.

It is at this point that we begin also to see even more noticeable modifications in the *Britannic*, for whatever applied to the *Olympic* would also apply to her younger sister, and it comes as no surprise to see the White Star Line publicity department's emphasis on the inherent strength of the new ship. The February 1914 edition of *Engineering* was also keen to emphasise the additional stiffening that had been put in place throughout the *Britannic*:

▲ A colourised cross section on the cover of the July 1914 edition of *Popular Mechanics* magazine, clearly emphasising the *Britannic*'s double skin. (Titanic Historical Society)

> This double bottom and double skin construction will not only exclude water from the interior of the ship in the event of the skin being fractured, but add enormously to the strength of the structure, because of the extent of stiffening members between the double bottoms and between the double skin.

In spite of the *Titanic* tragedy, work on Slipway No. 2 had continued to progress well. The hull had already been framed to the height of the double bottom by 12 March 1912; by 27 February 1913 the framing was complete; and on 20 September 1913 the hull was fully plated. Even then much still needed to be done, but by Thursday 26 February 1914 everything was finally in place for the launch of White Star's largest and finest vessel.

Perhaps it should come as no surprise that the launch would come on a typically cold and drizzly Belfast day, but despite the inclement weather, Lord Pirrie had arrived at the

⬆ A colourised postcard of the *Britannic* being launched at Belfast from Slipway No. 2 on 26 February 1914. (Titanic Historical Society)

⬆ Commemorative booklet cover for the launch of the *Britannic*. (Titanic Historical Society)

shipyard at 5.00am in order to oversee the final preparations, while thousands of locals gathered along the banks of the River Lagan eager to see the *Britannic* take to the water. At 11.10am the first warning rocket shot into the sky, signalling to any passing vessels in the Victoria Channel to stand clear, while the yard workers dislodged the remaining shores supporting the hull. With everything finally ready, at 11.15am a second rocket was fired as the launch trigger release valves were turned. Moments later, the 24,800-ton hull began to move down the sliding ways, the passage eased by 20 tons of tallow, train oil and soft soap. Eighty-one seconds later the *Britannic* was afloat, having reached a maximum speed of 9½ knots before being brought to a halt by the underwater anchors, the hull not even having travelled its full length in the water.

As with the launch of the *Olympic* and the *Titanic*, there had been no launching ceremony, other than the White Star burgee flying above the Arrol gantry while signal flags spelled out the word 'Success'. One

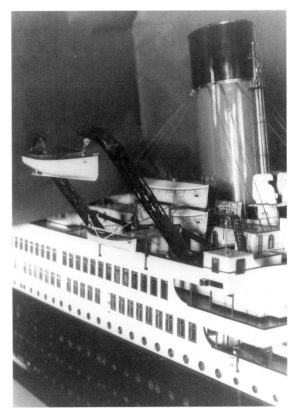

▲ The *Britannic*'s unique girder davits ensured a seat in the lifeboats for everyone on board. (Harland & Wolff)

shipyard worker, clearly unimpressed by the lack of observance, was moved to comment, 'They just builds 'er and shoves 'er in,' but given the unfavourable weather, perhaps it was understandable that the guests would be less concerned by the lack of ceremony and more interested in the celebratory lunch that had been arranged at the Grand Central Hotel in nearby Royal Avenue.

As the crowds slowly dispersed, the *Britannic*'s empty hull was quietly towed to the Harbour Commissioners' deep-water pier by the tugs *Herculaneum*, *Huskisson*, *Hornby*, *Alexandra* and *Hercules*, where the long process of fitting out would finally begin. Coming in the wake of the *Titanic* disaster, however, few were perhaps aware of just how much both the White Star Line and Harland & Wolff had riding on the success of their latest leviathan.

THE CALL TO ARMS

The intention had been for the *Britannic* to be in commercial service by the spring of 1915, yet come the early summer of that year she was still tied up at Belfast, lifeless and to all intents and purposes forgotten.

Over the preceding 18 months a lot had happened that no one in their worst nightmares could possibly have foreseen on the day the vessel had been launched. The outbreak of the Great War had cast a giant shadow over Europe, and by the autumn of 1914 most of the larger liners were redundant and surplus to requirement. At first the notion of utilising them as armed merchant cruisers had appealed to the Admiralty, but the vast size of the ships meant that they were unwieldy in confined waters, difficult to manoeuvre when carrying out escort duties, and incredibly expensive to run in terms of both their consumption of coal and the huge number of crew they required. It is therefore little wonder that by the spring of 1915 the *Mauretania*, the *Aquitania*, the *Olympic* and the *Britannic* were all tied up in port, to remain there until someone at the Transport Division could actually figure out what to do with them.

There was one exception: the *Lusitania* was the only one of the five British giant liners remaining in Cunard's reduced commercial service. But all that would change on 7 May 1915, when she was torpedoed and sunk off the Old Head of Kinsale by the German submarine *U20*. The *Mauretania* may well have taken the next scheduled crossing to New York on 29 May, but that same month Cunard agreed to charter the vessel to the Admiralty as a troopship. The agreed rate fell a long way short of the figure the Admiralty would have had to pay under normal circumstances, but the reality was that Cunard had little choice; they either compromised on the big ships or risked losing a larger number of smaller and infinitely more useful vessels instead.

So what had changed to persuade the Admiralty that it should even consider using the larger ships at all? The answer was Gallipoli. In April 1915 the Allies had invaded the Dardanelles in an attempt to force Turkey out of the war, resulting in a growing need for additional troops in the eastern Mediterranean. These men would arrive via the forward

---

▶ April 1913: The *Britannic* takes shape on Slipway No. 2 at Belfast. (Harland & Wolff)

WHITE STAR
ROYAL MAIL STEAMER
"BRITANNIC"

Nº 433

WELTE-PHILHARMONIE-ORGEL
auf S. S. Britannic der White Star Line

Allied base at Mudros, on the Greek island of Lemnos, and transporting them there was a task for which the larger ships were ideally suited. Even the Transport Division could appreciate the obvious logistical advantages and huge financial savings of converting the surplus larger ships, rather than a greater number of smaller ships. Even so, in May 1915 the director of transports still had his doubts:

These ships will accommodate large numbers – between 5,000 and 6,000 men each – but the risk of loss from submarine attack, owing to their great size and impossibility of taking them into closed harbours, is only justifiable if the emergency warrants it being taken.

Evidently it did, and one month later, on 18 June, the *Aquitania* was also requisitioned as a troopship.

Before long the nature of these ships' duties as transports would change considerably, and by September both of the Cunard vessels had been converted to hospital ships, in order to deal with the growing number of casualties. Once again this resulted in a lack of suitable vessels to transport combatants to the Mediterranean, and so on 1 September 1915 the White Star Line was finally notified that the *Olympic* was required for military service.

At 10.00am on 24 September, the *Olympic*, by now officially designated as Transport 2810, left Liverpool on her first trooping voyage to Mudros, leaving only one of Britain's four largest vessels still unemployed. In normal circumstance the *Olympic*, the *Mauretania* and the *Aquitania* might have sufficed, but as the summer wore on the casualty figures began to mount considerably. As if the increasing number of casualties from wounds was not bad enough, by September 1915 the number of men being laid low by sickness far exceeded the casualty figures from physical wounds. By the late summer of 1915 the Mediterranean Expeditionary Force was being decimated by diseases such as enteric fever (typhus) and dysentery, and in October alone the combined casualty evacuation figures reached the hitherto inconceivable total of 15,238 in a single month. With all of these invalids being transported through Mudros, even the *Mauretania* and the *Aquitania* were proving insufficient. In addition, the Inspector General of the British Expeditionary Force's own list of requirements for the evacuation of casualties from France advised that it was 'absolutely necessary that we should be prepared at short notice to meet an evacuation estimated at between 5,000 and 6,000 cases per day'. If the medical transports were not to be overwhelmed, there was only one possible solution.

As luck would have it, that solution was languishing in the docks at Belfast, ready for conversion to military service at a moment's notice. The *Britannic*'s size and speed made her ideal for service in the Mediterranean, especially as she and the other Olympic-class liners had been specifically built for the speedy transportation of thousands of passengers over great distances. Indeed, the *Britannic* was more than capable of making the journey between Southampton and Mudros, which had become the de facto centre of operations for all military transports and hospital ships throughout the Mediterranean. The Transport

◀ Harland & Wolff concept drawing of the *Britannic*'s even more elaborate first-class main entrance, with the intended German organ. (David Rumsey)

◀ The *Britannic* in her intended White Star colours, painted in 1914 by marine artist Charles Dixon. (Painting © National Museums Northern Ireland)

Division no longer had the luxury of dithering and, bowing to the inevitable, on 13 November 1915 sent official notification to Belfast that the *Britannic* was to be requisitioned as a hospital ship.

FOR KING AND COUNTRY

Although a long way from being complete by that point, the *Britannic* was still very close to being seaworthy. She had lain idle for months while Harland & Wolff concentrated on naval contracts, but by the autumn of 1915 the shipyard's workload had decreased enough for work to be restarted on some of the forgotten mercantile contracts. The *Britannic* had already completed her engine mooring trials in May 1915, but it would not be until early September that she could be placed in the Thompson Dock to have her propellers fitted. The conversion into a hospital ship, on the other hand, had changed everything, with the most urgent problem stemming from the fact that only five of the planned eight sets of girder davits had been installed. There simply was not enough time to install the complicated electric davits as per the original specification, so to cover the shortfall six sets of Welin davits, similar to those in the *Olympic* and the *Titanic*, were installed along each side of the boat deck, while two more were placed astern on the aft shade deck. Each set of conventional davits was capable of handling one rigid lifeboat and one collapsible, so that

▼ *Britannic* laid up, empty and forgotten, at Belfast. (Harland & Wolff)

▲ Detailed starboard elevations of the *Britannic* as she was intended for commercial service and as a hospital ship in her late-1916 configuration. (Cyril Codus)

▲ Captain Charles Bartlett (c.1902) with his son Charles Jr. Known to the family as Ellis, the latter would die aged only 15 during the torpedoing of the British battleship HMS *Goliath* in May 1915. (Alasdair Fairbairn)

by the time the work was completed there would be a total of 55 lifeboats on board. This number would later be augmented by a large number of emergency rafts positioned on the raised roof, which was above what would originally have been the first-class lounge.

Gone too was the shabby grey paint of the last two years, as the *Britannic* was freshly painted in the internationally recognised colours of a hospital ship, as required by the Hague Convention – a white hull, highlighted by a green band approximately one and a half metres in breadth running from stem to sternpost, broken in three places by large red crosses. The four towering funnels were also repainted, although not in the traditional White Star buff. Instead, they would be yellow, so that no U-boat skipper would have any difficulty identifying the *Britannic* as a hospital ship. For continued protection at night, a line of illuminated boxes ran from the forward length of the superstructure to the end of the aft shade deck, each giving off a green light, which, combined with the two large illuminated red crosses strategically positioned on each side of the boat deck, ensured that there could be no mistaking the nature of the ship's service.

The greater part of the work inside the hull involved converting the public rooms and open spaces into wards for 3,309 invalids; the staterooms on B deck were assigned to the medical staff, while the medical orderlies would be allocated to barrack rooms lower in the ship. By 8 December, four weeks and £90,000 later, the work was far enough advanced that the *Britannic* was finally ready to depart on her long-delayed sea trials. Two days earlier, having become responsible for the hugely expensive vessel's insurance the moment she left the dock, the Admiralty had officially informed the German authorities, via neutral

American diplomatic channels, of the *Britannic*'s status as a hospital ship. That same day, Lieutenant-Colonel Henry Concanon, one of the managers of the White Star Line, had also entered the *Britannic*'s details on the Liverpool register.

Twelve hours after leaving her berth the *Britannic* steamed back into the fog-shrouded waters of Belfast Lough, having successfully completed her engine trials, at which point the White Star Line duly took delivery of their new ship. The next step was to transfer the *Britannic* to Liverpool, where the process of fitting out would be completed, and it was at this point that the appointment of a captain became the company's most pressing concern. Despite the importance of the *Britannic*, not only to the war effort but also to the White Star Line, Harold Sanderson, the company's chairman and president of IMM since Joseph Bruce Ismay's retirement on 30 June 1913, was still unable to get the captain of his choice. Several months earlier he had attempted to have Captain Herbert Haddock, in charge of the *Olympic* before the war, reappointed to his old command, but his request had fallen on deaf ears as Haddock was considered to be of far greater use in his post at Belfast, coordinating what was commonly referred to as the 'Ghost Fleet', a flotilla of merchant vessels disguised as battleships to supposedly confuse and mislead the Germans. Seven weeks later Sanderson decided to try again, but the Admiralty's position remained unchanged, so the company chose instead to appoint Captain Charles Bartlett.

Charles Alfred Bartlett was certainly an appropriate choice. Having commanded the 21,035-ton *Cedric* for five years, he was used to big ships, and his tenure since 1 January 1912 as White Star Marine Superintendent at Liverpool meant that he had not only overseen the final delivery stages of the *Titanic*, but would also have been closely involved in the discussions regarding the modified designs of the *Olympic* and the *Britannic*. At the outbreak of war he had been transferred to patrolling duties in the North Sea, coordinating the operations aboard the 437-ton armed yacht HMY *Verona*, during which time his trawlers had even snared the German submarine *U14* in their nets, before subsequently sinking it with gunfire. Although patrolling duties were no less important to the war effort than the task of coordinating the ghost fleet, even if perhaps less exciting, Sanderson was reasonably confident that he would have no difficulty in obtaining the Admiralty's agreement regarding Bartlett's captaincy. By the evening of 11 December, Harland & Wolff had completed as much of the work at Belfast as was possible, and the *Britannic* finally departed from the city where she was built under the command of Captain Joseph Ranson, arriving safely in Liverpool's Gladstone Dock the following morning. Two days later, on 14 December, Captain Bartlett arrived on board to take command of the brand-new *Britannic*.

Even at this relatively late stage there was still a great deal to be completed, and work continued around the clock to install the necessary medical equipment and get the ship ready for sea. It would take another week before everything was ready, but eventually even the White Star ship's surgeon, Dr John Beaumont, gave his unofficial seal of approval, describing the *Britannic* as 'the most wonderful hospital ship that ever sailed the seas'.

At this stage only a handful of people knew that the *Britannic*'s ultimate destination would be the Mediterranean, but regardless of where she was bound, the ship's medical staff could at least take comfort in the thought that the conditions of service as a hospital ship were clearly laid down in the Hague Convention of 1907. Hospital ships were afforded the luxury of being exempt from deliberate attack or capture, with Article 4 of the Convention making it clear that hospital ships, even though they acted at their own peril, were intended solely for the relief and assistance of the wounded, sick and shipwrecked of the belligerents, without distinction of nationality. Governments undertook not to use a hospital ship for any military purpose, nor to use them to hamper the movements of the combatants, although the belligerents did still retain the right to search them and, if the military situation dictated, order them to leave the area. Hospital ships could only be seized if the circumstances were deemed critical enough to justify the action, although the

detention on 18 October 1914 of the German hospital ship *Ophelia* on suspicion of making illegal wireless transmissions and laying mines clearly indicates that the British were prepared to waive any hospital ship's rights of protection if the evidence justified it. Finally, the religious and medical staff were also considered inviolable and could not be made prisoners of war; in fact, the belligerents were also required to guarantee any medical staff falling into their hands the same allowances and pay that they would receive in their own navy.

THE CAMPAIGN AT SEA

The war at sea was also considered a more gentlemanly pursuit, or at least it was at first. At the outbreak of hostilities, German raiders and submarines were obliged to follow the agreed 'prize rules', whereby a passing merchant ship would be stopped and its captain permitted to abandon ship before it was sent to the bottom. The introduction by the British of Q-ships, vessels specially designed to lure submerged U-boats to the surface, persuaded the Germans that perhaps following such gentlemanly conduct was not to their advantage, and in February 1915 they commenced the practice of unrestricted submarine warfare, whereby any merchant vessel found in UK waters could be attacked without warning. The public outcry in America following the torpedoing of the *Lusitania* and the *Arabic* ultimately obliged the Germans to reconsider their tactics, and in September 1915 the unrestricted campaign was suspended, but it was an uncomfortable portent of things to come.

Fortunately, in the Mediterranean there was less chance of a mistake being made by an overly ambitious U-boat commander; in fact the evidence suggests that in this theatre at least the Germans were doing as little as possible to provoke a hitherto neutral America. In his five-volume treatise on the German war at sea between 1914 and 1918, Rear Admiral Arno Spindler detailed the considerable restrictions placed on a U-boat commander's freedom to operate in the Mediterranean between May and October 1916:

9 May 1916: The campaign against commerce is to be conducted above water. Men-of-war only and not armed merchant ships may be attacked submerged. Allow passenger steamers to pass.

17 June 1916: From now onwards in the Mediterranean armed cargo steamers may be

◀ *Britannic's* nemesis: the German mine-laying submarine *U73*.

attacked submerged when the armament has been observed with absolute certainty. Passenger steamers, even if armed, are to be spared in all circumstances. The only exception to this is the Aegean Sea north of Crete where large enemy passenger steamers may be attacked submerged, irrespective of armament because it may be assumed with certainty that they are transports.

15 July 1916: From now onwards [in] the whole of the Aegean Sea, and the routes for transports between Malta and the Cerigo Channel laid down by the British Admiralty, enemy cargo steamers recognised as troop or war material transports may be sunk from underwater even if their armament has not been observed.

Aids to recognising such steamers are:

Marked with numbers typical of transports, escort by men-of-war, wireless fittings.

Commanding officers are expressly informed that mistakes concerning the character of a vessel met with must not occur, and that if made, they will be held personally responsible.

▲ Kapitänleutnant Gustav Johannes Siess, commander of the *U73*. (Michail Michailakis)

12 October 1916: The campaign against commerce in the Mediterranean should be conducted in accordance with the Prize Regulations. Enemy cargo steamers, the armament of which is recognisable beyond doubt, may be attacked submerged in the area west of Gibraltar and in the Mediterranean. Passenger steamers are not to be molested in any circumstances anywhere even if they are armed.

Nor should the Mediterranean be looked upon as a quiet backwater in the war at sea. At the outbreak of hostilities the Austro-Hungarian KUK (*kaiserliche und königliche Kriegsmarine*) flotilla was relatively small, on top of which their submarines had only a limited range, so in April 1915 the Germans had dispatched their first submarines to the Mediterranean in response to the Dardanelles campaign. The *U21* in particular achieved considerable initial success by sinking the British battleships HMS *Triumph* and HMS *Majestic* within weeks, so between January and April of 1916 the Mediterranean flotilla also received an unusual reinforcement, in the form of six UB II-class submarines: the *UB42*, the *UB43*, the *UB44*, the *UB45*, the *UB46* and the *UB47*. These submarines had actually been constructed in sections

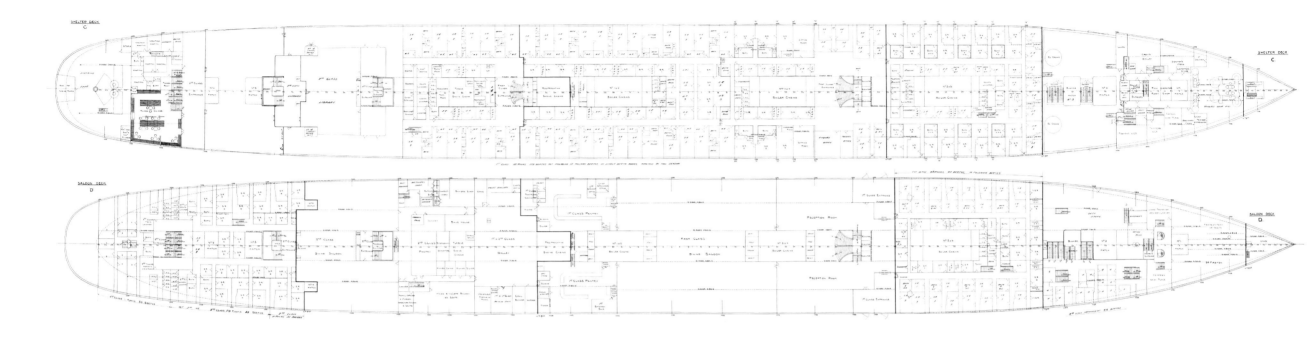

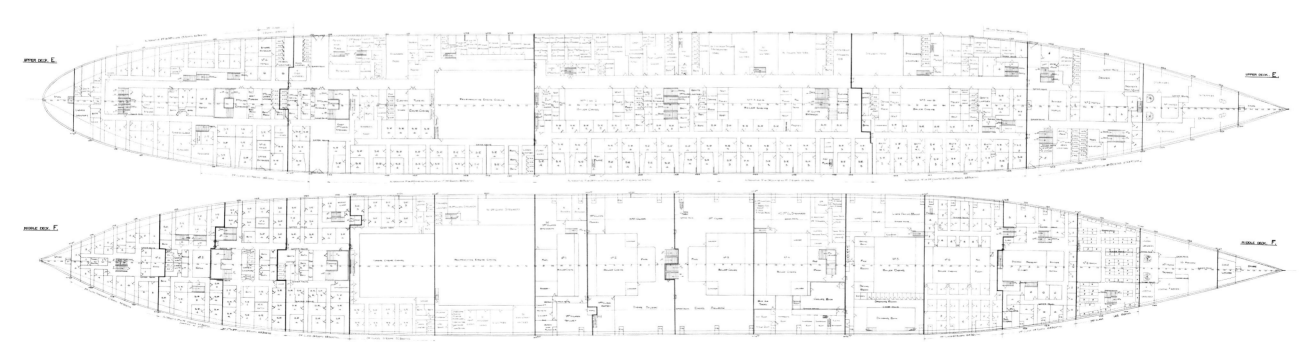

[Overleaf]

SS *Britannic*
Harland & Wolff Yard No. 433
<u>**Dimensions:**</u> **850 ft x 93 ft 6″ x 64 ft 6″ to Shelter Deck (C)**
All plans reproduced courtesy of Harland & Wolff Ltd.

Shelter Deck (C)
Saloon Deck (D)
Upper Deck (E)
Middle Deck (F)
Lower Deck (G)
Orlop Deck
Lower Orlop
Tank Top

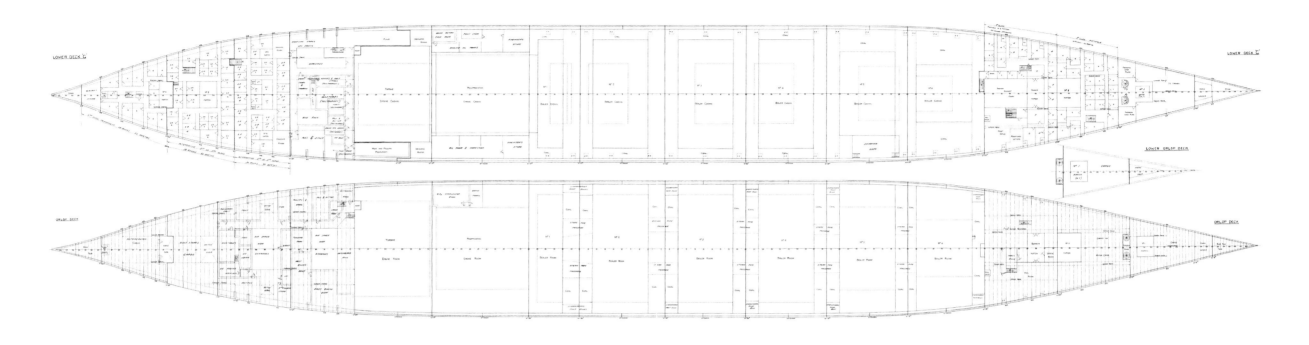

TANK TOP

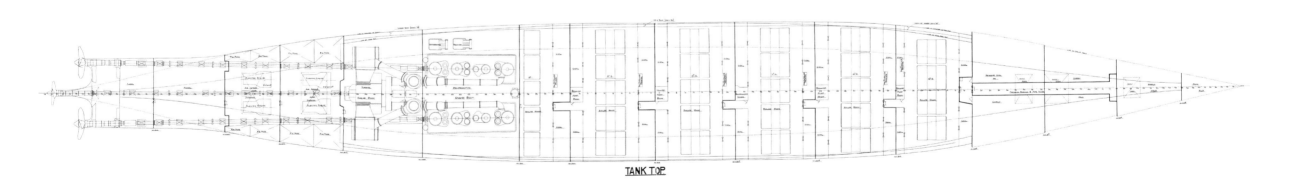

Nº 433.

S.S. 850'-0" × 93'-6" × 64'-6" TO SHELTER DECK "C"

by German shipyards before being taken by train to Pola, where they were reassembled and commissioned between 23 March and 4 July 1916.

For the purposes of our story, though, the German mine-laying submarine *U73* departed from Cuxhaven on 1 April 1916, bound for the Mediterranean. Under the command of Kapitänleutnant Gustav Johannes Siess, *U73* travelled around the Scottish coast and into the Bay of Biscay, before heading south along the Portuguese coast and breaking into the Mediterranean via the Strait of Gibraltar. Unable to lay his mine barrage off the French naval base at Bizerte due to poor weather and some unspecified technical issues, Siess proceeded instead to the British naval base at Malta where, sensing a golden opportunity, he laid 22 mines off the entrance to Valletta harbour, which would ultimately claim not only the 14,000-ton pre-dreadnought HMS *Russell*, but also several of the smaller vessels that would go to her assistance.

The success of the *U73*'s mine-laying activities in the Mediterranean was not lost on the German Admiralty, and throughout August and September 1916 the Pola flotilla would be reinforced by three additional mine-laying submarines, the *U22*, the *U23* and the *U72*. The sobering thought for any self-respecting commander of a hospital ship, however, was that while his vessel was in theory protected and safe from any deliberate attack, the simple fact was that a mine of any nationality was an indiscriminate weapon that cared little for political niceties.

THE MAIDEN VOYAGE

At 39 years of age, Dr Harold Goodman was already more than familiar with life's trials. After leaving school at 17, he had begun his medical training at St Bartholomew's Hospital in London, qualifying in 1899 and moving to Beckett's Hospital in Barnsley. He then took over a medical practice at Hemsworth, in addition to using the Warde Adlam Cottage Hospital to operate on his surgical cases, so the experience he gained from this hardened industrial background was now about to pay dividends.

Dr Goodman's latest assignment, taken up on 22 December 1915, was to His Majesty's Hospital Ship *Britannic*, the largest, if not quite the most luxurious, hospital ship in the world. Considering that his call to the colours was actually very recent – he had been appointed as a lieutenant in the Royal Army Medical Corps on 14 December 1915 – to find himself assigned to the *Britannic* was a remarkable stroke of good fortune. As his taxi pulled alongside the *Britannic*, safely secured in Liverpool's Gladstone Dock on that cold and frosty Tuesday morning three days before Christmas, he knew how fortunate he had been.

Goodman may well have been ready to do his bit for king and country, but unfortunately it seemed he would have to wait a little bit longer. At 11.00am the *Britannic* pulled out into the Mersey precisely on schedule, only to promptly drop anchor and remain curiously immobile for the remainder of the day. Despite the effort to get the ship ready in time, 200 Royal Army Medical Corps (RAMC) orderlies had still not arrived from Aldershot, and to make matters worse they were not liable to be on board for another 12 hours. All the crew could do was wait, so after settling into cabin 51, a two-berth stateroom that he was to share with a Lieutenant Anderson, Goodman would spend the afternoon getting to know his new home.

Given the *Britannic*'s huge size, this was almost certainly time well spent. Little survives in the official records detailing exactly how the converted *Britannic* was laid out, although Private Percy Tyler, a medical orderly in the RAMC, does provide a little basic information in his journal:

A deck was the company office, the officers and nurses quarters, and the officers wards. B deck aft was the promenade portion for the R.A.M.C., where also was the officers smoke room. Amidships were wards and for'ard some ship's quarters.

 C deck aft contained the isolation wards, the R.A.M.C. mess and parade ground. Amidships were more nurses quarters and for'ard wards. D deck held the patients large dining hall, wards and R.A.M.C. lavatories. E deck had K and H wards the two largest on the boat, and the main galley way which stretched from for'ard to aft known as 'Scotland Road'. Walking along her starting for'ard brought you to ship's quarters, and down two decks to No. 1 barrack room which held about 90 of the Corp staff; returning to Scotland Road brought you past more lavatories, scouts and stewards quarters. Passing on along the passage were crews quarters and passage ways to engineers rooms and the stokeholds, lifts etc. Halfway along and again down two decks, G deck was No. 2 barrack room; back again along the road and down again to F deck found No. 3 barrack room and down to G deck No. 4 barrack room aft. There were three passenger and three cot lifts all working from Scotland Road to the boat deck six decks up. G deck was well below the water-line but air was obtained by numerous electric fans which kept a cool breeze carrying through the rooms day and night.

◀ Colourised photograph of the *Britannic* in the colour scheme of a military hospital ship, taken during the initial stages of her service. (Ken Marschall)

Shortly before midnight the tardy orderlies from Aldershot began to arrive on board, and within 20 minutes the order was given to raise the anchor as the fully illuminated *Britannic* finally headed west into the Irish Sea, bound for an as-yet-unknown destination.

The Devil makes work for idle hands, as the *Britannic*'s first day at sea would demonstrate. Rumours abounded as to where the ship was actually headed, and for some inexplicable reason Australia seemed to be the leading contender. The monotony was briefly interrupted by the morning parade at 10.30, after which Lieutenant Colonel Henry Stewart Anderson, *Britannic*'s senior medical officer, made his daily rounds of the ship. By the time he had finished, Dr Goodman had been allocated to the 426 beds of F, L, M, N and V wards. This placed him in the forward starboard part of the ship on F and G decks, and straight away this location presented him with something of a problem as two of his wards were already taking in water due to a leaking porthole and the back pressure from a faulty valve in the ship's tank. On the bright side, at least Goodman's wards were all well served by the forward lifts.

To further add to the problems, practically everyone on board was feeling the effects of a strong squally south-west half-gale, so it was just as well that there wasn't much to do at that time. The following morning proved no different, with the conditions being so rough that breakfast was very thinly attended, although a midday lecture by Professor Squires and Dr Risk on the virtues of urea as an antiseptic at least provided a welcome distraction. More interestingly, Colonel Anderson's passing comment that the medical staff would only have six days to treat the wounded once they were on board provided everyone with the first real hint that *Britannic* was actually bound for the Mediterranean. At midday the daily run of 426 miles was published, and when it was learned that the ship had passed Cape Finisterre it seemed obvious that the *Britannic* was indeed headed for Gibraltar. Unfortunately for the medical staff, the Atlantic continued to make life as difficult as possible, with the ship sometimes rolling so badly that one of the tables in Goodman's cabin actually overturned. Christmas morning was equally squally, and following the 11.00am Church of England service in the saloon, which had been specially decorated with holly and mistletoe for the occasion, Colonel Anderson finally took the opportunity to inform the assembled medical staff of their embarkation duties.

And so the voyage continued. The daily run to midday on 25 December clocked up another 443 miles, and there was at least a little excitement when three small tramp steamers hove into view as the ship was passing Cape St Vincent, if only because they were the first vessels that had been sighted in days. Early the next morning the *Britannic*, illuminated by huge searchlights from the shore, slipped uneventfully through the Strait of Gibraltar and into the Mediterranean. Taking advantage of the much calmer conditions, at 11.30am

LIEUTENANT-COLONEL HENRY STEWART ANDERSON

A native of Lisburn, Co. Antrim, he joined the RAMC in July 1899, serving in South Africa, Burma, India and Malta prior to the war. Having joined the British Expeditionary Force in August 1914, attached to the 1st Battalion North Staffordshire Regiment, Anderson was invalided home from France the following January. He would remain in England until being appointed senior medical officer on the *Britannic* on 21 December 1915, serving two terms in that capacity. Following the loss of the *Britannic*, Anderson would go on to command the Citadel Military Hospital in Cairo from 1917 to 1919, followed by the Palestine General Hospital at Ludd, before retiring at the end of 1924. He died on 24 April 1961, leaving his body for medical research.

Captain Bartlett called all hands to their stations to carry out the ship's first emergency boat drill. The smoother seas also seemed to improve the ship's performance, as she covered another 455 miles in a 24-hour run. The engines seemed to be working up nicely, although the next day's run was not so encouraging, clocking up only 416 miles. Nevertheless, with the ship skirting the southern coast of Sardinia that afternoon, Italy was now less than a day away and, as if to celebrate the *Britannic*'s maiden arrival at a foreign port, that evening the first official ship's concert was held in the RAMC mess.

The morning of 28 December was hazy, but at 8.30am Dr Goodman was already up on deck gazing at the distant island of Capri, just as the *Britannic* was entering the Bay of Naples. He could clearly see the ruins of Tiberius' palace and the 700-foot drop into the sea – a sombre reminder of the Roman emperor's 'playful habit' of throwing his victims down from here to feed the lobsters – while the views of Vesuvius from the harbour were no less awesome. For the time being, however, this brief glimpse of Naples would have to suffice, as it seemed unlikely that the medical staff would be allowed ashore that day. Instead, all they could do was sit and watch the activities of the coaling lighters that lay alongside all

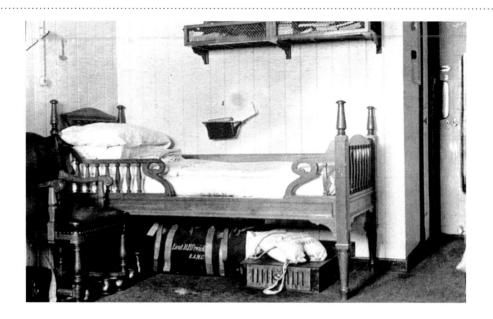

day. The following day looked set to be equally dull, but after they had lectured the orderlies and overseen the wards, which were getting straighter by the hour, doctors Goodman, Urwick, Anderson and Bachelor were suddenly given passes to go ashore in the ship's motor launch. Landing at the Arsenal step at 10.30am, they immediately proceeded to the local Thomas Cook bureau to change their money, but while the poor exchange rate came as a rather unpleasant shock, at least lunch at a Naples hotel made the trip ashore worthwhile. Sadly there were only a few short hours in which to escape the rigours of war, and by 4.00pm everyone was back on board as the *Britannic* headed south.

The call at Naples actually provided an interesting variation to the normal routine followed by the *Olympic*. Neither vessel was capable of completing the journey from Southampton to Mudros and back again without having to take on additional supplies of coal and water, and the differing nature of their service meant they took two completely different routes. As a troopship, the *Olympic* was full when she left Southampton, obliging Captain Hayes to get to Mudros as quickly as possible in order to offload the troops. After disembarking her troops the *Olympic* would then return to Southampton via the northern Italian port of La Spezia, where she would stop in order to take on enough fuel and water to be able to complete the voyage. For a hospital ship, however, the situation was very different. The *Britannic*'s task was to repatriate thousands of wounded servicemen, meaning that when she departed from Southampton she was practically empty. As a result, the outbound voyage was generally a relaxed affair, allowing Captain Bartlett to call in at the more southerly Italian port of Naples, where he would take on enough coal and fresh

▲ A typical doctor's cabin, located on B deck.　　▶ On-board concert programme.

46

— PROGRAMME OF CONCERT —

Held on Board

HOSPITAL SHIP "BRITANNIC,"

MONDAY EVENING, DECEMBER 27th, 1915,

Under the Patronage of

Captain C, A. BARTLETT and Lieut.-Col. H. S. ANDERSON

— PROGRAMME —

Song, "Show me the way to your heart" ...	Private Dixon
Musical Monologue, "Spotty" ...	Rev. T. W. Hancox, C.F.
Monologue, "The Groom's Story" ...	Capt. J. S. Morrow
Song, "The Sunshine of your Smile" ...	Sister Mason
Song, "Sincerity"	Private Lever
Miscellaneous Selection	Private Grates
Reminiscenses	Prof. W. St. C. Symmers
Song, "Till the Boys come Home"	Sister Brown
Song, Selected	Lieut Anderson
Song, "Juanita"	Sisters Henworthy and Elliot
Song, "The Home of the Hun" ...	Rev. W. Harrod, C.F.
Song, "Sweet be your Dreams"	Private Dixon
Musical Monologue, "The Caretaker"	Rev. T. W. Hancox, C.F.
Song, "When Irish Eyes are Smiling" ...	Sister Lincoln
Song, "The Tulip and the Rose"	Private Grates
Song, "In Sweet Content"	Private Lever

GOD SAVE THE KING.

Accompanist - Lieut. T. Heywood

M.C. - Sergt.-Major Debney

water to complete the journey to Mudros before heading non-stop back to England, usually a voyage of about six days.

IN THE FOOTSTEPS OF HOMER

Early the following morning the glowing volcanic island of Stromboli could be seen on the starboard horizon, and by 7.00am the snow-covered Sicilian volcano Mount Etna was in sight. At 8.00am the *Britannic* finally entered the Straits of Messina, where the ruins of the 1908 earthquake were still clearly visible to port, a sight that for Colonel Anderson would have awoken memories of his role in the British earthquake relief party which in January 1909 had been dispatched from Malta to assist with the rescue. At 9.00am came yet another embarkation drill, keeping everyone busy in the wards until lunch, but already it was

▲ Italian postcard of the harbour train station at Naples in 1915.

▶ *Britannic* anchored inside the Molo San Vincenzo, Naples.

clear that the tempo on board had completely changed. Mudros was now barely 30 hours away, and with the eastern Mediterranean crawling with enemy U-boats, the sudden increase in speed was very perceptible. That evening the medical staff were treated to another informal lecture in the lounge by Professor Squires, this time on Virgil's *Aeneid*, but just how successful it was in taking their minds off the approaching danger zone is anyone's guess.

The following morning the orderlies were finally given their duty watches. Colonel Anderson and Captain Bartlett made their final two-hour inspection of the wards to ensure that everything was in place, and at 3.50pm the *Britannic* passed through the outer defensive nets that guarded the Bay of Mudros, before anchoring inside the boom in 13 fathoms of water. The hospital ships *Dunluce Castle, Grantully Castle, Egypt, Gloucester Castle* and *Assegai* were already lying nearby and ready to transfer their cargos of wounded soldiers, so it was immediately clear that the next few days were going to be busy.

The whole aspect of Lemnos appeared to be very hilly and barren, with the shore and slopes covered with tents and encampments. To Harold Goodman it actually seemed pretty grim, but there would be little time to take in the surroundings as at 7.00pm, without any apparent warning, the P&O hospital ships *Assegai* and *Egypt* arrived alongside and immediately began to discharge their patients. For the first time Goodman began to appreciate just how large the *Britannic* really was, as the funnels of the other two ships, which seemed like lighters in comparison, only came up to the *Britannic*'s boat deck. To get

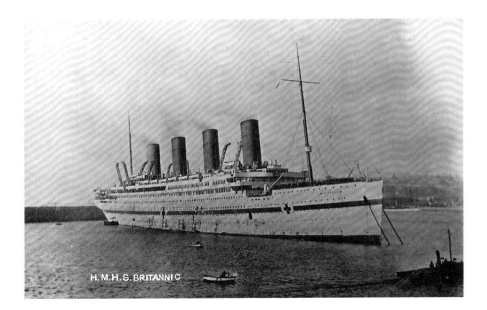

H.M.H.S. BRITANNIC

around this problem, the wounded came aboard on D deck via gangways from the smaller vessels' upper decks, which were at about the same level. It was a long process, meaning that for Dr Goodman there would be no dinner until 11.00pm, by which time the 94 beds of V ward were full, ten stretcher cases had been placed in F ward and several others were allocated to L and M. There was, however, one fly in the ointment. The unscheduled evening transfer had taken everyone completely by surprise, and with Colonel Anderson and Captain Bartlett still both on shore, the arrangements were probably not in accordance with their ideas, but that was a matter to be dealt with the following morning. For the time being, all the patients had been given either chicken broth or cocoa before bed at 11.00pm – not that they would have got very much sleep, for at midnight Mudros exploded in a cacophony of sound as the hundreds of vessels anchored in the bay sounded their whistles, continuing to sound off as they saw in the New Year.

The following morning would see no respite in the on-board activities. Throughout the morning patients continued to come aboard from the *Egypt* and *Assegai*, and the following day would find the hospital ships *Asturias*, *Killman Castle* and *Abdermain* alongside, along with a thousand wounded being transferred from the shore-based hospitals. As the transfer of invalids went on, the experiences of those who came on board proved varied. For Private R.E. Atkinson of the 29th Divisional Cyclist Company, who had arrived from Cairo on board the *Dunluce Castle* after being evacuated from Suvla Bay, it was like entering another world. Atkinson was amazed by the sheer size of the *Britannic*, remembering that

although he had boarded from the level of the *Dunluce Castle*'s well deck, he still had to go up five flights of stairs before reaching the *Britannic*'s boat deck. He was equally struck by the enormous width of the ship and the huge dining saloon that resembled Crystal Palace, noting that the ship's stewards looked just as white and sickly as those on the other boats. The on-board facilities, such as telephones, lifts and the swimming bath, made the vessel seem more like a small town. After being assigned to his ward and issued with his hospital suit – blue trousers and jacket with brown facings – without which no patient would be allowed on the top deck, he enjoyed a good dinner, which seemed to ensure that all was well with the world. But the following day Atkinson's wonderful world began to look a little tarnished as he continued to experience life on board and observe the transfer of the invalids:

> Grub is rotten, starvation, two slices for breakfast, dinner, stew in a basin, thought it was soup first course, but nothing else came up. Patients get nearly frozen waiting to get on from trawlers, some stretcher cases get douched with water from ship's side. Cocoa and hard biscuit for supper. Church in evening, gilt edge prayer books W.S.L. [White Star Line]

Meanwhile, the last of the injured continued to come aboard, although the process was not helped at all by problems with one of the ship's motor launches. At one stage its engine failed completely, and it was only by throwing the crew a rope attached to a buoy that the boat could be stopped from drifting off completely. By 3.00pm on 3 January the body of Private Arthur Howe of the 1st/5th Essex Regiment, who had died on board the previous morning from tubercular disease, had been landed, the errant motor launch had been corralled and the last of the patients were on board; six hours later the *Britannic*, by now making a good 20 knots, was 120 miles closer to home, and passed through the Kea Channel later that evening, where Harold Goodman recalled a good view of the island of Kea on the port side.

◀ A superb view of the *Britannic* at Mudros, detailing the workings of the ship's unique girder davits. (Imperial War Museum)

▶ Medical barges transferring invalids from the shore-based hospitals at Mudros.

BACK TO BLIGHTY!

The fast tempo of the voyage home would stand in stark contrast to the relaxed outward journey. With the ship filled with convalescent soldiers, the medical staff were suddenly busier than ever, while the ship's crew found themselves equally pressed. At 11.30am on 4 January the general alarm was sounded, and Captain Bartlett carried out the patients' first safety drill, as the medical staff were stood to their posts and the patients called to their boat stations. The drill was not just a consequence of the *Titanic* disaster, it was also a necessary precaution in the event that the ship was attacked at any stage of the voyage, so that everyone on board knew exactly where to go and what to do in an emergency. Even so, the *Britannic*'s odds of survival were getting better by the minute, as once she was past Malta she was considered to be clear of the major danger zone.

Even so, you could never take anything for granted in a war zone, and with the southern coast of Malta having been skirted and the coast of Tunisia in sight, at 6.30am on 5 January the hitherto calm on-board routine was dramatically interrupted when a man ran onto the bridge to inform the officer of the watch that someone had jumped overboard. Unfortunately, the option of stopping the vessel to go back and search for the unfortunate victim just did not exist. In peacetime they would without question have stopped, but with the Mediterranean crawling with hostile U-boats Captain Bartlett would have been foolhardy in the extreme to have exposed his command to the prospect of a submarine attack, regardless of the *Britannic*'s protected status as a hospital ship. His only option was to maintain course and speed, while carrying out as extensive a search of the ship as possible in order to find out who was missing. While the doctors checked their wards, the crew searched the ship from stem to stern, and by the end of the morning it was found that a naval rating named Samuel Jones, of Drake Battalion in the Royal Naval Division, could not be located. At 3.00pm that afternoon a formal court of inquiry was held on board to uncover what might have happened, but all that could be ascertained was that Jones was being invalided back to England due to a disordered action of the heart and pains in his chest. With no indication as to why he might have jumped, the court could only conclude that it was 'reasonable to assume that he is dead'.

There was, however, one positive result from the search, as three other patients who had also been reported missing from their wards the previous evening were found playing cards in one of the bathrooms. The ship's log makes no mention of any disciplinary action taken against the miscreants, but it is safe to assume that they were less than popular with the medical staff once they were returned to their wards.

And so the *Britannic* continued to head for home, passing Gibraltar at 10.00pm on the evening of 6 January, returning to the Atlantic and heading north along the Portuguese coast. With successive daily runs of 506 and 512 miles, soon she was safely off Cape Finisterre; as the ship passed the outbound *Mauretania* off the French island of Ushant on the evening of 8 January, the order was given to return the patients' military uniforms to them, confirming to everyone on board that they would be arriving back at Southampton the following day. Sadly, the last night at sea would not pass without incident, as at 2.40am, while the *Britannic* was steaming a little to the west of Guernsey, Rifleman Charles Vincent of the 8th Battalion Hampshire Regiment died of tuberculosis. With the home port less than 12 hours away Captain Bartlett was not required to conduct a burial at sea, so instead the body would remain on board before being landed for burial at Netley.

▲ Patient's medical card.

As she arrived off the Isle of Wight, observed by a hydroplane and with two minesweepers leading the way, the *Britannic* was carefully guided into the heavily defended Solent before two other patrol boats assumed the task of shepherding her up Southampton Water, towards her originally intended peacetime terminal in the White Star Dock. By 3.00pm, the six escorting tugs had safely completed the docking process, at which point the first of the 4,200 invalids could finally begin to disembark at the start of a process that would take over eight hours. With so many patients suffering from so many different ailments, their ultimate destination would be something of a lottery. Private Atkinson would find himself at Southwark Military Hospital, better known in peacetime as the Camberwell Infirmary, Dulwich, while Private Walter Goodwin of the 11th London Regiment (1st Finsbury Rifles), in spite of the on-board rumours that all choleric patients would be sent to Croydon, was instead horrified to find himself incarcerated over a hundred miles from home, at the Third West General Hospital at Ninian Park in Cardiff, Wales.

As for Harold Goodman, it would be well past midnight before he finally got to bed, but in spite of an early call the next morning, with the ship once again empty he was still able to obtain a seven-day pass until the following Sunday. Meanwhile, the *Britannic*'s work, for the time being at least, was done. Her maiden voyage may have been a far cry from that originally planned for the ship, but with over 4,000 invalids safely returned to British shores there could be no denying that it had been a success. For now, though, her corridors were once again eerily quiet, as the remaining medical personnel began to prepare for the next voyage, with little idea as to when it would be or even where it might take them.

TO HELL AND BACK

Although he had rushed back from his leave, by the time Harold Goodman was on board again, the rumours, if they were to be believed, suggested that the *Britannic* would not be going anywhere anytime soon.

The dynamics of the Mediterranean campaign had actually begun changing at the same time the *Britannic* was being converted into a hospital ship. Lord Kitchener himself had visited the Gallipoli beaches to assess the increasingly disastrous military situation, and after concluding that a general evacuation was the only realistic option, he officially authorised the withdrawal on 7 December. On the night of 18/19 December – four days before the *Britannic* departed on her maiden voyage – the beachheads at Anzac and Suvla had been abandoned, and by the time the *Britannic* was arriving back at Southampton the remaining Allied troops on the peninsula had also been evacuated from Cape Helles, having left Turkish soil for good.

The effect of this withdrawal on the casualty statistics can be seen almost immediately,

▲ Contemporary hand-tinted photograph of the *Britannic* as a hospital ship.

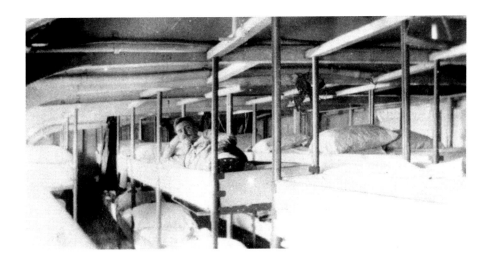

with the February 1916 figures being less than half those of the previous month. It was the beginning of a welcome and long-overdue respite, and by March 1916 the statistics were more or less back in line with those recorded in the spring of 1915, before the Gallipoli offensive had commenced. Suddenly the continued service of the larger hospital ships was in doubt, and with both the *Aquitania* and *Britannic* lying idle at Southampton it could only be a matter of time before the Transport Division, ever mindful of the ruinous costs of maintaining the larger liners in military service, would have to consider their options.

In the short term, both vessels remained on the payroll, and at midday on 20 January 1916 the *Britannic* was once again outward bound for Mudros. Following her now

▲ The typical wooden bunks in F ward. (Jonathan Mitchell)

▲ D ward. (Jonathan Mitchell)

established route to Naples, the ship passed through the Strait of Gibraltar during the early hours of 23 January, and by the following evening she was off the southern coast of Sardinia, on schedule to anchor at Naples the next morning to take on enough coal and water to complete the voyage to Mudros and then return home. By 7.00pm on the evening of 25 January the refuelling was complete and everything was ready for the *Britannic* to depart as planned the next day. However, the following morning found the ship still secured in the harbour.

The news quickly leaked out that Captain Bartlett had received new orders to await the arrival of the hospital ship *Grantully Castle*, but with four additional hospital ships also redirected to Naples in the coming days, the Italian port suddenly and unexpectedly found itself serving as the focal point of all British hospital ship activity in the Mediterranean. To further complicate matters, even the medical staff's established daily routine found itself subjected to unforeseen variations, with rumours of a planned visit by the Duke of Aosta coming to nothing after it was cancelled at the last minute because there were no patients

on board at that time. However, Sidney Churchill, the British Consul-General in Naples, ever mindful of the political advantages of having a hospital ship's *bona fide* status confirmed by representatives of a neutral power, had also made arrangements for the captain and medical staff of the American cruiser USS *Des Moines* to inspect the *Britannic*'s facilities on 26 January. Two days later the same invitation would be extended to Thomas Nelson Page, the American ambassador to Rome, who just happened to be visiting Naples with his wife and daughter, allowing Churchill to report back to London that the ambassador had expressed much pleasure at having had the chance to see over the ship.

◀ A colourised photograph of the *Britannic*, intriguingly showing the identification number G608. (Mark Chirnside, colourised by Cyril Codus)

▲ *Britannic* taking on patients from a smaller hospital ship at Mudros. (Michail Michailakis)

Politics aside, the inactivity could not last for ever. On the afternoon of 27 January the hospital ship *Grantully Castle* arrived along the *Britannic*'s port side to begin the transfer of her 438 invalids, with the hospital ship *Formosa*, carrying 393 patients, securing on the starboard side three hours later. Even so, the less frantic schedule at Naples only served to emphasise the reduction of military activity in the eastern Mediterranean, as one by one other diverted hospital ships arrived at Naples to transfer their cargos of wounded. The *Essequibo* arrived on 1 February with 594 invalids and the *Nevasa* arrived the following morning with an additional 593, but even when the *Panama* finally arrived on the morning of 4 February with another 319, the *Britannic* was still nowhere near filled to capacity. The reality was that after nine days in port, five subsidiary hospital ships had delivered a grand total of only 2,237 invalids. With no further business, at 3.15pm the *Britannic* weighed anchor and headed out into the Tyrrhenian Sea, bound once again for Southampton.

She arrived safely home on the afternoon of 9 February, but the following weeks remained full of uncertainty. On 22 February the ship was even moved to an anchorage alongside the *Mauretania* off Cowes in order to vacate her badly needed berth, but while the *Aquitania* remained in dock for the time being, with rumours of that ship having brought home only 1,500 patients on her previous voyage, few were speculating that the current situation would be allowed to continue for very much longer.

Behind the scenes, however, there was a great deal more activity. On 1 February, while the *Britannic* had been at Naples, a representative of the Neapolitan Principal Provincial Sanitary Authority had gone aboard to inspect the facilities, and the result of this visit was a formal objection from the Italian authorities, who were concerned about Naples being used for the transfer of patients due to the possible dangers of infection at the port. The Italians were not closing the door altogether on the British hospital ships, but instead they suggested that if the transfer of patients was to continue, then the port of Augusta, on the east coast of Sicily, would be more appropriate. Mindful of the logistical advantages of using a more centrally located port in the Mediterranean, especially since the casualty figures had been so drastically reduced, the Transport Division began to explore the possibility. Captain Bartlett was happy to confirm that the *Britannic* could anchor in ten fathoms of water without undue difficulty, but he was less sanguine at the potential risks caused by the anchorage being particularly exposed to strong winds from the south-east. For his part, the senior naval officer on Malta regarded Augusta as being totally unsuitable due to the lack of jetties and the possible difficulty of transferring patients from ship to ship in heavy weather, but undeterred by the logistical issues, the Transport Division concluded that until the system at Mudros could be re-established, Augusta would suffice as the temporary port for the transfer of invalids in the Mediterranean.

After two monotonous weeks anchored off Cowes, on 3 March there was a brief moment of excitement on board when eight doctors, 15 nurses and 60 medical orderlies were suddenly transferred to the hospital ship *Morea* for an emergency trip across the Channel to Le Havre, but 48 hours later they were back on board, having safely returned another 840 invalids from France. Shrove Tuesday found both Captain Bartlett and Colonel Anderson called to Southampton, but any expectations they might have had came to naught and for the next ten days the freezing *Britannic* continued to ride quietly at anchor. It seemed as if the monotony would never end when suddenly, after more than five weeks of inactivity, on 18 March all leave was cancelled without warning, and recall telegrams were sent off to the medical staff already on leave.

BACK TO THE FRONT

Two days later the *Britannic* was once again outward bound, and as usual the medical staff had been given no official notification as to the ship's destination. By now, however, they could at least be reasonably confident that it would still be somewhere in the Mediterranean, so it came as no surprise when the ship duly arrived at Naples in the early hours of Saturday 25 March to take on coal and water as usual. The on-board routine was interrupted the following afternoon when the Duke of Oporto, living in exile in Italy since the Portuguese revolution of October 1910, arrived on board for an official visit. Included in the duke's retinue were a number of Italian boy scouts, eager to be shown around the ship by the eight British scouts who were living on board. Aged between 15 and 16, the *Britannic*'s scouts had actually been taken on board at the instigation of Captain Bartlett, who, although known to be something of a disciplinarian, was keen to help broaden their horizons. The young scouts had their own allocated duties, ranging from operating the lifts and taking messages through to learning physical drill, boat drill, swimming and Morse code and semaphore signalling, but on this occasion they would be serving as young ambassadors and entertaining the Italian representatives of the scout movement.

At 4.00pm on Monday 27 March the *Britannic* was once again headed south towards the toe of Italy, but it was only at this point that the medical staff were finally informed that in less than 24 hours they would be arriving at Augusta, where, as it happened, three hospital ships were already awaiting their arrival. Although no doubt ignorant of the drawbacks involved in using the Sicilian port, the medical staff would at least have been aware that using Augusta would mean avoiding the more hazardous voyage to the eastern Mediterranean where the U-boats were more active. The fine weather the following morning, as the ship entered the Strait of Messina, further enhanced the positive mood,

▲ Close detail image of *Britannic*'s aft-port girder davits.

and by 10.00am, only 18 hours after departing Naples, the *Britannic* dropped anchor in the new operational hub for the Mediterranean hospital ships.

The official files contain practically no information on the *Britannic*'s one and only call at Augusta, which, in view of the Transport Division's previous determination to experiment with the port, seems a little odd, but fortunately we have Dr Goodman's diary entry for Tuesday 28 March, which seems to suggest that the routine worked well:

> Most glorious morning. The bay is entered past a lighthouse, the houses on north side reach down to water's edge, the water a lovely clear blue. Found hospital ships awaiting us at anchor, the *Glengorm Castle* [and two more]. We came to anchor and were surrounded by numerous boats selling oranges. Commenced embarking patients off the *Dunluce Castle* on port side (alongside) at 10:15 about. The *Egypt* appeared and came into bay and drew alongside at 12.15 p.m. on starboard side where I was on duty as embarkation officer with Taylor and Walsh. We got 486 all told. Embarking going on aft by barge and lighter – Canadian Hospital and equipment, so taking in at four gangways at the same time. Finished at 7 p.m. with deceased officers baggage checking off, which stored in No. 3 hatch forward. Bed at 11 p.m. While we disembarked the *Egypt* the *Glengorm Castle* took *Dunluce*'s place and was disembarked and on barges the *Valderia* sent patients and the Canadian Hospital with 120 orderlies and staff to the after disembarkation ports on E deck and their equipment to the after hatches by crane.

The following morning provided a brief respite, which gave Captain Bartlett the opportunity to send one of the ship's motor launches to the south side of the bay to collect sand from the beach for cleaning the wooden decks. As well as being known to his crew as 'Iceberg Charlie', on account of his apparent ability to smell icebergs – something perhaps that might have been very useful on the *Titanic* four years earlier – another sobriquet that he enjoyed was 'Holystone Charlie', due to his partiality for nice clean decks. Later that afternoon the ABs could busy themselves with cleaning the woodwork under the hot Sicilian sun while the rest of the Canadian field hospital equipment was taken aboard, but at 9.00am the following morning the on-board routine returned to normal as the hospital ship *Formosa* arrived alongside. Once again Harold Goodman had been allocated to embarkation duty, but due to the change in on-board accommodations he instead found himself redistributing the patients in L, M and N wards, who needed to be moved in order to make room for the orderlies of the 1st London Field Ambulance.

By 3.00pm the *Britannic* had weighed anchor and was once again headed for home, having experienced the amenities of Augusta for barely two days. Although the passage was wet and stormy, it would also be largely routine, until 1.15am on 4 April, when Private Robert Pask of the 8th Battalion South Wales Borderers died from diabetes as the ship was passing near to the island of Guernsey. Less than 12 hours later, the *Britannic* would be safely secured in the White Star Dock, at which point Pask's body would be landed at Southampton for burial at Netley, but, unlike previous arrivals, this time the *Britannic* was met by Surgeon-General Sir Benjamin Franklin. This was clearly no ordinary homecoming, and not surprisingly, speculation started to spread quickly as to what it could mean. Twenty-four hours later the rumours were confirmed – the *Britannic* was to be decommissioned.

Despite the disappointment, in reality the news had been long expected by the medical staff. The Mediterranean casualty figures had dropped so much that it was all but impossible for the Transport Division to justify the costs of maintaining the larger vessels in service, with the result that the *Mauretania* had been paid off on 1 March, while the *Aquitania* was set to follow suit on 10 April. So confident were they that there was no chance of the ships being recalled in the short term that £150,000 had also been advanced to Cunard to cover the cost of converting the two vessels back to civilian service. Now it was the *Britannic*'s turn.

Declining Colonel Anderson's offer of a transfer to the hospital ship *Dover Castle*, Harold Goodman chose instead to remain aboard the *Britannic* for what little time was left to help tie up the inevitable loose ends, which for the most part seem to have focused on the military's apparent obsession with lists. According to Goodman, those final days were spent as follows:

5th: Twelve hours solid checking in linen and bedding into stores in D ward and 1st London Amb. News that the ship is out of commission and all to be disbanded. Offered H.S. *Dover Castle* by Coln. – refused it as want to finish work begun if no good even.

6th, 7th: Checking all the time from 6.30. Mrs. Howard called to see me on evening of 6th and had a chat in Matron's cabin. All sisters and matrons disembarked yesterday. Urwick, Maclagan and self left on ship.

8th: We are put on as Board of Survey for amm stores on ship in military charge. Men hard at work all day disembarking quantities of stores onto quay for checking. More linen checking for me.

9th: Same thing all day. I searched A B C D E F G H wards late at night with two sergeants.

10th: Checked all stuff in sheds. Received in all oddments collected on board and balanced accounts with ship's people, showed surplus on nearly all stuff issued – good egg – but useless work really as it doesn't matter a d… apparently. Hear I am promised 7 days leave.

By 11 April the work was done. At 4.00pm Colonel Anderson, along with doctors Goodman, Urwick and Maclagan, stood at the end of the White Star Dock to watch the ship that had been their home for almost four months pull away and steam slowly towards her temporary anchorage off Cowes. For a while the vessel would remain on the active roster at half rate – which, in the *Britannic*'s case, equated to the princely sum of five shillings per gross ton – but with the military situation in the Mediterranean stabilised, the Transport Division finally came to the only possible conclusion that it could. The *Britannic* was officially discharged from military service on 6 June, although she would still remain on the books at half rate until 20 July. The White Star Line would also receive a one-off payment of £76,000 to cover the cost of reconditioning the *Britannic* for civilian service, but in view of the subdued level of passenger traffic on the North Atlantic, which was likely to remain that way for the duration of the war, the reality was that there was still no demand for ships of her size.

In the meantime, the *Britannic* had returned safely to Belfast on 18 May, her crew having been paid off three days later. Now lying empty and seemingly forgotten alongside the Thompson Wharf, she would not be going anywhere for the foreseeable future.

BACK IN THE ROUTINE

As August 1916 drew to a close, the *Britannic* remained idle at Belfast, but while the military situation had stabilised in the Mediterranean, elsewhere it was a very different matter.

The German offensive against the French at Verdun had begun on 21 February and was still going strong after six months; the Russians had launched a full-scale offensive of their own against the Austrians in Galicia; the British offensive on the Somme had begun on 1 July; while in the East the Arab Revolt, which would ultimately make the reputation of one Lieutenant Thomas Edward Lawrence, was in its infancy.

At sea there had also been a monumental change. Less than two weeks after the *Britannic* arrived back at Belfast, the British and German battle fleets finally clashed at Jutland.

Although on the face of it the battle had proved inconclusive, the reality was that the German High Seas Fleet would remain largely bottled up in port for the rest of the war, with the Germans taking the decision to focus less on their capital ships and more on their increasingly dangerous U-boat fleet.

Matters were also escalating in the Balkans, with the Allied forces at Salonika taking a more active role in supporting their Romanian and Serbian allies. Gradually the casualty figures began to rise, but this time the biggest single issue was malaria, with the medical authorities in Malta predicting that the number of malarial cases would become increasingly frequent as the summer wore on. Sadly their fears would be proved all too correct, and on 21 July the *Aquitania* was duly recalled to service to help deal with the rising numbers. With the *Olympic* and *Mauretania* by now allocated to trooping duties between Canada and Britain, the Transport Division's options to deal with the growing crisis were limited, and sure enough, on Monday 28 August the *Britannic* was once again requisitioned as a hospital ship.

It was not long before the ship was back at Southampton, and on 4 September Captain Bartlett once again assumed command. Within five days the depleted medical stores and equipment had been replaced, and the ship was once again anchored off Cowes, after which there followed a couple of weeks of relative inactivity. Behind the scenes, however, the War Office was juggling a number of options, and the *Britannic*'s imminent departure for the Mediterranean provided the ideal opportunity to transport some nurses to foreign postings. One of those passengers would be the famous writer and pacifist Vera Brittain, at that time a 22-year-old nurse who in 1915 had volunteered to serve in the Voluntary Aid Detachment. Having previously served at the 1st London General Hospital, on 15 September Vera was suddenly informed that she was being posted to Malta and was ordered to report aboard the *Britannic* on 23 September. From the entries in Vera's journal, it is clear that the *Britannic*'s huge size made quite an impression on her:

> To us who have never been on a liner before, her size was almost terrifying, especially when I looked over A deck after night had fallen and noticed her height from the water. We waited for a long time at the bottom of the ship's main staircase while berths were being appointed; after all the staff was settled we got ours – inner cabins without portholes as we were only passengers. We were however lucky to get a cabin at all as most of the people who came next day had to go into wards.

◄ The *Britannic* at Mudros.

⬆ Deck cricket on the promenade deck.

▲ The only known internal image of one of the *Britannic*'s first-class staircases.

The following morning Vera took the opportunity to explore the lower wards on the ship, although the sight of the swinging iron cots and the stuffiness of the lower decks only added to her relief at not being permanently posted to a hospital ship. The afternoon was spent attending a church service and writing a last letter home before the ship departed, but at 5.40pm the *Britannic*, shadowed at first by destroyers and several seaplanes, headed out into the Channel.

By the following morning the ship was headed into a particularly stormy Bay of Biscay, and the landlubbers of the medical staff experienced their first taste of seasickness. Even when the ship was in the Mediterranean Vera recalled it being an uncomfortable passage, including a thunderstorm which, if anything, seemed even worse than the Biscay crossing, but the morning of Friday 29 September found the *Britannic* entering a relatively calm, if overcast and wet, Bay of Naples. There followed two days of bunkering, allowing the passen-

▲ Rev. John Fleming on the boat deck. Note the life rafts stowed on the raised lounge roof.

gers time to experience the customary delights of the Italian port for themselves, but with the coaling complete by the Sunday afternoon, the *Britannic* was once again headed for Lemnos, where she would arrive two days later.

Although it had been nine months since the *Britannic*'s last visit to Mudros, the level of activity seemed unchanged. Almost immediately the hospital ship *Galeka* was alongside, as the first patients were embarked, but it would not be until 9.00pm that the transfer was completed, at which point it was time for the nurses to be transhipped. If Vera felt that parts of the *Britannic* were cramped and stuffy, then the conditions inside the 440-foot *Galeka* would come as an even greater shock; ahead of her lay a four-day voyage to Malta in a cramped ward, during which she and 16 nurses would contract a mysterious on-board virus.

By 5 October the *Britannic* was once again headed for home on an otherwise routine voyage, which was sadly interrupted after only a few short hours by the death of Corporal Joseph Seddon of the 1st Battalion Manchester Regiment. With the ship still six days from her destination, the established procedure was to bury the body at sea, and a service was held on the stern at 10.30pm as the ship was passing south of Cape Matapan. The remainder of the voyage would be uneventful, and the *Britannic* would arrive safely at Southampton on 11 October, having quickly re-established herself on the Southampton-to-Mudros run.

Without anyone realising it, however, the first clouds to cast a shadow over the ship's reputation were already lurking on the horizon. It had all begun innocently enough when, on 13 October 1916, the Transport Division had made the seemingly innocuous request to the Admiralty for the *Britannic* to transport additional medical personnel and stores to Mudros on her next trip. Three days later the request was duly approved, with the proviso that in future the only medical personnel permitted to travel to their destinations in a hospital ship would be nurses, but in view of the *Britannic*'s imminent scheduled departure, on this occasion the orders were confirmed. Over the next two days the *Britannic* subsequently took on 2,762 packages of medical stores and 168 tons of other stores destined for Egypt, Malta, Salonika, Mesopotamia and India; in addition to the ship's medical staff, also on board would be another 484 medical personnel, destined for various theatres of war.

▲ The *Britannic*'s upper decks and superstructure towering above the boat deck of the hospital ship *Guildford Castle*.

The departure at 4.30pm on 20 October would be a particularly noisy one, with rousing renditions of 'Keep the Home Fires Burning' and 'Best Luck Go With You' from troops on nearby transports serenading the ship as she headed south towards the Solent, before arriving safely at Naples on 25 October. As ever, some of the medical staff were issued with the much-sought-after shore passes, but their attempts to charter a train to visit Pompeii went completely awry, with the train eventually leaving at 3.15pm and taking the better part of two hours for a journey that normally took only 45 minutes! Even with their visit massively curtailed it would be well past 6.00pm before they were back on board, by which time their passes had expired and dinner was finished. The captain was wary about allowing the medical staff onshore again for that particular trip, so the next day everyone remained on board as the bunkers were replenished with some 3,000 tons of coal, and shortly before 5.00pm the *Britannic* was headed out into the Tyrrhenian Sea.

THE FOG OF WAR

Once again the ship made it safely to Mudros, arriving just after breakfast on the morning of 28 October. Up to this point the voyage had gone without a hitch, but the arrival alongside of the hospital ship *Wandilla* would change everything. Among the patients was a 24-year-old Austrian national named Adalbert Franz Messany. Messany, an opera singer by profession, had been detained at Luxor in Egypt immediately on the outbreak of the war. At the end of the year he had been transferred to Malta, where he would remain for the next 22 months, but when he developed a severe case of tuberculosis the Allied authorities had decided that he was eligible for repatriation. In itself this was not difficult to arrange via the established diplomatic channels in Holland, and with hospital ships required to provide relief and assistance to the sick and wounded of any nationality, transporting Messany back to England aboard the *Britannic* would have been quite appropriate.

Over the next 48 hours the *Britannic* took on a total of 3,022 invalids from a procession of hospital ships, but as the men came aboard, the unsupervised Messany was able to observe the procedures, particularly noticing the khaki-clad troops of the RAMC, who looked practically identical to combat troops, and numerous packages being transferred from the *Britannic* to the smaller hospital ships. Shortly after midday on 30 October the *Britannic* was once again bound non-stop for Southampton, but while Messany had at first been confined in the ship's mortuary, the death of Corporal George Firth Hunt of the RAMC on 2 November meant that he had to be transferred to one of the wards to allow for storage of the body. He would remain there for the rest of the voyage and, amazingly, would be only minimally supervised. Messany seemed to be free to roam around much of the ship, where he was quick to notice that many of the officers had been permitted to retain their side arms, while unguarded conversations with a number of the patients, in particular Private Harold Hickman of the Welsh Hussars and Private Reginald Taplay, would cause further problems. Finally, when the *Britannic* arrived safely back at Southampton on 6 November, Messany continued to observe the repatriated soldiers going ashore, by now no longer in their hospital suits and back in uniform, as well as many of them marching away from the ship in military formation.

Messany's repatriation to Austria was confirmed at the end of December, and by 5 January 1917 he was back in Vienna where, given that he had been in Allied hands for almost two and a half years, the Austrian authorities were understandably eager to debrief him. As Messany spoke of his journey home, the uniformed medical orderlies he had observed being transhipped at Mudros suddenly took on the aspect of potential combatant soldiers, while the Austrian authorities also became equally suspicious of the unidentified stores that he had seen being carried in the ship's hold. Perhaps most damaging of all was Messany's interpretation of his chats with Private Taplay and Private Hickman, who he alleged were not ill and had claimed to be translators being transferred to France. With his additional references to uniformed soldiers being ordered to stay below decks while being on different rations, as far as the Austrians were concerned there was a persuasive *prima facie* case to suggest that all on board the *Britannic* was not as it was supposed to be.

From the propaganda standpoint, Messany's statement was political dynamite, so perhaps it is no coincidence that just prior to their reintroduction of unrestricted submarine warfare, the German authorities included Messany's observations in a document published on 29 January 1917, listing 22 alleged cases of Allied abuses in the use and operation of hospital ships. By 1 February the German submarines were once again targeting all shipping in the war zone without warning, as the unrestricted U-boat campaign for which the German High Command had been arguing for so long finally stepped up a gear.

In the overall scheme of things, Messany's observations were probably of little substance, but the British authorities were nevertheless determined to lay to rest what they considered to be damaging and scurrilous charges regarding their operation of hospital ships. Perhaps the most concerning charge of all alluded to the reference to 2,000 troops being ordered to remain below decks and out of sight, yet it also proved to be the easiest to refute. Of the 3,022 invalids embarked at Mudros, the records confirmed that only 367 of the men were actually classified as what was known as 'cot cases'. Regarding their rations, the cot cases may well have been on different rations to the walking wounded, the reality being that every patient's diet was regulated where necessary, as per the instructions contained on their medical cards. Nor was there any truth in the allegation that patients were not allowed

on deck in their uniforms, as each man was issued with a blue hospital suit as soon as he went on board the *Britannic*. As long as they followed the instructions of the medical staff, every patient had the absolute freedom to use their allocated area of the open deck as they wished.

The small matter of the officers retaining their pistols was a little more tricky to explain. According to regulations, the only personnel permitted to carry side arms on any hospital ship were the military police. No other weapons were permitted on board, although one concession seems to have been that if the pistol in question was the personal property of an officer, rather than one issued by the government, then they would be allowed to retain it. During the earlier stages of the war these side arms had actually been secured in a separate location of the ship, to be returned to their owner when back at Southampton, but nine months on, the procedure seems to have become rather more lax. Although the Admiralty continued to maintain that the conveyance of weapons belonging to wounded officers was not considered to be a breach of the rules, the future practice, perhaps tellingly, was also 'under consideration'.

As for Private Hickman and Private Taplay, they were anything but translators being transferred to France. Upon his return to England, Hickman had been sent to a hospital near Nottingham, where he would be treated for malaria before being discharged to sick

▲ The enclosed promenades on A Deck served as the officers' wards.

furlough on 19 December. Private Taplay, on the other hand, was suffering from dysentery and had been sent to the Second Western General Hospital in Manchester, where he would remain until 7 March 1917. Both men were subsequently interviewed in order to counter the German claims, but while they both recalled having spoken with Messany, not surprisingly each had a somewhat different recollection of what was actually said. Both men denied ever having claimed to be translators, with perhaps the only explanatory factor being that they both had an 'L' patch sewn onto their tunic sleeves, which was a common enough identification in Salonika for any soldier who could speak a foreign language.

As far as the British were concerned, the German allegations had been effectively seen off, but more important events were already unfolding in the Mediterranean. On the morning of 28 October 1916, the day on which the *Britannic* had made her last arrival at Mudros, 160 miles to the south-west the German submarine *U73* was lurking beneath the dark blue waters of the Kea Channel. Once again under the command of Kapitänleutnant Gustav Siess, on this particular mission the German submarine had been tasked with laying mines in areas that would obstruct the movement of any Allied naval or military vessels in the Aegean. The previous day Siess had chosen to lay his first barrage of 12 mines off the Greek island of Phleva, in the Saronic Gulf, and now, with his awareness of the volume of traffic passing through the Petali Gulf, the island of Kea was very much in his sights. Siess's war diary confirms that he was certainly aware of the presence of hospital ships in the Kea Channel – in fact, he had abandoned at least one torpedo attack on an unidentified approaching steamer when he saw the red crosses painted on its side – but this did not deter him from laying two mine barrages off Port St Nikolo between 8.07 and 8.27 that morning. He remained in the area for the next six hours to observe the effects of his handiwork, but by early afternoon the volume of traffic passing through the Kea Channel had thinned out enough for Siess to consider moving on, confident that before long one of his mines would claim a suitably large victim. Fortunately, on this occasion the *Britannic*'s southerly passage through the channel some 30 hours later would prove uneventful, and the ship would arrive safely back at Southampton on 6 November, having navigated a particularly stormy English Channel in the final stages of the voyage.

The stormy weather, however, had apparently taken a greater toll on the *Aquitania*, meaning that the *Britannic*'s last stay at her home terminal would be reduced to only six days. Sure enough, at 2.23pm on Sunday 12 November the *Britannic* was once again outward bound for Mudros, arriving at Naples five days later to take on coal and water as usual. The

▶ A stormy departure day at Naples. (Jonathan Mitchell)

plan had been to depart from Naples the following morning, but throughout the day the weather became increasingly stormy, to the point where the prospect of manoeuvring a ship the size of the *Britannic* through the narrow harbour entrance became impractical without risking possible damage to the ship. Rev. John Fleming, the *Britannic*'s Presbyterian chaplain, later recalled just how hazardous the situation had been:

> We had hoped to leave the following morning, but during the night a great storm broke, with much damage to the shipping, and we were held fast prisoners. All the anchors were out, weighing together 37 tons, and in addition twenty great hawsers fixed the hinder part of the vessel to the quay; yet so violent was the storm that the vessel was in danger.

By Sunday afternoon the weather had finally cleared just enough for the *Britannic* to slip past the Molo San Vincenzo and out into the open sea. Ahead lay her now established terminal on the island of Lemnos, where Captain Bartlett fully expected to arrive safely two days later, unaware that closer to their current location, less than 800 miles away, his ship would have a historic rendezvous with destiny.

JOURNEY'S END

At 7.52am, on the morning of Tuesday 21 November 1916, the *Britannic* was four miles south of Angalistros Point on the island of Makronisos. This long, finger-like island marked the northern extremity of the Kea Channel, while ten miles to the south-east the larger island of Kea marked its southern boundary. Setting the established course of N48°E (magnetic) to pass through the channel, up on the bridge Chief Officer Robert Hume and Fourth Officer Duncan McTavish maintained the watch. Back in the wheelhouse, James Vickers, a 15-year-old boy scout who was acting as one of the messengers, found himself thinking about breakfast – indeed, most of the nurses were already in the lounge sitting down to theirs, which, for Nurse Ada Garland, was the pear compote. Sheila Macbeth, on the other hand, had opted for the porridge. Both had been late for breakfast that morning, but there were others who were even more tardy. Rev. John Fleming was still in his cabin, staring at the town of Ioulis, perched precariously high up in the hills of the island of Kea, while in Barrack Room 2, down on G deck, Private Percy Tyler of the RAMC was stretched out on his bunk, polishing his tunic buttons before the morning parade.

The apparent calm was shattered at 8.12am, when John Fleming heard a noise sounding 'as if a score of plate-glass windows had been smashed together'. To Ada Garland it was more of a 'loud report which seemed as if something ran against the side of the ship', while Sheila Macbeth referred simply to a loud bang. Nearly everyone remembered how the ship began to shudder immediately after the initial explosion, but after that, people's memories differed. Ada Garland and Sheila Macbeth both remembered everyone standing up immediately after the explosion, Ada recalling a loud clatter of falling plates and glasses, with the stewards ready to dash out of the room before suddenly coming to their senses and telling everyone to sit down as they had only run into a barge. Sheila, on the other hand, remembered things differently, with Major Harold Priestley of the RAMC calmly telling the nurses to sit down again as the siren had not sounded, so that they continued to eat their breakfast in 'a most unnatural silence'. Stewardess Violet Jessop, no stranger herself to disaster at sea after escaping from the sinking *Titanic*, recalled a dull, deafening roar, after which the ship gave a long drawn-out shudder, shaking the crockery on the tables and in the pantry where she was working just violently enough to smash a few plates and glasses as they fell to the floor.

Elsewhere in the ship people recalled different sensations. Private Percy Tyler, industriously polishing his buttons down on G deck, wrote of a violent bump, which sent him forward a few paces and back again before the ship began to shudder, while 15-year-old boy scout George Perman, working one of the aft lifts, did not recall hearing the actual explosion. In fact, his first inkling that something was wrong was the subsequent extended violent shudder running throughout the ship.

Higher up and much closer to the bridge, things were a lot more perceptible. Fifth Officer Gordon Fielding, barely ten metres aft from the point of the explosion, was still in his cabin shaving when, he recalled, 'I was thrown very forcibly across the cabin with sundry articles of gear on top of me. The boat lifted twice, and everything seemed to dance, and the fumes from the explosions temporarily blinded me.' Seaman Archie Jewell, another *Titanic* survivor, was closer still, having himself just gone on duty in the area of the explosion; he noticed not only how the ship shook all over, but also the sight of the water rushing in and the 'smell of powder'. Private John Cuthbertson was so close that he was actually swept away by the massive inrush of water into the forward barrack room on G deck, before finding himself washed up a broken staircase two decks up, while down in Stokehold no. 11, Bert Smith, a stoker, felt the full force of a massive explosion just in front of the boiler

◀ Angalistros Point on the island of Makronisos; *Britannic*'s final landmark before entering the Kea Channel.

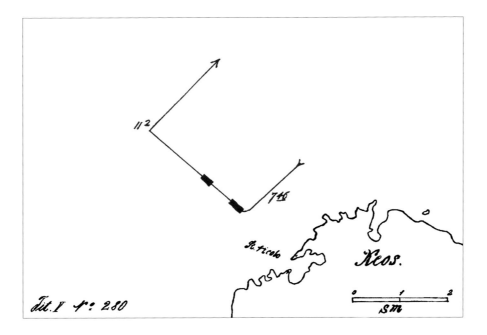

room where he was on duty. Staggering back into the forward firemen's tunnel, through which he had passed only moments before to go on duty, he was suddenly deluged by the full weight of inrushing water, which swept him back towards the boilers, before somehow grabbing hold of the walkway handrail and holding on just long enough to make it to the emergency staircase in the vestibule.

Oblivious to the drama unfolding on the lower decks, the nurses continued to quietly eat their breakfast, but the suppressed calm could not last long. Moments later, although no one can recall exactly how long, the alarm began to sound, at which point Ada Garland described hearing the order, 'Ladies go to your cabins put on your life-belts and go up to the boat deck!' Violet Jessop went into a little more detail:

> As one man, the whole saloon rose from their seats. Doctors and nurses vanished to their posts in a trice. The pantry where I stood, holding a teapot in one hand and a pat of butter in the other, was cleared too, as men dropped what they were doing

◀ An illustration by artist William Barney showing how the *U73*'s mines were set particularly deep in order to bag a larger vessel.

▲ *U73*'s plan of the two Kea Channel mine barriers laid on 28 October 1916. (Titanic Historical Society)

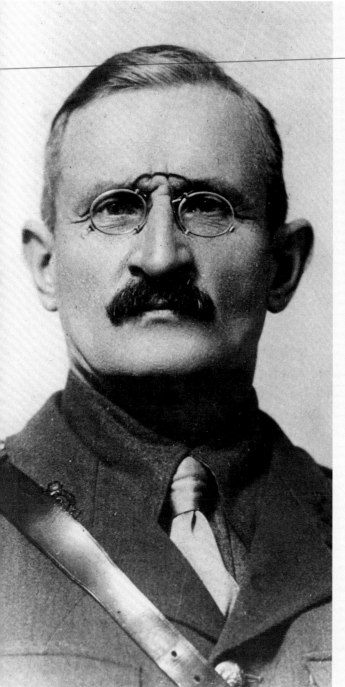

LIEUTENANT JOHN CROPPER

Lieutenant John Cropper was born in Yorkshire in 1864 and was educated at Charterhouse school. After working as a medical student at Bart's Hospital, London, he obtained his medical degree at Cambridge University in 1891, specialising in ophthalmic surgery. He would later work with the Church Missionary Society in Turkey, Palestine, the Sudan and Uganda, becoming a Fellow of the Society of Tropical Medicine and Honorary Surgeon and Assistant County Commissioner of the Monmouthshire Red Cross Society.

In 1895 Cropper married Annie Walker, daughter of Thomas Walker, the civil engineer who built the Severn Tunnel. When not working Cropper was an acknowledged artist, at one time receiving a Royal Academy Medal, as well as a keen motorist, owning one of the first cars in Monmouthshire and winning first prize in the 1909 Tortoise Race at the home of Charles Rolls, co-founder of the Rolls-Royce company. That same year he also patented an improved handheld vulcanising device for repairing rubber tyres by dry heat.

In 1914 Cropper volunteered for the RAMC, serving with the BEF in France, while in 1915 his wife oversaw their hospital for the wounded at Sudbrook. Cropper would serve two terms aboard the *Britannic*, being first appointed to the ship in December 1915. Posted back to the *Britannic* for her second tour of duty, on 11 October 1916 he renewed his contract with the RAMC for a further year, but on the day of the sinking, having given his lifejacket to another man, he would be one of the unfortunate occupants of the two lifeboats destroyed by the ship's port propeller. John Cropper's body was never recovered, and his name is commemorated on the Mikra Memorial at Thessaloniki.

and jumped over presses with the agility of deer. In seconds, not a soul was to be seen and not a sound had been uttered.

Up on the bridge the situation was confused to say the least. On the *Titanic*, Captain Smith had had the benefit of a much slower rate of flooding, along with the invaluable advice of designer Thomas Andrews to help him formulate a plan of action. Captain Bartlett had no such luxury. Rushing to the bridge, he immediately gave orders for the ship's engines to be stopped and for the watertight doors to be closed. Gradually the damage reports began to find their way to the bridge, confirming that the explosion had occurred in the vicinity of the bulkhead between Holds 2 and 3. In itself, the scale of the damage ought to have been well within the *Britannic*'s margin of safety, but unfortunately the firemen's tunnel had been seriously damaged in the blast, and the watertight doors at either end of the vestibule leading into the forward boiler room had failed to close. To further complicate matters, the watertight door between Boiler Rooms 6 and 5 had also failed to close, resulting in five – possibly six – watertight compartments open to the sea. With the water level in the two boiler rooms deep enough for them to have to be evacuated within a couple of minutes of the initial blast, the immediate situation was much worse than that faced on the *Titanic*.

Immediately after the explosion, the *Britannic*'s course had fallen off a couple of points before she came to a dead stop, as the ship swung around to a northerly heading. However, Captain Bartlett's order to make for the nearby island of Kea, in an attempt to beach the ship, was easier said than done. For reasons unknown, the steering gear had failed, meaning that it was only possible to turn the ship by using the propellers, but before long the *Britannic* had assumed a southerly heading as the ship slowly began to move towards the apparent safety of the island of Kea. It being only three miles distant, this probably seemed like an attainable goal, but even so, Captain Bartlett had still ordered the standard call for assistance to be sent, signalling 'SOS. Have struck mine off Port Nikola'.

And so the exodus began, as the nurses returned to their cabins to gather what few items they could carry. For Ada Garland it was her coat, rug and lifebelt, while for Sheila Macbeth it was an eiderdown, a pillow, a lifejacket and her Gieve inflatable waistcoat. Violet Jessop, after having helped a nurse who had been lying ill in her cabin, returned to gather her coat, a ring, a clock and even a bread roll from the breakfast table; recalling how much she had missed having a toothbrush on the *Carpathia* after the *Titanic* had gone down, she also made absolutely sure that this time she would not make the same mistake.

In spite of the urgency there was no sense of panic among the medical sisters, and Violet clearly recalled a sense of subdued composure:

There was a hubbub of conversation on the decks below. Doors stood ajar, revealing sisters and nurses hurriedly collecting belongings and little treasures, commenting with relief at the fortunate absence of wounded on board, while they tried hard to smother their feelings of concern at Matron's command for haste.

Elsewhere on the ship there were other cases of British sangfroid displayed by many of the troops on board. Down in Barrack Room No. 2, Private Percy Tyler had quietly resumed the task of polishing his buttons without any undue concern, and he remained there for a full five minutes before someone rushed in to say that the captain had sounded the alarm, at which point he threw on his lifejacket and looked for as many spare belts as he could carry before heading up to the boat deck. Fifteen-year-old scout George Perman immediately ceased operating his lift and headed for the boat deck, while Henry Pope, another scout, headed for his station in the purser's office down on C deck. In spite of Pope's youth, Purser Claude Lancaster would always remember his cheerful words: 'It's been a big explosion, sir, but I don't think it will do us much harm.'

How little he knew! The damage caused by the explosion was wreaking havoc in the forward part of the ship. Down in Boiler Rooms 6 and 5 the deluge of water was so great that after barely two minutes it was impossible for the firemen to continue to work, while higher up in the focsle one man came rushing out of a cabin door in a blind panic, running straight into Archie Jewell, striking him accidentally over the eye and cutting his head open.

CAPTAIN HARRY DYKE

Born in Liverpool in 1869, Dyke's first position with the White Star Line was on the SS *Bovic* in 1900. By March 1913 he had risen to the position of assistant captain aboard the *Olympic*, before assuming that role aboard the *Britannic* on 20 December 1915. Dyke would remain in the ship for both tours of duty, and was responsible for operating the aft starboard girder davits on the day of the sinking. The *Britannic* would be his last seagoing position, leaving the White Star Line shortly afterwards.

Although he had blood all over his face, it was only when Jewell was up on deck that someone thought to bandage up the wound, so that he recalled being 'like old Nelson only one eye!'

Fortunately, up on the boat deck there was still a semblance of order. On the starboard side, Captain Harry Dyke, *Britannic*'s assistant commander, was busily arranging the loading of the lifeboats under the aft girder davits, while Sixth Officer Herbert Welsh, who had been on board for less than two weeks, was looking after the lifeboats under the Welin davits along the middle section of the boat deck. On the port side, Fifth Officer Gordon Fielding had assumed responsibility for the two sets of aft girder davits, with Third Officer Francis Laws taking care of the Welin davits on that side of the ship. Up to this point Captain Bartlett's order had simply been to load and lower the lifeboats, but as long as the *Britannic* was still moving forward there could be no question of releasing them into the water. It was not long before Mrs Elizabeth Dowse, the ship's matron, had ensured that every one of her nurses had been accounted for, but even after they had been placed safely in their lifeboats by Captain Dyke, Sheila Macbeth later recalled in her diary:

> We were kept hanging over the side for a long while… We did not realise that while we were hanging over the side of the ship, the whole of the fore part of her was under water – we might have been more frightened if we had seen it.

Meanwhile, the RAMC orderlies remained calmly in the enclosed aft promenade deck, their designated parade ground, before being taken up to the boats in groups of 50. Even so, there were still one or two signs that discipline was not being maintained on all parts of the ship, as Captain Dyke, leaving the nurses in their boat literally hanging over the side of the ship, had to use his megaphone to call back a group of firemen who had already taken one of the boats located on the poop deck, ordering them to pick up any swimmers already in the water.

As the *Britannic* continued to move slowly forward, Lieutenant Colonel Henry Anderson later recalled that the ship seemed to be moving in a wide circle to the right. Whether this indicated that the ship was still experiencing steering problems is uncertain, but in view of the deteriorating situation, Captain Bartlett was concluding that the time had come to stop the engines and release the boats. According to the journal of Fifth Officer Fielding, the order to abandon ship finally came at about 8.35am, but somehow during the crucial minutes leading up to the accident the chain of command broke down:

8:30am: Two of the boats in charge of the third officer were lowered into the water (without his knowledge, with the use of the automatic releasing gear) as these boats (heavily laden) must have dropped some six feet into the water, they must have been stove in and were helpless so far as controlling them was concerned. The strong set of the tide carried them direct to the *Britannic*'s propellers. These two boats were smashed up by the propellers, and the people in them badly mutilated and many killed.

▲ A dramatic image painted by artist Ken Marschall in 1997, showing the *Britannic* sinking barely three miles from the safety of Kea. When researching this project the distant headland was photographed in particular detail to ensure that the image was as historically accurate as possible. (Painting © Ken Marschall)

VIOLET CONSTANCE JESSOP

One of the best-known White Star Line personalities, **Violet Constance Jessop** was born in Argentina on 2 October 1887. Her first position as a stewardess was for the Royal Mail Line aboard the SS *Orinoco* in 1908, before she joined the White Star Line two years later. On 14 June 1911 she was posted to the *Olympic*, and was aboard when the ship collided in the Solent with the armoured cruiser HMS *Hawke* on 20 September 1911. Seven months later she would survive the sinking of the *Titanic*, after which she would return to sea until the outbreak of war, when she became a VAD nurse. A poisoned hand forced her to leave the nursing service and return to the sea, and on 12 November 1916 she was posted to the *Britannic* for her one and only voyage, ending in the Kea Channel only nine days later.

After her traumatic escape Violet would spend the next four years ashore, working for the London branch of the Banco Español del Rio de la Plata, but she would return to the *Olympic* in June 1920 and later transfer to the new *Majestic*. Leaving the White Star Line at the end of 1925, Violet would continue at sea with the Red Star Line between 1926 and 1934, before returning to the Royal Mail Line until the outbreak of the Second World War. After five years in the censor's office vetting the Spanish mail, she returned to the Royal Mail Line in 1948 for her last two years at sea aboard the *Andes*, retiring at the end of 1950 to the village of Great Ashfield in Suffolk. She died on 5 May 1971, and is buried in the churchyard of All Saints, Hartest. (Margaret Meehan)

A stewardess in one of these boats was carried completely round the propellers, and beyond a few bruises and the clothing almost torn off her, she was not injured. This same woman was one of the *Titanic* survivors and stated her present experiences were much worse than those of the *Titanic*, and I could well believe her. The men in my boats saw this disaster, and I might say they ceased cursing about not being released.

That stewardess was Violet Jessop, although her account differed somewhat to Fielding's. In her memoirs she recalled being told as she arrived on the boat deck that the boats with the nurses had gone; she could also see other boats pulling away from the ship, even though the *Britannic* was still moving. Her lifeboat – number four – was quickly filled, but it was only as the boat began to be lowered that she became aware of the increasing list to starboard:

…our lifeboat, hooking itself on an open porthole, whose circular, brass-rimmed glass jutted out, tilted us considerably; then, righting itself, started gliding down rapidly, scraping the ship's sides, splintering the glass in our faces from the boxes, which formed, when lighted, the green lighted band around a hospital ship's middle, and making a terrible impact as we landed on the water.

EDWARD IRELAND

Edward Ireland was a 16-year-old scout from Liverpool. For his bravery displayed at the sinking of the *Britannic* he was later awarded the Scout's Cornwell Badge for Courage. Ireland later became a 2nd Lieutenant in the RAF and was killed, aged only 19, on Thursday 31 July 1919. His flight from Cranwell aerodrome to Liverpool should have been routine, but while taking off against a slight headwind the Bristol aircraft side-slipped and crashed to the ground, killing both Ireland and the pilot, Lieutenant William Roberts. Edward Ireland is buried in Toxteth Park Cemetery, Liverpool.

As if the bumpy journey down the side of the ship wasn't bad enough, things were about to get a whole lot worse for the occupants of lifeboat number four. Glancing back along the ship's side, Violet could not fail to notice the ship's port propeller, which by now was breaking the surface. As the *Britannic* continued to move forward, try as they might to get clear, the lifeboat's occupants could only stare helplessly as the huge propeller, 23 feet in diameter, drew closer and closer. Finally they could wait no longer. Violet continued:

> Not a word, not a shout was heard, just hundreds of men fleeing into the sea as if from an enemy in pursuit. It was extraordinary to find myself in the space of a few minutes almost the only occupant of the boat; I say almost, for one man, a doctor, was still standing in silence beside me. I turned around to see the reason for this exodus and, to my horror, saw *Britannic*'s huge propellers churning and mincing up everything near them – men, boats and everything were just one ghastly whirl.

In spite of all her years at sea Violet had never actually learned to swim, but she knew that she either had to take the plunge or suffer the same fate. As she leapt overboard, the weight of her coat began to drag her down for what seemed like an eternity, before she began to rise. Suddenly she felt something very solid strike her on the back of her head as she reached out instinctively to free herself from her predicament:

> I touched something – an arm – that moved as mine moved! My fingers gripped it like a vice, but only for a second, until my almost senseless head remembered what is said of the people drowning, that they retain their hold after death, bringing death to another. With that cheering thought, I let go.

When Violet finally came back to the surface, her first sight was the brains of one unfortunate medical orderly trickling onto his khaki tunic, his head completely split open. Young George Perman had a bird's-eye view of the entire tragedy, having also been in the lifeboat before managing somehow to grab hold of a dangling rope, which may well have saved his life. As the propellers did their gruesome work, George recalled seeing red blood being splattered along the ship's white side, while the sight of dead bodies, severed limbs and the cries of the wounded would never be forgotten. But for Captain Bartlett's timely order up on the bridge, a third lifeboat would have suffered a similar fate, but fortunately the propellers were stopped just in time, allowing Captain Thomas Fearnhead and the few remaining occupants of that boat just enough time to push against the now motionless propeller blades and get clear of the ship.

The timing of the order to stop the ship bordered on the miraculous, as at this stage Captain Bartlett had no idea that any boats had been sent away. It was actually because the forward boiler rooms were by that time so full of water that he made the decision to send the boats away, but with the ship now motionless, a few of the closer lifeboats could give

MAJOR HAROLD EDGAR PRIESTLEY

Born in London on 24 January 1879, Priestley was commissioned in the RAMC in July 1905, going on to serve in the UK and Gibraltar. At the outbreak of war he was assigned to 6th Field Ambulance, leaving for France on 18 August 1914, before being captured only nine days later during the retreat from Mons. In spite of his protected status as a medical officer, Priestley was detained at Halle before being transferred in February 1915 to Wittenberg prisoner-of-war camp in Saxony, where typhus was rampant. Many of the British medical personnel also succumbed to the disease, while the Germans declined to enter the camp, instead passing in food and supplies via a chute. Thanks to the efforts of Priestley and the British medical officers, by mid-1915 the situation had improved considerably and efforts to have him repatriated, by then seriously ill with pleurisy, were taken up by the British Red Cross and the neutral American government. Priestley was eventually repatriated via Holland on 23 February 1916, remaining on extended sick leave until 2 November, when he was posted to the *Britannic*.

After the loss of the *Britannic*, in January 1917 Priestley was posted to the hospital ship *Egypt*, before serving as medical officer in charge of inbound troops Western Approaches at Bristol. In 1922 he was posted to Singapore Military Hospital, returning home in May 1926, before a final foreign posting to the Ram Hospital in Lahore, India. He retired due to ill health in August 1932, dying on 16 March 1941 from pulmonary and renal tuberculosis.

what assistance they could to the injured, as the nurses helped to fish them out of the water, before tearing up their aprons and pillowcases for use as bandages and slings.

THE LAST MINUTES

By 8.35am the *Britannic* was finally stationary and the evacuation could begin in earnest. Fifth Officer Fielding quickly sent away his first three boats, in spite of his forward set of davits becoming inoperable, and was in the process of loading *Britannic*'s port motor launch when First Officer George Oliver and Colonel Anderson arrived, having been ordered to coordinate the rescue of any swimmers in the water. Ten minutes later Fielding lowered what would be his final lifeboat before the starboard list made any further working of the davits on the higher port side of the ship impractical, at which point he moved forward to the middle of the boat deck to assist Major Priestley's party in throwing life rafts and deck-chairs over the lower starboard side.

ROBERT FLEMING

Robert Fleming was born in Ireland, joining the White Star Line in July 1881, being appointed 6th Engineer of the first *Britannic*. His first appointment as chief engineer was to the SS *Bovic*, assuming that position aboard the *Olympic* in 1911. Appointed to the *Britannic* in November 1915, Fleming served two tours of duty aboard the ship. According to rumours among the survivors at Athens, Fleming allegedly kept the engineers at their posts courtesy of his pistol. He was one of the last to leave the ship, walking off the starboard bridge wing just before Captain Bartlett. Following the loss of the *Britannic*, Fleming was posted to the 32,234-ton *Justicia*, which was torpedoed off Malin Head, Ireland, on 20 July 1917. *Justicia* would be Fleming's last ship and he would retire at the end of that year. He died in 1925.

▲ Anton Logvynenko's interesting underwater view of how the *Britannic*'s bow would have made contact with the seabed while the stern was still above the surface.

Despite the rapidly deteriorating conditions, even at this late stage it seemed as if the *Britannic* might still be saved. After the engines had stopped the ship appeared to be settling more slowly in the water, so that at 8.45am Captain Bartlett restarted the engines in the hope that he could reach the tantalisingly close shoreline. Once again the *Britannic* began to move forward, but as the bow was pushed deeper into the water by the forward momentum, reports began to arrive on the bridge that the water had risen to the level of D deck. On hearing that news, Bartlett could only resign himself to the inevitable, finally giving the order for those still working below to come up on deck.

The final moments of the *Britannic*'s fleeting life were almost entirely concentrated on the lower starboard side of the boat deck, as the davits continued to work virtually to the end. Percy Tyler left the ship in the third-to-last boat, supposedly designed for 60 people but actually holding 80, while Rev. Fleming made it away in the penultimate boat at 8.55am. Although there was still room, Major Priestley turned down his place in order to make one last search for any men still left behind, while Fielding and Welsh prepared the next boat for lowering. Priestley returned just in time to take his place, and at 9.00am the final lifeboat, containing Purser Claude Lancaster, who not only carried the ship's papers but also, according to legend, a spare uniform, was ready for launching. Even then, however, Priestley would only step into the boat after the last of the eight men in his party was aboard. No sooner had they touched the surface than Fielding and the two brakemen slid the remaining short distance down the falls, dropping into the boat and moving away from the listing ship before it toppled over onto them altogether.

Even at this late stage a few stragglers remained on board, as Captain Bartlett ordered the remaining bridge personnel, including two scouts, to swim for it, at the same time signalling for the remaining engine room personnel to come up on deck with a final series of long blasts sounded from the ship's whistle. By now safely clear, Fifth Officer Fielding was still close enough to see the ship's stern towering some 150 feet into the air, and to see Captain Bartlett, Assistant Commander Dyke and Chief Engineer Robert Fleming still standing near the bridge. One at a time they calmly walked along the bridge wing and into the rising water; following the tradition of the sea, Captain Bartlett was the last of them to leave the ship.

Still the *Britannic* was not quite finished, as slowly the hull began to settle back before finally completing its roll to starboard. One by one the huge funnels crumpled at the base and fell into the sea, while Violet Jessop, still struggling in the water, had time for one last unforgettable view of another sinking Olympic-class liner. As the *Britannic* made her final plunge, the last thing she remembered was 'the noise of her going resounding through the water with undreamt-of violence'.

The Last Voyage of His Majesty's Hospital Ship "BRITANNIC"

By
Rev. John A. Fleming, M.A., C.F.
United Free Church, Stepps, Glasgow

Rev. Fleming's recollections of the *Britannic*'s last moments were no less dramatic:

> Gradually the waters licked up and up the decks – the furnaces belching forth fierce volumes of smoke, as if the great engines were in their last death agony; one by one the monster funnels melted away as wax before a flame, and crashed upon the decks, till the waters rushed down; then report after report rang over the sea, telling of the explosion of the boilers. The waters moved over the deck still, the bows of the ship dipping deeper and deeper into the sea, until the rudders stood straight up from the surface of the water, and, poised thus for a few moments, dived perpendicularly into the depths, leaving hardly a ripple behind.

By 9.07am it was all over, the only remaining sign that the *Britannic* had ever existed being patches of smoke, the scattered lifeboats and drifting wreckage in the Kea Channel. In less than one hour a single German mine had sent Great Britain's largest and finest ship to her premature watery grave.

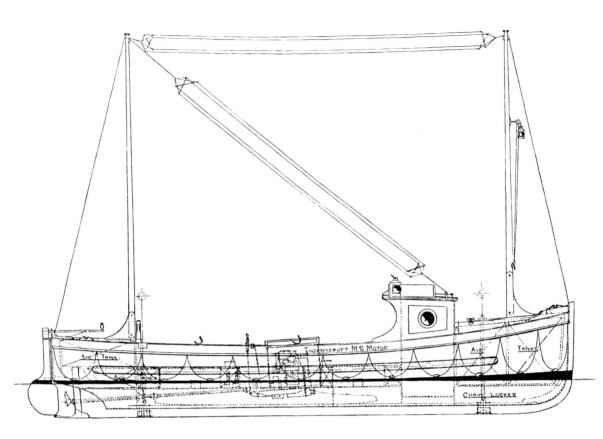

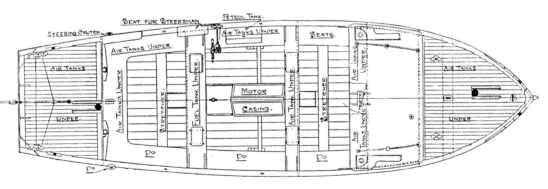

◀ The cover of the short booklet written by Rev. John Fleming. Originally published by Marshall Brothers in 1917, it is the only record of the sinking published at that time.

▲ The *Britannic*'s two Thornycroft motor launches would prove invaluable in rescuing swimmers from the water, before transferring the nurses to Port St. Nikolo on the nearby island of Kea to arrange for the treatment of the more seriously wounded.

AFTERMATH

As the *Britannic's* stern slipped beneath the tranquil waters of the Kea Channel, the survivors may not have realised it at the time, but they probably had much for which to be grateful. When the *Titanic* had gone down four and a half years earlier the ship had been hundreds of miles out to sea, on a dark and bitterly cold night. Many of those who survived the sinking process but who then found themselves in the water more likely died from exposure in the ice-cold water than from drowning, while those in the life-boats still had to endure an anxious wait of nearly two hours in the increasingly choppy Atlantic waters before the first of them could be rescued. The *Britannic*, on the other hand, had sunk in broad daylight, in the calm, warm waters of the Aegean and in clear sight of land. In that the Kea Channel was also a busy shipping lane, it was only a matter of time before the first rescue vessels had arrived on the scene.

In fact the *Britannic*'s initial call for assistance had been received almost immediately, although the specifics of the location, according to the report of the commanding officer of the HMS *Scourge*, had been less than ideal, simply stating that the ship had struck a mine off 'Port Nikola'. The position given was not necessarily incorrect, but the imprecise detail had created some confusion as there were a number of points in the Aegean named after St Nikolas. The *Britannic*'s radio receiving apparatus had also been unable to receive any transmissions, with the result that none of the requests for clarification from any of the rescue vessels were picked up by the ship's radio operators. The wireless damage was almost certainly caused by the initial explosion, but it is interesting that somehow this communications issue later helped to fuel rumours that the Germans had deliberately interfered with the ship's transmissions in order to impede the rescue.

Fortunately there was one ship to hand whose crew knew exactly where to look. The armed merchant cruiser HMS *Heroic*, en route from Mudros to Piraeus, had actually passed the *Britannic* as she was entering the Kea Channel less than an hour before, and quickly turned back to give assistance. The British destroyer HMS *Scourge*, under the command of Lieutenant Commander Henry Tupper, was also nearby, escorting the Greek steamer *Sparti*, which had struck another of the mines laid by *U73*, this one off Phleva island near Piraeus. Within minutes, both of these vessels, along with the French tugs *Goliath* and *Polyphemus* and a trawler, were headed at full speed towards Kea.

In the channel itself the situation was bordering on chaotic, with lifeboats and swimmers, some horribly mutilated by the ship's propeller, scattered across a wide area. Many of the boats lacked a trained seaman to help with the rowing, while others were so overcrowded that it was impossible for the occupants to free the oars secured in the bottom of the boat without capsizing. For the several hundred survivors in the water, however, the problems faced by those in the lifeboats seemed relatively trivial. Fortunately, the life floats – each capable of supporting about 20 people in the water – and deckchairs thrown overboard by Fifth Officer Fielding's party helped to alleviate the immediate situation, but as Captain Bartlett – according to Violet Jessop, still dressed in his pyjamas – was picked up out of the water by Colonel Anderson in the *Britannic*'s port motor launch, he could at least set about restoring a semblance of order.

Furthermore, unlike the situation on the *Titanic*, the *Britannic*'s passengers were not just civilians or families travelling with children, but instead were trained military and medical personnel, which was exactly what was required at that particular moment. This

---

◀ A *Britannic* lifeboat lies close to the open shell door of the HMS *Heroic*.

time the lifeboats had returned to pick up survivors while the nurses quickly set about ripping up their pillowcases, blankets and even lifejackets so that they could be made into practical dressings and slings. One of the swimmers was Violet Jessop, trying hard to shut out the horrific scene of carnage surrounding her, as most of the bodies from the two smashed lifeboats drifted away in the current. The propeller blade had also inflicted a deep gash to her leg, but as she was pulled into the motor launch, Violet's memories were of one badly injured man with both of his severed arms seemingly hanging by only a few pieces of skin, yet he was still able to smile knowing that he was lucky not to have been killed. Those who were beyond help could only be lowered back over the side to make space for the living. It was little better on shore, where it was reported that injured survivors had already been landed, so with no indication as to when help would arrive, Matron Elizabeth Dowse made sure that several nurses were taken ashore in one of the motor launches to assist the wounded.

Almost immediately several Greek fishing boats were on the scene rescuing survivors from the water, and by 10.00am, barely an hour after the *Britannic* had gone down, HMS *Scourge* and HMS *Heroic* had arrived in the Kea Channel. Over the next 90 minutes the lifeboats converged on the two British vessels as the survivors were taken aboard. At first the transfer proceeded smoothly enough, but as the morning wore on, the southerly Sirocco wind began to make itself felt, pitching the lifeboats up and down as the waves continued to rise. Ada Garland remembered having to leap onto the decks of the *Scourge* at the precise moment her boat reached its highest point, before being taken below deck. Once she was there, the cramped conditions and lack of air, along with the cries of the wounded and the smell of the blood, became too much for her, but after being revived by a welcome shot of brandy she was taken topside, where she could recover in the fresh air.

By about midday the two rescue ships were almost full to capacity. On board the *Heroic* the 494 survivors still had a limited amount of space, but for the 339 survivors crammed into the smaller destroyer, things were not nearly so comfortable. Fortunately, the destroyer HMS *Foxhound*, under the command of Lieutenant Commander William Shuttleworth, arrived on the scene at 11.45am and proceeded to conduct a further sweep for survivors in the channel, allowing the *Heroic* and the *Scourge* to set a north-westerly course for the 40-mile journey to Piraeus.

THE STRAGGLERS

Meanwhile, the situation in Port St Nikolo was grim. Both motor launches and two of the lifeboats had made it safely to the island, where the severely injured passengers were being

BELIEVED TO BE
12423 SERJEANT
W. SHARPE
ROYAL ARMY MEDICAL CORPS
21ST NOVEMBER 1916 AGE 39

HIS MEMORY LIVES ON

attended to by the available medical staff. Once again Violet Jessop was on hand, remembering one man in an RAMC uniform with part of his thigh missing and one foot gone altogether. Having had some prior medical training as a VAD nurse, she did her best to comfort him, but sadly Sergeant William Sharpe was beyond help, dying from his injuries on the quayside shortly before noon. After an hour searching the channel, HMS *Foxhound* finally dropped anchor in the harbour and immediately began to take on the survivors. By 2.00pm the scout cruiser HMS *Foresight* had also arrived on the scene, by which time Captain Shuttleworth had taken on board a total of 193 survivors, 22 of them seriously injured. Not wanting to lose any time, at 2.15pm *Foxhound* duly weighed anchor, leaving Commander Worsley and the crew of the *Foresight* to arrange for the burial of Sergeant Sharpe and the recovery of the motor launches and lifeboats in the harbour.

As the rescue flotilla headed for Piraeus, Sheila Macbeth later recalled the thrilling adventure of a journey on a destroyer, as the *Scourge* flew over the waves, her nose parting the flying spray, whereas for Violet Jessop, more used to the ocean-going life, her fondest memory was of one of the crew on HMS *Foxhound*, seeing how wet she was from her experience, asking if she would like to take a bath while her clothes were dried in the engine room. The race to get there first was won by the *Heroic*, arriving at Piraeus at 3.45pm and immediately

▲ The headstone on the grave of Sergeant William Sharpe, who died on Kea at about midday on 21 November 1916. His body was later moved to the New British Cemetery on Syra in 1921.

Ξενοδοχεῖον Ἀκταῖον — Φάληρον.
Palace Hôtel Actéon — Phalère.

proceeding alongside the British flagship HMS *Duncan* to begin the transfer of the survivors. Barely 15 minutes later, HMS *Scourge* was also in port, but with over 800 survivors
the *Duncan*'s limited on-board facilities were on the verge of being overwhelmed. The
situation was greatly eased by Admiral Gabriel Darrieus, commanding the French Third
Squadron, who provided additional boats from the French ships to ferry the uninjured
survivors to shore.

Once the 1,032 survivors were ashore, the quandary of finding accommodation for them
fell to Lieutenant WH Rogers, the port control officer at Piraeus. Captain Bartlett and
Colonel Anderson would have to remain aboard the *Duncan* in order to assist with the
inevitable inquiry into the *Britannic*'s loss, although Anderson's familiarity with the ship
from December 1908, when the *Duncan* had transported him from Malta to Messina as part
of the British earthquake relief party, might have made things easier for him. Even so, the
available space aboard the ageing battleship was limited, and the only workable option was
to accommodate most of the survivors either ashore or in one of the available transport

▲ Postcard of the Aktaion Palace Hotel. (Michail Michailakis)

▶ The official telegram informing Sheila Macbeth's family that she was safe. (Jonathan Mitchell)

vessels. With most of the local hotels closed up for the winter, the choice of accommodation became something of a lottery, and not surprisingly it would be the nurses who found themselves with the pick of the available space, comfortably installed in the Aktaion Palace Hotel at Phaleron. Even then, their arrival came as something of a shock to the hotel manager, who, having misunderstood the original request for rooms, had prepared accommodation for 18 nurses instead of 80! The medical officers were lodged in the nearby Phalére Hotel, a less-than-ideal choice according to Rev. Fleming, who later recalled that the hotel staff were not supporters of the Greek Prime Minister Eleutherios Venizelos, who was backing the Allied cause. As supporters of the Greek King Constantine, coincidentally educated in Germany and married to the Kaiser's sister, their political sympathies lay elsewhere, and it would seem that their British guests were left in no doubt as to exactly where that might be.

The hardships suffered by the medical staff would not have unduly troubled the *Britannic*'s crew or RAMC medical orderlies, for whom the remaining accommodation was not nearly so comfortable. The more fortunate ones found themselves berthed either on board the *Duncan* or in one of the French warships, but for 300 men, the ex-Greek depot ship *Kanaris* turned out to be an insalubrious choice. Percy Tyler would certainly not recall the ship with any great affection:

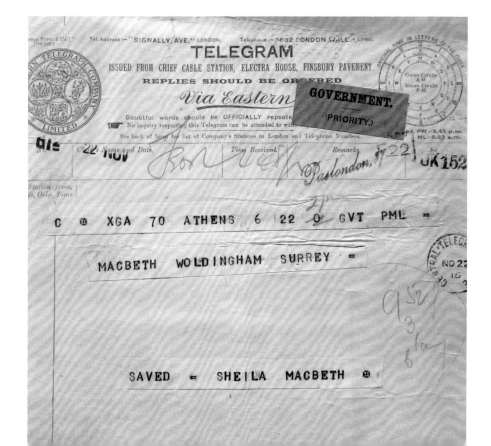

Ours was a very poor boat, which smelt from end to end as much like a sewer as could be, and looked very much as though it had never had a clean up since it was launched… It was also very unfortunate that our two scouts were with us and for their own sakes we made them sleep up on deck with us, sleeping below was out of the question from a health point of view and the language of the crew was not fit for them.

Gradually the activity in Piraeus began to settle down. At 6.30pm the *Foxhound* was finally able to proceed alongside the grain wharf, where Major Priestley was overseeing the ambulances transferring the wounded to the nearby Russian Hospital. Unfortunately, the shortage of vehicles meant that the destroyer would not depart again until after midnight, but gradually a measure of calm continued to return to the Bay of Salamis, and as the evening wore on the bodies of Private Arthur Binks and trimmer Charles Phillips, who had died while aboard the *Heroic*, along with the body of fireman Joseph Brown who had died aboard the French tug *Goliath*, were transferred by motor launch to the *Duncan*.

Meanwhile, the situation was complicated by problems with the Greek and Russian medical staff, who, although they were more than capable of handling the casualties, unfortunately did not speak any English. Luckily some of them spoke a little French, although

▲ Piraeus in November 1916. (Jonathan Mitchell)

that in itself was bad news for Sheila Macbeth who, because she knew a little of the language, had been able to speak with some of the staff at the hotel to obtain some soap for everyone. Sheila's linguistic abilities had not gone unnoticed, and barely half an hour after retiring for the night, she found herself being hauled out of bed and driven to the hospital, along with the assistant matron and two charge sisters. She could look forward to a long night, during which George Honeycott, one of the ship's lookouts, would become the last casualty to die from his injuries.

Working late into the night, Captain Bartlett and Colonel Anderson set about the difficult task of completing the casualty list following the sinking. Of the *Britannic*'s nominal roll, the final breakdown of the ship's personnel present at Salamis and Piraeus amounted to 652 ship's company, 304 RAMC and 76 nurses. This poignant calculation effectively confirmed that 30 of the 1,062 on board that morning were listed as either dead or missing. The fact that only five of those listed were confirmed as dead may have given some limited grounds for hope, but the cruel reality was that the Kea Channel had been carefully searched before the rescue ships had returned to Piraeus, and the chances of any further survivors being found were minimal at best.

In the end the final calculation for the number killed on the day of the *Britannic*'s sinking would come in at 21 of the ship's crew and nine officers and men of the RAMC, a total of 30 souls, although that figure would increase to 31 when Spencer Genn, one of the ship's stewards, would die from his injuries six months later in England. Even so, it could have been worse. Had the explosion occurred on the return journey, with the ship's wards packed with thousands of sick and wounded, the potential number of killed or injured does not bear thinking about. In the end the casualty figure for the doomed *Britannic* was mercifully small.

Compared with the *Titanic*, she really was the lucky one!

THE END OF THE BEGINNING

Even though the Transport Division was 1,500 miles from Athens, it would have found the morning of Wednesday 22 November 1916 a very difficult one. It was suddenly faced with the task of repatriating the thousands of wounded who still needed to be evacuated from Mudros, yet it would be two weeks at least before the *Aquitania* could complete the journey to Lemnos. With the shore-based hospitals already overflowing, the only option to relieve the pressure in the eastern Mediterranean was to order the immediate return of the hospital ships *Warilda*, *Herefordshire*, *Wandilla*, *Llandovery Castle*, *Dover Castle* and *Glenart Castle* to England, carrying as many casualties as possible.

▲ The medical staff touring the Parthenon before being repatriated. (Jonathan Mitchell)

The situation was further complicated when on 23 November the hospital ship *Braemar Castle* fell foul of another mine laid by the *U73*, this time in the Mykoni Channel. Employing the same tactics that Captain Bartlett had tried, Captain Ernest Mais had fortunately managed to beach his ship on the Blade Rocks on the nearby island of Tinos, although it would later transpire that by even entering the Mykoni Channel, where mines had already been reported, he had violated his sailing orders. In spite of his actions in saving his ship, three men had died as a result of Mais's error and he would never command a military transport vessel again.

As the crisis continued to escalate, back in Piraeus the political situation was growing equally tense. The French were only days away from presenting King Constantine of Greece with a seven-day ultimatum, demanding the immediate surrender of military material and the demobilisation of the Greek army as a guarantee of Greek neutrality – something to which Constantine could not possibly agree – and with the serious prospect of an armed intervention occurring, the last thing that the British wanted was to have over a thousand *Britannic* survivors spread throughout Piraeus.

By the afternoon of 22 November things were beginning to get back to something like normal. As the bodies of Arthur Binks, Joseph Brown, George Honeycott and Charles Phillips were laid to rest in the nearby cemetery at Drapetsona, the work of concluding the inquiry into the *Britannic*'s loss and repatriating the survivors was quietly moving forward. The most important undertaking was to find out exactly how the *Britannic* had met her fate, but with the limited time available, combined with the fact that the survivors were scattered around Piraeus, the task would not be an easy one for Captain Hugh Heard and Commander George Staer, HMS *Duncan*'s commanding officer and chief engineer respectively. The evidence was also conflicting, with Thomas Walters, a steward, and Henry Etches, a baker, both convinced that they had seen the wake of a torpedo. In addition, an engineers' writer named Thomas Eckett had reported seeing an object in the water resembling a periscope, but while none of the men actually physically saw a torpedo, the *prima facie* evidence pointing to a potential German war crime was mounting.

But was it really that straightforward? Certainly no one on watch on the bridge had reported sighting any wake, and even Walters and Etches disagreed on both which side and which end of the ship they had seen their torpedoes. Captain Bartlett's initial distress call had also specifically stated that the *Britannic* had struck a mine, and as if to further muddy the waters, as lookout J Conelly was going off duty at 8.00am he had reported two 'suspicious objects' in sight.

Considering the many weeks it took to complete the inquiry following the sinking of the *Titanic* and the thousands of words that went into it, the three-day *Britannic* investigation

and subsequent 726-word report were a model of the succinct and clipped style so typical of the military:

H.M.S. 'Duncan',
24th November 1916.

Sir,

Having enquired into the circumstances attending the loss of the Hospital Ship 'Britannic', we have the honour to make the following report. It must be premised that the enquiry was necessarily incomplete owing to the shortness of time at our disposal and the difficulty of finding witnesses scattered over the whole fleet.

2. The following is a brief description of structure of 'Britannic' in the region of the

◄ The nurses outside the Aktaion Palace Hotel, Piraeus. (Jonathan Mitchell)

▲ The graves of Brown, Binks and Honeycott in Piraeus Naval and Consular Cemetery at Drapetsona. The grave of Trimmer Charles Phillips lies nearby, as no body was found when the graves were regrouped in the late 1920s. (Michail Michailakis)

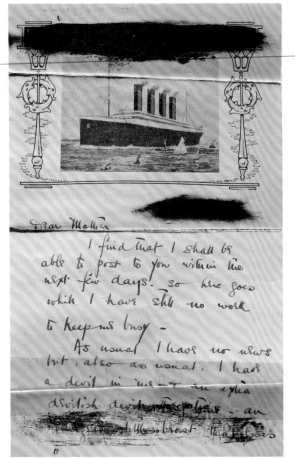

explosion. Rough sketches are attached. Forward of Bridge were situated the Fore Peak and Nos 1, 2 & 3 holds, No 3 hold being a reserve coal Bunker, Water tight bulkheads separating these compartments. No 6 Boiler Room was immediately under Fore Bridge & No 5 Boiler Room being immediately abaft No 6. A W.T. tunnel ran from forward bulkhead of No 6 and under Nos 3 & 2 holds to No 1 hold, compartments over which were situated Fireman's quarters.

Unless therefore the W.T. doors in this tunnel were closed the boiler rooms were in free communication with Nos 1, 2 & 3 holds in the event of Tunnel being damaged.

The Watertight doors were automatic in action and could also be closed by means of handles abaft doors or from deck plates on E deck.

3. There was one explosion only. This took place on Starboard side low down and in the vicinity of the bulkhead between 2 and 3 holds, breaking this bulkhead and thus filling Nos. 2 & 3 holds. Whether the bulkhead between Nos 1 & 2 holds was broken is not certain, but it is probable. Anyway No. 1 hold also filled either in this way or through the tunnel.

4. It appears that the bulkhead between No. 3 hold & No. 6 Stokehold was not broken, but water from the holds gained free access through the W.T. door between stokehold and tunnel which was not closed, the tunnel having been broken.

▲ A clumsy attempt by the censor to conceal the name of the *Britannic* in one of Sheila Macbeth's letters home. (Jonathan Mitchell)

5. Water also had free access to No. 5 Stokehold through the W.T. door between 5 and 6. It is clear that this door was not wholly, although there is evidence to show that it may have been partly, closed.

6. There seems to have been a period of 1 to 2 minutes from the time of the explosion until the water in the stokeholds was too deep for work to be performed, when these doors might have been closed. This would have secured the two boiler rooms, measuring about 35′ x 90′ in area, from incursion by water. This might have saved the ship, but without plans of the whole structure it is impossible to offer an opinion.

7. We are confident that no water penetrated abaft No. 5 stokehold in the lower part of the ship.

8. A further means for the admission of water was by side scuttles. The W.T. doors before the stokehold seem to have been closed except in the tunnel. The scuttles on F deck should not have been open as it was contrary to orders at that time, but there is evidence that these orders were occasionally disobeyed. Many of the scuttles on E deck were open.

The ship taking a list of about 25 degrees to starboard and getting down by the bows would quickly bring these under water. Direct evidence shows that about 15 minutes after the explosion, the scuttles on E Deck (normally 25′ out of water) on a line between the foremost funnels were awash, and water was coming along this deck from forward.

9. Question of mine or torpedo. The water was deep, probably over 100 fathoms and there is a current through the Zea [Kea] Channel. This against the mine theory.

Three persons gave good evidence of having seen

(a) A Periscope

(b) The wake of a torpedo immediately before the explosion and in its direction. This man F. Walters, Deck Steward having been an Officers Steward in the Navy had seen torpedo practice. He did <u>not</u> pretend to have seen the torpedo.

(c) The wake of a torpedo on port side apparently missing aft. It is to be noted that the sea was glassy smooth.

On other hand there is no evidence of a column of water having been thrown up outside the ship.

The effects of the explosion might have been due to either a mine or a torpedo. The probability seems to be a mine.

We have the honour to be,

Sir,

Your Obedient Servants,

H. H. Heard.
Captain.

G. H. Staer.
Engineer Commander.

Although the report concluded that the *Britannic* had probably been sunk by a mine, the announcement in the press on Thursday 23 November 1916 of the ship's loss had quickly led to accusations of Germany's 'disregard for the laws of nations' and allegations of 'German barbarity'. For added effect, the *Daily Mirror* even reported every effort having been made to save over 1,000 sick and wounded, in spite of the fact that the wards had been empty at the time. Then again, with rumours circulating among the actual survivors about the ship's engineers being kept at their posts until the last minute by Chief Engineer Robert Fleming's pistol, it seems clear that even the crew were not above embellishing their stories.

The Germans, not surprisingly, were having none of it, as their official communiqué made clear when published in *The Times*. Needless to say, they were quick to justify their suspicions about the large number of people on board, and hence about the possible misuse

▶ The medical staff at Fort Manoel, Malta, before being repatriated to England. (Jonathan Mitchell)

of the *Britannic* as a transport, but to the charges of the ship being deliberately attacked, they could have only one response:

> Inasmuch as the ship carried distinguishing marks of a hospital ship, in accordance with regulations, there can naturally be no question of a German submarine in connection with the sinking.

RETURN OF THE WANDERERS

As the diplomatic gamesmanship continued, the political crisis in Athens was fast coming to a head, though for the shipwrecked survivors there were other more pressing concerns. The nurses were largely concerned with looking after the wounded at the Russian Hospital, while the *Britannic*'s destitute crew were having to fall back on the American government's Serbian relief stores for the barest of essentials. However, at least the process of evacuating survivors could begin on 24 November, when the *Britannic*'s 605 surviving officers and uninjured crew went aboard the auxiliary transport RFA *Ermine*. Accompanied by HMS *Foxhound* on the first leg of the journey, the *Ermine* reached Salonika the following evening,

and at 7.00am on the morning of 26 November she went alongside the battleship HMS *Lord Nelson*. Vice Admiral Cecil Thursby, commanding the British naval forces in the eastern Mediterranean, himself took the opportunity to interview the men who had been on watch at the time of the sinking, but not surprisingly he could obtain no fresh information. Holding a further inquiry would have meant detaining a number of key personnel in Greece, so on the assumption that there would be a more thorough investigation once the crew were back in England, later in the afternoon the survivors were transferred to the transport ship HMT *Royal George* – minus two firemen who had failed to return after going ashore, and who were still absent when the *Royal George* departed at 3.30pm the following afternoon, leaving Captain Bartlett with no option but to list them as deserters who would face the full wrath of the naval authorities when they finally turned up.

At about the same time that the *Royal George* was departing from Salonika, the *Britannic*'s medical staff, together with the wounded survivors, were boarding the hospital ship *Grantully Castle*, departing from Piraeus barely two days before the royalist government of King Constantine would reject the French ultimatum, resulting in the Noemvriana bloodshed in Athens.

The two groups of survivors, however, would end up taking very different routes. The *Royal George* reached Marseilles on 2 December, and from there Captain Bartlett went ahead via a scheduled overland train to the north. Everyone else remained in Marseilles for another two days before being packed into unheated train carriages, which, given the particularly cold winter, did not bode well for the journey. The meagre rations of bully beef, bread, cheese and black tea did little to improve conditions on the 50-hour journey, and even when they did finally reach Le Havre, the men still had to endure a five-mile march to the rest camp and a freezing night under canvas without the luxury of even a blanket. As the *Britannic*'s former crew waited to board the transport *Caesarea* the following afternoon, one man was so weakened by the ordeal that he collapsed and fell into the freezing harbour. The *Caesarea* finally docked at Southampton at 9.00am on 8 December. After being welcomed home by Captain Bartlett, the men were granted the customary two-week survivor's leave.

The medical staff had a more convoluted journey home. The *Grantully Castle* arrived alongside Malta's Hamilton Wharf shortly before midday on 30 November, and the nurses were then quartered in different hospitals on the island, Sheila Macbeth ending up at St George's Hospital, where she would be fortunate to come across several friends, while

▷ An announcement concerning the post-war sale of the *Britannic*'s unused panelling.

G. R.

BY DIRECTION OF THE LORDS COMMISSIONERS OF THE ADMIRALTY.

Messrs. W. P. GRAY & MacDOWELL, LTD., will realise by AUCTION SALES at BELFAST (as per Catalogues) the First of which will be held on

THURSDAY, 3rd, and FRIDAY, 4th JULY, 1919,

The Complete Magnificent and Costly Unused Interior

SALOON AND OTHER DECORATIONS, FITTINGS, FURNISHINGS, & ARISINGS

appertaining to the palatial

WHITE STAR LINER, "S.S. BRITANNIC."

THE FITTINGS, &c., to be disposed of represent approximately £500,000, and offer an exceptional opportunity to Ship Builders, Hotel, Restaurant, Picture House, and Entertainment Concerns, Contractors, Shop Fitters, Furniture Manufacturers, Wood Workers and Others of obtaining FINE SPECIMEN RICHLY CARVED

WALL and CEILING PANELLING, in choice selected Walnut, Mahogany, Sycamore, Oak, and other Hardwoods; FIBROUS PLASTER and LINCRUSTA ADORNMENTS, with Ornate finishings of various period reproductions, as follow:—

First Class Main Entrances and Stairways — Panelled in Polished Oak, Georgian period, staircase having wrought iron-work of French design.

Children's Playroom — Size 44 feet x 18 feet. Panelled in Walnut, Modern design.

First Class Gymnasium — Size 44 feet x 18 feet. Panelled out in Oak, Modern design.

Reading and Writing Room — Size 44 feet x 24 feet. Panelled in Georgian period, finished White Frieze, richly carved.

First Class Lounge — Size 60 feet x 60 feet. Two Bays each side. Handsome Bookcase at the after end and Fireplace at the forward end. Panelled and Framed in Polished Oak, Louis XV. period.

First Class Smokeroom — Size 40 feet x 60 feet, with vestibule, 30 feet x 18 feet. A reproduction of one of the state apartments in Hampton Court. Panelled in Cedar of Lebanon with Lime Tree carvings after Grinling Gibbons.

First Class Restaurant — Size 90 feet x 44 feet. Panelled and Framed in Italian Walnut, relieved with gold, Louis XVI. period.

Restaurant Reception Room — Size 30 feet x 34 feet. Panelled and Framed in the same period, but finished White.

First Class Reception Room — Size 84 feet x 90 feet. Panelled and Framed Jacobean period, handsomely carved and finished White; special stained glass to windows.

First Class Dining Saloon — Size 114 feet x 90 feet. Panelled and Framed finished White, in Jacobean period; handsome Oak Carved and Inlaid Sideboards at each end.

Second Class Main Entrance and Stairways — Handsomely carved in Polished Oak, finished fielded panels.

Second Class Dining Saloon — Size 70 feet x 90 feet. Finished in Polished Oak, Jacobean design, with handsome Carved Sideboard at the forward end.

Second Class Smokeroom — Size 34 feet x 60 feet. Panelled and Framed in Oak, Jacobean period.

Second Class Library — Size 34 feet x 60 feet. Panelled and Framed in Sycamore, handsomely carved, Colonial Adam's design.

Second Class Gymnasium — 19 feet x 19 feet.

About 70 Decorated Bedrooms — (Deck) 10 ft. 6 ins. x 15 ft. In the following styles—
"A"—Modern, White panelling, Oak Dado; "B"—Louis XVI., handsomely carved in Polished Oak; "C"—Adam's, in White; "D"—Louis XV., Oak; "E"—Louis XV., Grey; "F"—Empire, White and Gold.

One Sitting Room — Louis XVI., in Oak, size 14 feet x 22 feet.

One Sitting Room — Regence, in Polished Mahogany, relieved with Gold, size 14 ft. x 22 ft.

Also Several Hundred Thousand Square Feet PINE PANELLING, PITCH PINE QUARTERING, CANARY and DEAL MOULDINGS, &c.

70,000 Square Feet MAHOGANY CORRIDOR PANELLING; 50,000 Square Feet OAK PANELLING; and about

4,000 FITMENT WARDROBES, DRESSING CHESTS, SIDEBOARDS, BOOKCASES, and other FURNITURE, easily convertible for various utility purposes.

CATALOGUES, giving full particulars and admitting to View and First Sale. Price 2 each, from

W. P. GRAY & MacDOWELL, LIMITED,

Auctioneers and Valuers,

Belfast Auction Rooms, 40, Chichester Street.

Phone 99.   Wires—"Realize."

Violet Jessop would even have the added bonus of being able to visit her brother William, who coincidentally was in one of the island's hospitals recovering from malaria. The men of the RAMC were also billeted in hospitals, but Private Percy Tyler later recalled that after several days in Fort Manoel Hospital they were transferred to the All Saints Convalescent Camp, about five miles outside Valletta, to await transport to England. One week later, the first 77 of their number were homeward bound, with the remainder boarding the transport HMT *Huntsend* on the morning of 10 December for a circuitous six-day voyage to Marseilles. On 17 December the RAMC staff took the same train journey that the *Britannic*'s crew had been forced to endure two weeks earlier, finally reaching Le Havre at 3.30am on 20 December. Spared the privations of the rest camp, that same evening they went aboard the HMT *King Edward*, arriving safely back at Southampton the following day after a stormy crossing.

Once again the nurses – not that they would have realised it at the time – almost certainly had the best of it, remaining at All Saints until a suitable vessel was available to take them home. After 17 days on the island they were suddenly rushed aboard the HMHS *Valdivia*, which proved much less homely than the *Britannic*. Originally the ship was supposed to steam directly to Southampton, but the plan came to naught due to a lack of fresh water on board. A brief pause at Gibraltar proved fruitless, with no water being available, and by the end of the voyage supplies were practically exhausted. Somehow the nurses managed to hold things together – only just – until the ship finally arrived at Southampton at 9.00am on 26 December. They were then packed off to London on a scheduled train to Waterloo Station, where they would be met by the Matron-in-Chief, who ordered them to return home and await further orders.

Although the survivors were all safely home, this was not quite the end of the *Britannic*'s story. On 23 January 1917 the Admiralty advanced £1,750,000 to the White Star Line until Harland & Wolff were able to complete the final accounts for the construction of the *Britannic*, which would eventually come to a total of £1,947,797 5s. Even then, with monies outstanding for the loss of other vessels, it would not be until after the war that the accounts with the various shipping companies would be fully resolved, the stress of the delay no doubt eased by the available prize tonnage that would restore Great Britain's decimated merchant fleet at the end of the war. That end came on 11 November 1918, when the Armistice ending the fighting on the Western Front finally came into force. Two years to the day – almost to the hour – after the *Britannic* was sunk, the German High Seas Fleet rendezvoused with the British Grand Fleet in the North Sea for one last time, this time sailing into internment and ultimately to self-destruction in the British naval base at Scapa Flow.

And so, like many of the vessels lost in the war, and having never seen a single day of commercial service, the *Britannic* faded from memory. The few physical fragments that did remain were scattered to the four winds after the war, as the Admiralty auctioned off the warehoused wooden panelling, which would no longer be needed. Unlike her elder sister, there are no memorials to those lost in the *Britannic*, except for the war memorials at Tower Gate and in Thessaloniki, and it is curious that until the centenary of her loss even the Belfast slipways made no mention of the *Britannic*, although they had long commemorated the construction of the *Olympic* and the *Titanic*.

However, the *Britannic* would not be destined to go gentle into that good night. Over the

◀ The Mercantile Marine Memorial, Tower Hill, London.

1–3. Details of the *Britannic* panelling purchased for the old La Scala Cinema in Dublin. (John Hynes)

4. *Britannic*'s organ, rediscovered, restored and on display at the Museum für Musikautomaten at Seewen, Switzerland. (David Rumsey)

5. The old Harland & Wolff drawing office where the Olympic-class liners were designed, now a fashionable cocktail bar of the Titanic Hotel.

years, important items and pieces of information giving hints of what could have been have started to come to light. Some of the panelling sold off in the Admiralty auction has been given pride of place in several private homes in Belfast and Dublin; the long-lost organ has been found and restored and is now on display in the Museum für Musikautomaten at Seewen, in Switzerland, while the *Titanic*'s once-forgotten sister has now been the subject of no less than eight documentaries. As interest in the *Britannic* has continued to grow in recent years, it has become increasingly clear that everything that happened up to the end of the war was merely a curtain raiser.

▲ The Cross of Sacrifice at Mikra, Thessaloniki, commemorating those killed in the Aegean with no known grave.

PART 2

EXPLORING THE *BRITANNIC*

REDISCOVERY

By the time I had begun to show an interest in the *Britannic* she had been lying at the bottom of the Kea Channel for more than 70 years. Nor can I even claim the honour of having been the individual who inspired the world to find and explore the wreck of the *Titanic*'s lost sister.

In truth, it all began some 17 years before I was even on the scene, the origins buried in an obscure article in an issue of the American magazine *People Weekly* dated 15 September 1975. Flicking through the pages of human-interest stories about Elizabeth Taylor and Richard Burton, Valerie Harper's marriage to Richard Schaal and a story on General George Patton, Connecticut resident William Harris Tantum IV came across an article on Jacques Cousteau, the 'grand old man of the sea', who was working in the Aegean on behalf of the Greek Ministry of Tourism in an attempt to discover evidence of the lost continent of Atlantis. To most readers, this innocuous article would have been of little more than passing interest, but to Bill Tantum, then vice

president of the Titanic Historical Society, it provided the first tangible opportunity to locate and film an Olympic-class liner. Even more conveniently, the Cousteau Group was at that time headquartered in Westport, Connecticut, barely 20 miles from Tantum's hometown in Riverside.

Figuring that rejection of his idea was the worst that could happen, he decided to contact Cousteau's Westport office, if only to see if he could rouse the captain's interest in his plan. Much to his surprise, the captain not only responded, but the answer came quickly. In everything, timing is always essential, but in this case Cousteau was literally on the verge of commencing an extended series of sonar operations for the Greek government for two hour-long programmes, and was already in discussions with the Massachusetts Institute of Technology about using their side-scan sonar to locate a number of deep wrecks. Once located, they would be explored using the *Calypso*'s *Soucoupe* submersible, so the prospect of adding the *Titanic*'s sister ship to the list was sure to be extremely attractive.

Known affectionately to Cousteau and his team as 'Papa-Flash', Dr Harold Edgerton of the Massachusetts Institute of Technology was just the man to spearhead the search. It did not matter that Edgerton's main interest was in the Lepanto wrecks, which Cousteau would also be surveying, or that he was just a long-standing friend. In fact, Cousteau and Edgerton had been collaborating since 1952, and over the years had compiled an arsenal of state-of-the-art under-water cameras, lighting systems and exploration technology. In 1967 Edgerton's sub-bottom profiling equipment had also been instrumental in locating the resting place of the *Mary Rose* in the Solent, and his subsequent development of side-scan sonar, whereby the angle of the sonar beam was shifted sideways in order to survey much larger areas, made it easier to detect objects rising above the seabed. Edgerton's side-scan sonar had also helped locate the wreck of the USS *Monitor* in August 1973. If anyone could help to locate the *Britannic*, surely it was Harold 'Doc' Edgerton.

On 5 November 1975 some 620 pounds of delicate sonar equipment, packed into 12 cases, left New York on a flight bound for Greece. Edgerton would make the same journey 24 hours later, enabling sonar technician Parviz Babai to have everything unpacked by the time he arrived. Edgerton's to-do list looked ambitious, with initial targets pinpointed in the Bay of Corinth, Lepanto, Patras, Cephalonia, Chalkis Bay, Marathon, Santorini and Crete, but tucked away further down the list was item no. 6, the *Brittanic* [sic], which, according to Edgerton's notes, was a large ship in 80 metres of water, about 170 kilometres from Athens. In theory, locating the *Britannic* would not be difficult as the position was clearly marked on the charts, but as it would turn out,

◀ Jacques Cousteau (left) poses with sonar technician Parviz Babai (middle) and Dr Harold 'Doc' Edgerton (right) aboard the *Calypso* in November 1975. (© 2010 MIT. Courtesy of MIT Museum)

finding the wreck would be a lot harder than anyone had expected. Far from X marking the spot, the *Britannic* was actually nowhere near the recorded position, obliging Cousteau to widen his search area as the *Calypso* travelled up and down the Kea Channel.

French diver Robert Pollio kept a journal of his time on the *Calypso* during the 1975 and 1976 season, and recalled how the ship carried out a monotonous but nonetheless systematic sonar search of the Kea Channel, similar to the 'mowing the lawn' technique used by Robert Ballard almost ten years later when looking for the *Titanic*. For several days the *Calypso*'s depth sounder continued to record the monotonously featureless seabed, but on Thursday 13 November a huge object, estimated to be 200 metres long and rising to an approximate depth of 80 metres, suddenly appeared on the screen. Normally this would not have been a problem, but Parviz Babai knew that the sonar towfish was being towed at a depth of 100 metres. Fortunately Albert Falco, *Calypso*'s long-time captain and lead diver, had also seen the contact, and was able to alter course just in time to prevent the towfish slamming into the side of the wreck, while the deckhands frantically pulled on the winches to raise it clear of the unidentified object. Either luck or the gods must have been on their side, as the sonar towfish cleared the wreck just in time, avoiding not only a collision but, more importantly for Cousteau and Edgerton, the cost of a new and very expensive towfish.

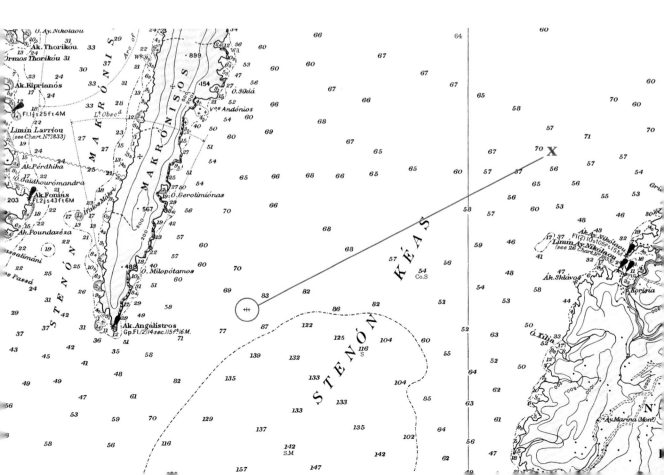

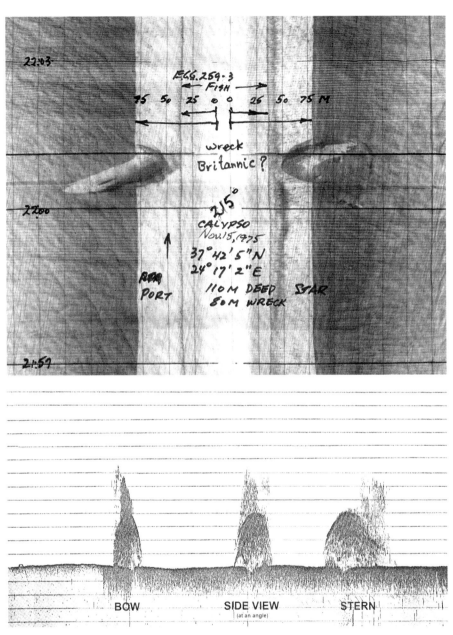

◀ Cousteau's corrected position of the wreck would result in years of speculation and conspiracy theories.

▲ Edgerton's side-scan of the relocated *Britannic*. The question mark suggests that Cousteau was still not absolutely certain that it was the *Britannic*. (© 2010 MIT. Courtesy of MIT Museum)

▲ Printout of the *Calypso*'s surface sonar of the wreck. (Titanic Historical Society)

The target was large enough that it could surely only be the *Britannic*, although the fact that it was located at the not inconsequential distance of 6.75 nautical miles (12.5 kilometres) from the charted position still left considerable room for doubt. Had they but known it, this location tallied almost exactly with the position recorded in the *Britannic*'s log book – namely, three miles north-west of the Port St Nikolo light on the island of Kea – but the November winds in the Aegean can be especially high, and those of 1975 were no different, making it impossible to launch the *Soucoupe* in order to obtain a positive visual identification. With a busy schedule, the *Calypso* was unable to linger in the area for too long, but even so, on the basis of the side-scan sonar image dated 15 November 1975, Cousteau was confident enough in his own mind that the *Britannic* had indeed been relocated, and on 3 December the corrected position was forwarded to the British Ministry of Defence.

On the face of it, the results were better than anyone could have expected, particularly considering that but for the chance reading two months earlier of a brief article in a human-interest magazine, practically no one would have even remembered the story of the *Britannic*. In the overall scheme of things, Tantum's purchase of the magazine probably represents the best 50 cents ever spent in the field of *Titanic/Britannic* research, but for the time being all that could be done was to wait until the following summer.

INTO THE BLUE

In the meantime, a lot of groundwork still needed to be carried out. The wreck had been located, but it was about 30 metres deeper than expected, meaning that the *Calypso*'s on-board diving equipment would not be sufficient for the extensive deep diving operations that would be required. As if to prove the point, on 10 July 1976 the briefest of exploratory dives was scheduled to enable a small four-man dive team to obtain the necessary images to positively identify the wreck, but problems with nitrogen narcosis (a condition resembling drunkenness brought on by breathing nitrogen under pressure) and with the increased pressure causing the camera light bulbs to implode meant that in the end only lead diver Albert Falco was able to reach the wreck. The sight of the unique girder davits was enough to confirm once and for all that they had indeed found the *Britannic*, but in the early summer of 1976 the *Calypso* was by no means sufficiently equipped to support a manned diving operation in 110 metres of water. A lot of preparation still needed to be done if the *Calypso* was to be able to return to the Kea Channel in the autumn, by which time the infamous Meltemi wind would hopefully be past its summer peak.

▶ *Calypso* alongside the quay at Korissia in September 1976. (Peter Nicolaides)

Cousteau would finally return to the Kea Channel in mid-September, by which time the diving equipment needed to handle the logistical issues of a dive of up to 110 metres had been taken on board. For the safety of the divers, this effectively meant the use of a special gas mix known as trimix, used in commercial diving at depths where helium is needed to replace some of the nitrogen to lessen the threat of nitrogen narcosis. The use of mixed gases in deep diving was by no means new, however. As far back as 1919 a British-born inventor named Elihu Thomson had speculated that inert gases, such as helium, might be a suitable alternative to nitrogen in a diver's breathing supply, and in 1924 the US Navy had begun to research the use of helium–oxygen gas mixtures, which had no detrimental effects on either the animal or the human test subjects; it was also noted that decompression time, known in the diving world as off-gassing, was shortened with the use of such gas mixtures as the human body can dissolve the helium more quickly. The salvage of the submarine USS *Squalus* in 1939 from a depth of 75 metres off the New Hampshire coast proved that breathing a helium–oxygen mix at depth was both practical and advantageous.

However, while the use of the mixed-gas diving technology that Cousteau was about to utilise was by no means new in the world of commercial diving, its incorporation into open-circuit diving technology to explore a shipwreck was groundbreaking.

With the season's Antikythera dives concluded, the *Calypso* returned to Marina Zeas (Piraeus) to take on board the necessary equipment, before returning to the Kea Channel to begin a more detailed exploration of the wreck. Between 24 September and 10 October 1976 a total of 68 manned dives were made to the wreck, although in terms of bottom time – time actually spent on the wreck itself – each diver was limited to no more than six minutes before having to return to the submerged three-seat Galeazzi decompression chamber, where they could complete their

▲ Sheila Macbeth Mitchell, on board the *Calypso* before her dive. (Peter Nicolaides)

two and a half hours of decompression in relative warmth and comfort before returning to normal surface atmospheric pressure. Finally, to complete the logistics, the expedition also carried the SP-350 *Soucoupe*, *Calypso*'s three-man submersible, affectionately known as 'Denise', which would be on hand to support the dive team and provide additional lighting as they descended to film the wreck.

With everything in place, at the age of 66, Cousteau was about to embark on one of the deepest dives of his career. Incredibly, someone 20 years his senior would be there to show him the way. Eighty-six-year-old Sheila Mitchell, formerly Nurse Sheila Macbeth, who had survived the sinking of the *Britannic* almost 60 years earlier, had responded to his requests for a *Britannic* survivor to join him in Greece, and had flown from Edinburgh to Athens specially for the occasion. At her third attempt Sheila would finally succeed in lowering herself into the *Soucoupe* for her own private tour of the *Britannic*, her presence on board providing a tangible and touching link to the human elements of the programme's story. An interesting calculation also confirms that in 1976 Cousteau set yet another record, with the combined age of the two oldest divers on his expedition being an astonishing 152 years!

Over a 17-day period Cousteau's divers amassed something in the region of 400 minutes on the wreck itself, which was in such robust condition that people were already beginning to speculate that the wreck of the *Titanic*, if and when it was found, would be equally well preserved. Much of the pine decking on the *Britannic* was gone, although the teak decking in the working areas of the focsle seemed to be in remarkably good condition. Structurally, the iron hull looked to be completely intact, and when the divers ventured inside the superstructure, they were able to retrieve a number of well-preserved metal artefacts, including a sextant, the base of a bridge engine telegraph and the brass band of the ship's wheel. In truth, these trophies shed no light whatsoever on the all-important questions about how and why the *Britannic* had been sunk, although Cousteau had already given some consideration to that particular question. On the afternoon of Tuesday 5 October Bill Tantum boarded the *Calypso*, ready to assist where he could with his structural knowledge of the *Titanic*. Not one to waste time, that same afternoon Tantum lowered himself through the *Soucoupe*'s tight hatch, ready for his appointment with the wreck whose exploration he had first proposed one year earlier.

Tantum's commentary as he made his dive was recorded on tape and set down for posterity by the Titanic Historical Society. Inevitably his description of the wreck contains references to the abundant sea life, the broken portholes, the intact propellers, and his journey forward along the promenade deck toward the bridge, but it would be his observations on the forward part of the hull that would later become so controversial. Although he didn't realise it at the time, Tantum's description of what he saw would serve to feed the multitude of conspiracy theories that would later surround the wreck:

From the No. 2 to the No. 3 bulkhead, right straight up to the deck, she is opened up like a can opener. All her ribs and sections of her keel are blown completely away; they are not even there. The ribs that are there are bent and blown out. It looks to me like either a mine or a torpedo hit her in the reserve coal locker, which at this voyage, they had been using coal from Naples – and as you know, coal dust is probably one of the greatest explosives in the world – just blew her all the way through. She's blown completely through, right from starboard to port, port to starboard! The only thing holding the bow to the rest of the hull is the deck and some deck plates. Incidentally, the bow is bent – it is not like the rest of the hull – straight and laying on its side. It is bent at an 85° angle the other way. In other words, when she first touched bottom with her bow, it twisted and as she went a little bit, as the survivors and witnesses stated, that she first went to the port, then she went over to the starboard and then she went back over to the port again and rolled over. The water rushed into the funnels and the funnels broke off simultaneously and she went down on that angle on her starboard side.

▲ Petros Vrontamitis (left), president of the local community of Korissia, with Jacques Cousteau (middle) and Bill Tantum (right) aboard the *Calypso* in October 1976. (Titanic Historical Society)

▶ Cousteau and Tantum's summary of their exploration data. (Titanic Historical Society)

As the fragments were gradually woven together, all of a sudden the arrows were beginning to point in a decidedly troubling direction. Combined with the sheer scale of the apparent blast damage, the fact that the wreck had been found some distance from her charted position seemed to indicate that something more substantial than a single explosion caused by a mine or a torpedo had occurred. At one stage in Cousteau's completed *Britannic* documentary Tantum would even speculate that, before firing his torpedo, a U-boat commander may have seen RAMC orderlies dressed in their khaki uniforms and assumed that the *Britannic* was being used to carry combat troops. If Tantum was right, then it was possible that both the British and the Germans had been playing fast and loose with the regulations, the British by transporting a clandestine

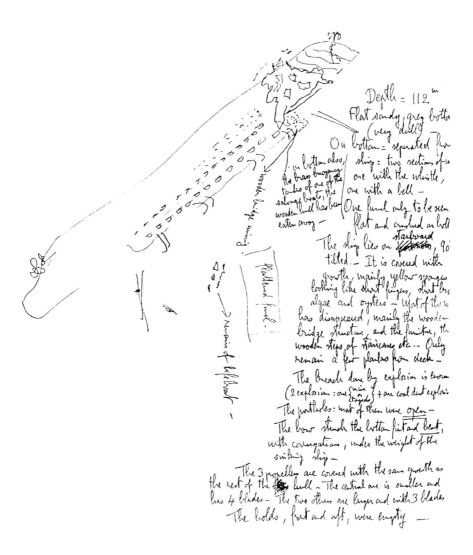

cargo of combatants and war materials, and the Germans by torpedoing a clearly marked hospital ship protected by the Articles of War. At times it almost seemed as if the evidence surrounding the *Britannic*'s fate was being manipulated to explain what Tantum was seeing – or thought he was seeing – for there is no record in any of the official reports or survivors' testimonies of the *Britannic* first listing to port, then to starboard, and then back to port before rolling over. Nor, indeed, was there any mention of a secondary explosion; in fact the official report stated unequivocally that there had been 'one explosion only'.

If Cousteau had hoped to resolve once and for all the historical and political issues that had originally arisen out of the loss of the *Britannic*, unfortunately the 1976 expedition only succeeded in raising more questions than answers. To any self-respecting conspiracy theorist, the mystery of the misplaced shipwreck, the controversial secondary explosion, and the fact that the hull had apparently been blown through completely and that the ribs and plating on the port side were bent in an outward direction could mean only one thing – that a clandestine cargo of munitions had exploded inside the hull, with the British authorities deliberately misplacing the wreck in order to prevent the evidence from ever being discovered. Had the Germans' 1917 allegations been right after all?

Inevitably the newspapers couldn't wait to speculate on the more sensational side of the story, but to be fair to Cousteau, the final programme, *Calypso's Search for the Britannic*, left the viewer in absolutely no doubt about his feelings on the matter when it eventually transmitted in the USA on 22 November 1977. He personally never gave any particular credence to the munitions theory, and by the time he and his team had concluded their planned dives they had found no evidence whatsoever of any illicit cargo in any of the holds. The discovery of deposits of coal on the seabed near the area of the breach persuaded Cousteau, no doubt spurred on by Tantum's exploding-coal-dust theory, that the initial blast had simply touched off a secondary and far more devastating explosion in the *Britannic*'s reserve coal bunker.

By the end of 1977 the *Britannic*, which for almost 60 years had lain undisturbed and all but forgotten on the bottom of the Kea Channel, was suddenly back in the headlines, and on the face of it the wreck was finally beginning to give up some of her secrets. For the next 20 years, however, Cousteau's expedition would remain the only detailed exploration of the wreck from which historians would be able to draw any evidence, and being located at such an extreme depth, not to mention right in the middle of a particularly busy shipping lane, there seemed little chance of anyone being able to pick up where Cousteau had left off until the available underwater

▶ Painting of the wreck done in 1991, based on an interpretation of Bill Tantum's 1976 data.

(Painting © Ken Marschall – THS Collection)

technology was a lot more accessible. Until such a time, the findings of the 1976 expedition would continue to be discussed and argued within the *Titanic* world, and would continue to be embellished over the course of the next 20 years in order to bolster the evidence that best suited the more controversial agendas.

As the *Calypso* departed the Kea Channel in October 1976 for pastures new, Jacques Cousteau was quite confident that he knew everything there was to know about the *Britannic*. But did he? Then again, with Cousteau's superior track record in exploration, would anyone even consider disagreeing with the grand old man of the sea?

11

IN THE FOOTSTEPS OF COUSTEAU

The questions concerning whether the *Britannic* was mined or torpedoed, and whether she was carrying troops or munitions – even though Cousteau had already confirmed that her cargo hold was indeed empty – would endure for the next 20 years, reigniting the old allegations which had lain dormant since the end of the First World War. In many ways the *Britannic*, particularly with the focus on a mysterious internal explosion, had suddenly become a conspiracy theorist's dream, made even more sensational by the *Titanic* connection, but without following in Cousteau's footsteps it would be all but impossible to directly question his version of events.

In the late spring of 1995 it finally seemed that this might actually happen and – incredibly – that I might even be involved. It had all started out as a relatively simple research job. This was no great chore for me as from time to time my work in the film industry involved researching the occasional documentary project, so when I was called by Lisa Wolfinger from the Varied Directions documentary company in Portland, Maine, at first I remained strangely detached. Quite why I was so removed from it all I am not sure, as by that time I had been researching the *Olympic* and *Britannic* for a good five or six years. The occasional documentary enquiry was not unusual, even if it rarely resulted in anything tangible, but this call seemed different. Lisa was involved in the early stages of planning the documentary treatment of an expedition to the *Britannic* by Dr Robert D. Ballard, the man who in 1985 had co-led the expedition that had located the wreck of the *Titanic*; ten years on, he now wanted to celebrate the tenth anniversary of that discovery by exploring the wreck of her less-well-known sister ship. The deal was not yet signed with the broadcaster, Nova-WGBH, but there was enough initial interest to begin the preliminary research, and the fact that I was the only person in living memory to have published a book on the *Britannic* meant that sooner or later they would find their way to my door. Amazing as it seemed, suddenly I was considered to be 'the expert'!

As the spring moved into summer I was happy enough to carry out some provisional film archive research in the UK, but I had little or no thought of being on the voyage itself until, in a telephone conversation, Ken Marschall, one of Bob Ballard's historical advisers, suggested that if I was in Greece when the expedition began they *might* be able to find me a place on board the research vessel. It was a tantalising suggestion. Even if I wasn't quite ready to fly to Greece on a wing and a prayer, it was enough for me to start thinking on it over the next few days, particularly as Cathy Offinger, Bob Ballard's logistical organiser, had given her approval provided

Nova said that I was essential to the project. I suspected that it would be quite a job to persuade anyone that my presence was essential, and a cramped and stuffy viewing room in the basement of the British Film Institute was probably not the ideal venue in which to broach the subject with Lisa, but I knew it was the only chance that I would have to discuss it face to face. As we mulled over the reams of black and white archival footage on the noisy 35mm Steenbeck editing table, no doubt aided in her decision by my offer to waive my paltry researcher's fee, Lisa gave an encouraging response: 'No problem if you want to come to Greece, but as you are in the film business would you mind helping out the cameraman as he usually works alone?' I should have seen that one coming, but I had no problem with the thought of loading the occasional camera magazine if it meant that I would be on the trip. I am reasonably certain that it is the only time that a focus puller, which was my grade in the camera department back then, has ever been regarded as 'essential' to any project.

▲ Dr Robert D. Ballard and Cathy Offinger, holding the THS memorial plaque.

Even then, it was not quite a done deal. A last-minute hitch threatened to result in the expedition's cancellation even before it had started, as the Greek gods threw a particularly hefty spanner in the works in the form of the Greek government's concern at rumours of unexploded munitions being inside the wreck. For several days the final clearance still remained elusive, but fortunately the assurances of the historical team, and, I suspect, also the American Department of Defense, saved the day. The official permission was duly authorised, but only on the understanding that no internal penetration of the wreck would be allowed. It was a major disappointment, but at least we knew that we were definitely going.

On the other hand, the extended run-up to the expedition had allowed me plenty of time to augment the suggested dive plan with a few targets of my own. Needless to say, everyone wanted to carry out a detailed video inspection of the exterior, including extensive photography of the entire hull, in order to put together a detailed photomosaic of the wreck, but having wanted to explore the wreck for so long, it's curious that my main contribution to the project was actually to propose that we look further afield, in an attempt to find evidence of the German mine sinkers. If they could be found, it would surely resolve the mine *vs.* torpedo controversy once and for all, so I was especially pleased when the plan got Bob's official approval, but with the proviso that it would only happen after the filmmakers had obtained their required images of the *NR-1* (the nuclear submarine being used as part of the expedition, about which more later) and the wreck. The mine anchors weren't going anywhere, so I was happy enough with the agreed order of battle.

Although we would be following in Cousteau's footsteps, we would actually be using radically different technology. Not being an advocate of manned diving operations, Ballard instead favoured the use of remote technology when working in deep water, made possible by the success of the remote operated vehicles (ROVs) used on the *Titanic* in 1986. Nine years on, Ballard brought with him two ROVs – the older *Phantom* being used for video and stills, and the newer *Voyager*, on loan from Perry Tritech, equipped with a new 3-D camera system being developed at NASA's Ames Research Center in California. The use of ROVs also meant that we did not have to deal with the issues of diver narcosis and decompression that Cousteau had faced back in 1976. But in August 1995 our real ace in the hole was the fact that our base ship, the *Carolyn Chouest*, also happened to be the support vessel for the US Navy's nuclear submarine *NR-1*. If there were any *Britannic* myths to be disproved and questions to be answered, surely we now had the equipment to resolve them once and for all?

The toys at our disposal were undeniably impressive, but coordinating everything would prove

▶ Launching the ROV *Voyager*.

more problematic. Although under charter from the Edison Chouest company, the *Carolyn Chouest* was still serving as a naval auxiliary, meaning that everyone on board was effectively under military orders. This was not necessarily as draconian as it sounds – in fact, we were generally free to go anywhere on board except the radio room, which, because it contained the highly secret naval codes, was probably the most secure location on board. For safety reasons, no one was allowed to venture alone onto the ship's fantail at night without first advising the officer of the watch up on the bridge. More importantly, when you had finished whatever you were doing, you then had to report back to the bridge so that they knew you had not fallen overboard, avoiding sparking a major search and rescue alert. The only real drawback of working on a naval vessel was the difficulty of obtaining information from the liaison department. This may well have been because we were not regarded as military personnel, which of course we were not, but I will confess to having felt a degree of smugness when providing them with Cousteau's corrected positional fix on the wreck, as their charts were still 20 years out of date!

Even so, there could be no doubting Ballard's technology. The *NR-1* (*Nuclear Research 1*) was a nuclear-powered submarine, which brought with it a host of advantages, not least the fact that the submarine could maintain a 24-hour presence over the wreck for the seven days that

we would be in the Kea Channel. Even to be operating a nuclear submarine in Greek waters required the permission of the Hellenic Navy; indeed, so unusual was the application for diplomatic clearance that the paperwork was handled through the office of the Hellenic Navy General Staff, rather than by the usual Greek cultural authorities. The logistics for supporting such a

▲ The SSV *Carolyn Chouest*.

▲ The *NR-1*, a unique nuclear-powered submarine that would allow us to survey the exterior of the
Britannic in hitherto unimaginable detail.

▲ The chart table on the *Carolyn Chouest*'s bridge, with the converted *Titanic* model that would guide the
ROV pilots.

vessel, which, in order to save time, had been towed 140 miles from Souda Bay on Crete to the Kea Channel, were also considerable. Although not originally intended for documentary film-making, *NR-1*'s silicon intensified target (SIT) cameras, augmented by a bank of powerful thallium iodide underwater lights, had been specially developed for all manner of military and scientific research applications. At night the thallium iodide lights bathed the wreck in a ghostly green hue, making them less useful from the point of view of filming in colour, but when working at depth, where the wavelength of light decreases across the visible colour spectrum, the enhanced ability of the green light to penetrate the water column meant that we would be able to illuminate far greater areas of the wreck than we would by using standard incandescent lighting.

The *Carolyn Chouest* finally arrived in the Kea Channel at 8.45am on 29 August 1995, but as preparations began for the first dives, a small caique approached from the direction of Port St Nikolo carrying a port police official who wanted to know why we had stopped in the middle of a busy shipping lane. A quick word from the Greek naval liaison officer assigned to the expedition confirmed that we had the required permits, and once he knew that the paperwork was in order, the official was happy to go about his business, pointing out as he left that we were actually in the wrong place and that the *Britannic* was several miles from that particular spot. Amazingly, almost 20 years after the wreck had been relocated, the charts for the area still had not been updated, but I assured Bruce Kay, the captain of the *Carolyn Chouest*, that the position that I had provided to Bob was up to date. Trusting the UK Hydrographic Office coordinates, preparations for the first dive continued and at 1.30pm Bob finally transferred to the *NR-1*, along with the NOVA cameraman Nick Doob and sound technician Dan McIntosh.

THE EMOTIONAL ROLLERCOASTER

Someone once told me that diving is not a spectator sport, and the ensuing hours on the *Carolyn Chouest* bitterly proved the point. As the minutes slowly ticked by, the lack of any information left me seriously wondering if my confidence in the Hydrographic Office position had been misplaced. Had Cousteau got his position wrong? Had I sent the very expensive *NR-1* off on a wild goose chase to the wrong end of the Kea Channel? Was the *Britannic* even located in the channel at all? My growing self-doubt was not helped at all by the strange pinging, whistling sound that seemed to reverberate throughout the ship, which we soon found out was in fact caused by the radio waves from the *NR-1* travelling through the water and bouncing off the hull of the *Carolyn Chouest*. Judging by the amount of acoustic noise, someone was evidently saying quite a lot, but unless you were in the radio room itself, the one part of the ship from which we were banned, there was no way of knowing what was happening. The more I listened to the din, the further away the *Britannic* seemed to get; in the end I could take it no longer and made my way up to the bridge to see if anyone actually knew what was going on. Spying Al Murray, the officer of the watch, standing to one side, I walked over to him, hoping that he could put me out of my misery. 'Any news, Al?' I asked sheepishly.

'Not much. They've been on the wreck for a couple of hours now; it's about 90 feet high!'

To Al it all seemed like no big deal, but his reassuring response was exactly what I needed to hear. Suddenly my anxious visions of Bob coming back on board, his multi-million-dollar submarine having found nothing, and telling me exactly where I could stick my coordinates evaporated. My confidence, which only seconds before had been at rock bottom, suddenly came flooding back. Determined not to show any more self-doubt and to maintain a degree of outward calm, I made my way down to a quiet corner of the conference room where I could finally begin to relax. Ever so slowly, snippets of information finally began to find their way down to the saloon, and by the time night fell we knew that the wreck was on a heading of 253°, that she was largely intact, and that the visibility was in the region of 40 feet.

The following morning, at precisely 11.36am, *NR-1* finally resurfaced and the tapes were quickly brought aboard. The first night of operations had seemingly gone without a hitch, and

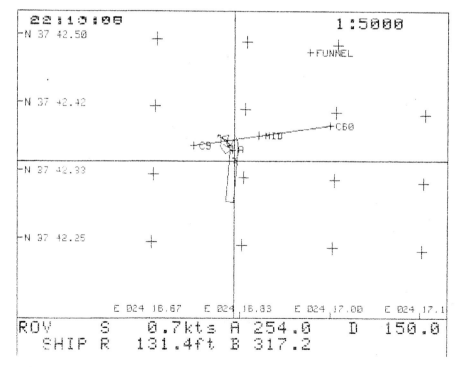

▲ The US Navy's printout of the wreck's location.

as Ken Marschall and Charlie Smith, Bob's on-board video technician, transferred to the zodiac for the next dive, Kirk Wolfinger, the producer from Varied Directions, was keen to make an immediate start on reviewing the SIT camera footage. The results did not disappoint, even if the multitude of fish attracted by the *NR-1*'s lights more often than not totally obscured the impressive views of the wreck, but the fact that the *Britannic* lies on her side also meant that the orientation of the footage was rotated by 90 degrees. The sight of five grown men staring at a video screen with their heads all tilted to one side probably raised more than a few eyebrows from passers-by, but it was only after developing an acute pain in the neck that I decided to release the ratchet straps holding the monitor in position in order to turn it on its side.

For the most part we were thrilled with the footage: in a single night we had covered the entire wreck from end to end. But the first inkling that not everything had gone quite to plan came a short while later, when it transpired that the stills cameras on the *NR-1* had not been loaded before the dive, so we had spent the entire night snapping away without any film in the magazines. No one seemed to know exactly how it had happened, the most logical assumption being that due to a breakdown in communications, before attaching the cameras to the *NR-1* the divers had assumed that they were already loaded. Fortunately not everything had depended on that one dive, and there was still enough time to load the cameras and reattach them to the *NR-1* before she submerged that afternoon.

However, that would turn out to be only the first of a series of technical glitches that would bedevil the expedition for the next few days. The plan for the second day had been to commence the first ROV operations that evening, even though we would actually spend more time filming the *NR-1* to provide footage for the Navy's publicity department, as with the Cold War now over, it was felt that US voters needed to see where their hard-earned tax dollars had been spent. However, problems with the dynamic positioning equipment (SDP), without which the *Carolyn* could not maintain an exact position over the wreck, meant that *Phantom* couldn't be launched until shortly before midnight. Even then we had to wait for another hour while the *NR-1* powered up her lighting system, after which we then spent the better part of three hours grabbing images of the submarine for the documentary. It was not until 4.30am that we were finally able to start filming the *Britannic*'s promenade deck, cargo cranes and forward well deck, and by the time *Phantom* was back on deck we had been on the go for exactly 24 hours, proving once again that wreck exploration is sometimes not as glamorous as you might think. For myself, I was puffed

▷ North-running side-scan sonar emphasising the shadow of the *Britannic*'s counter with the rudder turned to port. (Dr Robert D. Ballard)

▷ *NR-1*'s full-length sonar of the wreck. (Dr Robert D. Ballard)

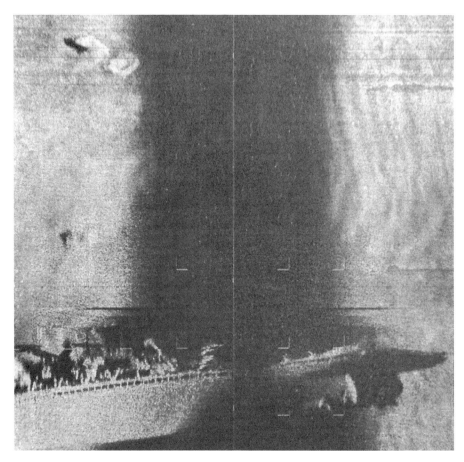

up by a feeling of self-importance as the officially designated dive log keeper – I suspect largely because no one else really wanted to do it.

In spite of the technical problems, in the first 36 hours we had already obtained the first substantial images of the wreck, and with the *NR-1* now allocated to other tasks we could at last concentrate on the ROV footage that would be so crucial for the programme. It would also give us something to do on board the *Carolyn*. But while the plan looked sound enough on paper, from the moment I sat down in the lab at the beginning of day three it was downhill all the way. First of all, the ship's SDP apparatus failed again, and to make matters worse, Randy Ledet, the specialist technician who was the only one who could put it right, had gone ashore to Kea to catch the morning ferry to Piraeus. The captain dashed ashore in the *Carolyn*'s Z-boat to search for Randy in one of the quayside bars in St Nikolo before the ferry departed, and about an hour later, much to his annoyance, Randy was back on board to rectify the fault.

Things got worse, however. Having been told by Kirk that I would be getting a dive in the *NR-1*, barely an hour later I heard that because I was not an American citizen I was not allowed to go aboard the nuclear submarine. This made no sense at all, as only four days earlier I had been all over the submarine, installing the strip lights in the observers' viewing pad for Nick's cameras. No one had raised any questions at the time, although thinking back on it I did recall the slightly quizzical look on one officer's face when he heard my ever-so-British accent and asked me if I was an American citizen. He had shrugged and seemed to accept the situation before leaving, but without realising it I had created a major security issue before we had even left Souda Bay. I later heard that Lieutenant Commander David Olivier, the officer commanding the *NR-1*, had been none too pleased to discover that some foreign civilian had not only walked straight through his security, but had boarded a US Navy nuclear submarine and then proceeded to take photos! That clearly wasn't going to happen again, and it meant that I was no longer going to get my dive. Cathy tried to cheer me up by saying that Bob's relationship with the Pentagon should resolve the problem, but with Labor Day weekend coming up, I wasn't hopeful that it could be sorted in time.

As if to further darken my mood, the technical problems began to mount. Focus issues on one of *Voyager*'s 3-D cameras forced the early recovery of the ROV, and until the problem was fixed all I could do was continue to analyse the SIT camera footage. Fortunately things picked up the following day, with *Voyager*'s repaired cameras obtaining impressive images of the stern and propellers, while *Phantom* took hundreds of stills along the boat deck between the bridge and casing of what would have been funnel number three. Perhaps it was appropriate that everything should come right on that particular day, because it left everyone in precisely the right mood for the party that night in the dining saloon to celebrate the tenth anniversary of finding the *Titanic*. I couldn't think of anywhere more appropriate to have been at that time than directly above the wreck of her sister ship.

The party may have been fun, but the technical problems continued to bedevil the expedition. As we prepared for the evening's operations, Bruce Kay passed on the news that somehow the *NR-1* had accidentally dropped the memorial plaque that was to be laid on the wreck, and that they had been ordered to retrace their movements in order to find it. The window for exploring the minefield was diminishing before my eyes, and when *Phantom* developed a ground fault while we were exploring along the promenade deck, it was enough to cancel the night's activities altogether. The following day, problems with a bearing in one of *Voyager*'s motors curtailed yet another dive, and when the American VIP guests began to arrive from Athens, I realised that my chances of being able to locate the minefield on this trip were looking doubtful. Facing up to the disappointment, I grudgingly accepted that as we had been given free use of the *NR-1* it was not unreasonable for the American VIPs to be given a tour. However, although I didn't realise it, my work that day was not quite done. To pass the time while the submarine was submerged, Kirk asked if I would film a sequence with Rear Admiral Richard Mies, who was commanding the American Mediterranean submarine flotilla. It was a relatively straightforward sequence, even though I continued to distinguish myself by not knowing my east from my west, but the plan to locate the remains of the minefield definitely got his interest. As the liaison officer quickly

▲ The cake specially baked for the tenth anniversary of the discovery of the wreck of the *Titanic*. The fact that we were diving on her sister ship at the time made it a particularly appropriate venue for the celebration.

▲ Myself at the helm of the *NR-1*, supposedly keeping a low profile while on board.

▶ Souvenir certificate of my first *Britannic* dive.

▶ The first mine barrier survey.

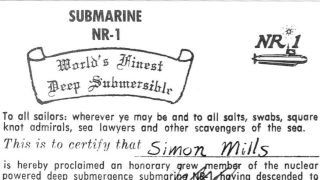

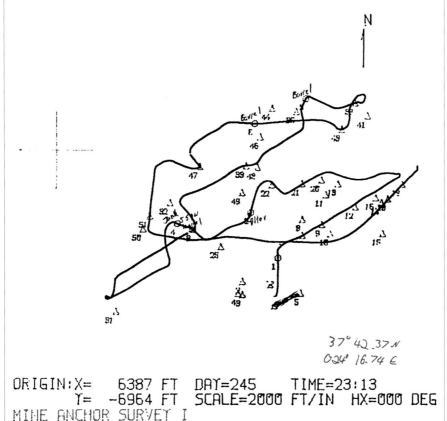

ORIGIN:X=   6387 FT   DAY=245   TIME=23:13
        Y= -6964 FT   SCALE=2000 FT/IN   HX=000 DEG
MINE ANCHOR SURVEY I

disappeared to pass on the orders to investigate the area more thoroughly, I dared to hope that it still might not be too late.

I had already resigned myself to the fact that I would not get a chance to see the wreck with my own eyes when all of a sudden Bob walked up to me to say that he had had a word with the admiral, and he had given his approval for me to go aboard the *NR-1*. I was given ten minutes to pack an overnight bag, and nine minutes later I was in the Z-boat and on the way over to the *NR-1*. Because of my apparently dubious nationality, Bob's instructions were for me to make sure that I stayed in the viewing pad for the entire night so that there was less chance of me seeing anything that might be regarded as sensitive. I thought it better not to mention to the

admiral that actually I had already seen the reactor when I had been on board to set up the lights in Souda Bay, or that the reactor technician on duty had even given me a friendly wave through the glass window in the steel door. Once I was aboard it no longer mattered, and immediately after the obligatory on-board familiarisation – as though I actually needed it – I dropped down into the viewing pad directly beneath the con, from where the submarine was steered, and where, true to my word, I would remain for the rest of the night.

For all the disappointment of missing the earlier dives, in the end I could not have picked a better one on which to be present. With camera sequences planned from the focsle to the propellers, I was effectively given the grand tour of the *Britannic*, even if the view through the *NR-1*'s 6-inch starboard viewport was limited at best. We were still working to the instructions from the surface, but shortly before midnight the ROVs were recovered and we were finally sent on our way to see if we could find the mine evidence in the remaining few hours. With Bob's impossible challenge to shoot off the entire roll of film, we headed in a south-westerly direction to a position where, if Kapitänleutnant Siess had got his calculations right, we would hopefully locate the physical evidence to prove once and for all that the *Britannic* had not been deliberately sunk by a torpedo.

Sadly, the bottom of the Kea Channel is no longer the pristine environment it once was. At one stage the submarine's instruments were picking up so many contacts on the seabed that it was impossible to know which one to check out first. On the one hand I was delighted that my strategy to locate the minefield appeared to be viable, but as the night wore on, almost imperceptibly the external background light began to change from pitch black to an intensely dark blue. As the view continued to brighten, I instinctively knew that we were not going to locate the mine anchors in the available time, and when the order was given to surface at 5.00am, as I watched the seabed slowly drop away I knew that we had missed our chance. At 6.00am on Monday 4 September 1995 the *NR-1* broke the surface, signalling the end of our expedition.

REFLECTIONS

As the *Carolyn Chouest* headed south and back to Souda Bay, I could only reflect on what we had achieved. For me, the lack of time to locate the minefield had struck a particularly raw nerve, not to mention the fact that we had not been permitted to go inside the wreck, but we had still covered the exterior of the wreck and the surrounding area in more detail than Jacques Cousteau would ever have dreamed possible. The hours of video imagery would provide an invaluable

◀ The 1995 team. (Eric Sauder)

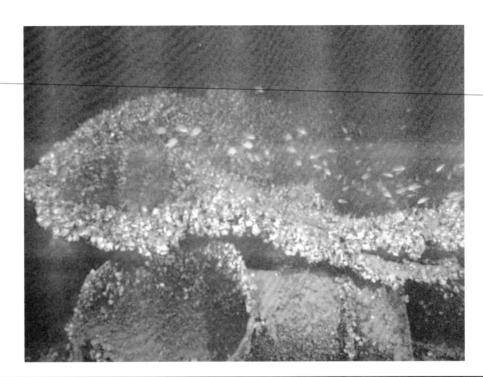

resource for analysis and would certainly keep me occupied for the next several months, with the vast scale of the damage to the hull just forward of the bridge attracting particular attention. In fact it did not take us long to conclude that the hull had not been blown through by a huge internal explosion, as Cousteau and Tantum had postulated back in 1976, and although it was true that the extensive damage was way beyond that capable of being caused by a single mine, there was now little doubt that it had largely been caused when the focsle came up against the resistance of the seabed as the weight of the main hull, part of which was still above the surface, continued to provide a significant downward force. The analysis of the 1995 video confirmed that it was the stresses exerted in this area of the hull during the sinking process that had eventually caused it to give way; as the focsle then settled forward onto the seabed, this would have had the additional effect of further prising the hull open like an egg, causing the deck plating below the forward well deck to collapse inwards in a tangled mass.

The last hours of any expedition are generally an anticlimax, as everything begins to wind down and the ship returns to port. After we had finished packing away the equipment there was the obligatory meeting in the ship's conference room, where we were all sworn to secrecy until after the programme had been transmitted, though at the same time we all knew that we would be up to our necks in post-expedition analysis for the next four months. In truth, it is the kind of research that anyone even half-interested in the *Britannic* would have been happy to do, but at the same time, when you are working on a programme for the general public, you also know that there is so much more technical and specialised detail that will eventually have to be left out.

It was with a combination of pleasure and frustration that I first watched *Titanic's Lost Sister*, which aired in America on 28 January 1997. The documentary nicely summed up the extent of the additional knowledge that we had gained on the 1995 expedition, but the much-hoped-for companion article in the *National Geographic* magazine ultimately had to be abandoned because every single one of the thousands of photographic stills taken on the voyage had been ruined by an unidentifiable stock defect. In the end the pictures, all sent to the magazine, simply did not meet its high technical standards, and with that, the chance to create the detailed photo-mosaic was also lost. When *Lost Liners* was finally published later that year, barely a handful of indistinct wreck images, all taken by Ken Marschall through one of the *NR-1*'s viewports, found their way into the book's *Britannic* section, the official 1995 *Britannic* expedition images having sadly disappeared into a forgotten and dusty corner of the *National Geographic* photographic archive in Washington, DC. They are probably still there...

◀ Two of the photographic images affected by the mysterious stock fault. (Dr Robert D. Ballard)

▲ Updated painting of the wreck of the *Britannic* from 1995. Compare this image with the one on page 127 in the previous chapter. (Painting © Ken Marschall)

All of that, however, was still to come, and as we left the Kea Channel to return to Crete, I reflected on the path that had led me to that particular point. A few years earlier I had written a brief book on the *Britannic* and it had been enough for Nova to agree to take me on their 1995 expedition, but I could content myself with what we had discovered, and with the knowledge that I had helped to formulate the plans for the exploration of the wreck. I had also been privileged to get a dive in the *NR-1* and see the *Britannic* with my own eyes, which was surely about as good as it could possibly get. But while I continued to obsess about the things that we had failed to achieve on that trip, the realist inside me seemed to be telling me that I would probably never return to the wreck.

By September 1995 I honestly thought that I was done with the *Britannic*; I had little idea that actually she had not even started with me!

12

THE IMPOSSIBLE DREAM

The ten months that followed the Ballard expedition are still something of a blur. Immediately after returning from Kea I found myself on a six-month shoot in Rome on *Daylight*, an improbable piece of Hollywood hokum with Sylvester Stallone in a flooded New York traffic tunnel, followed by two months in London on *London Suite*, a new Neil Simon teleplay. Something must have gone very right on that project as that summer I then found myself working for the same production company, appropriately enough on a television adaptation of *Twenty Thousand Leagues Under the Sea*. Truth be told, ours was not a particularly faithful treatment – in fact, I am pretty sure that Jules Verne would have been spinning in his grave if he could see what our screenwriters were doing to his literary classic – but the fact that I was once again working on a project with a seagoing theme meant that my thoughts were, perhaps inevitably, beginning to drift back to the *Britannic*. Never in my wildest dreams, though, was I prepared for what was to come.

I still remember it as if it were yesterday. Wednesday 31 July 1996 was a gloriously sunny day, perfect for filming our exterior *Nautilus* sequences in the paddock tank at Pinewood Studios. It was so hot that when the unit had broken for lunch I had decided to remain alone on the set, stretched out on one of the camera rostrums above the tank. It was an oddly tranquil setting, with none of the usual noise or hubbub to suggest that I was actually in the middle of the largest and busiest film studio in the UK. All I could hear as I dozed was the noise of the water gently overflowing into the spillway, but suddenly the peace was interrupted by the sound of my phone ringing. I recall being incredibly annoyed by the unwanted interruption to my lunchtime snooze, but I decided to answer it anyway, as a polite voice on the line asked, 'Is that Simon Mills?'

'Yes, can I help you?'

'My name is Bamford; I'm calling about your letter...'

Suddenly I was wide awake. A few days earlier I had been speaking with Paul Louden-Brown, a friend and fellow White Star Line researcher, who had told me that Mark Bamford, of the JCB family, had apparently obtained from the British government the rights to the *Britannic*. The revelation had confused us both, as we had always been under the impression that the wreck was still owned by the government, an understandable enough conclusion as we even had a letter from the Ministry of Defence confidently stating as much. Paul's comment had got me curious – so much so that I had decided to contact Mr Bamford to get to the bottom of it.

The discussion about the ownership issue did not last very long, as Mark quickly confirmed that he had obtained the legal paperwork to the UK government's legal title as far back as July of 1977, not to mention the legal title to 19 other shipwrecks! After that we seemed to go off on a bit of a tangent, as he began to ask me about Pinewood and to talk about the Norman Wisdom movies filmed at the studio in the late fifties and early sixties, for which I sensed he had a particular fondness. Eventually the conversation came back to the wrecks, but I was totally unprepared when he casually said, 'I haven't done anything with the wrecks in years, so I'm clearing the books if you want to buy them!'

It was not at all what I had in mind when I had written my letter only a few days earlier, but as I tried to gather my thoughts, while at the same time trying to appear cool, calm and pro-fessional, I responded by saying, 'That's very good of you, Mark, but I'm really not sure what I would do with 20 shipwrecks.' And then I said it: 'I might be interested if we were just talking about the *Britannic*.'

◄ Myself pictured in 1992 alongside the 50-foot *Titanic* model on Malta, which was specially built for Lew Grade's 1981 movie *Raise the Titanic* before being reused as a hospital ship in the 1991 TV mini-series *The Burning Shore* – four years before I bought the wreck!

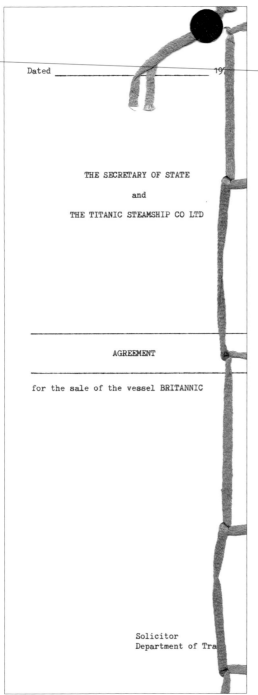

THE SECRETARY OF STATE

and

THE TITANIC STEAMSHIP CO LTD

AGREEMENT

for the sale of the vessel BRITANNIC

Dated _____ 19

Solicitor
Department of Tra

I still have no idea what prompted me to say it, but I recall Mark's last words to me as he rang off: 'All right, you now have first option on the *Britannic*!' After that, all I could do was sit beside my camera in a virtual state of shock, contemplating the fact that this phone call would probably be the most expensive lunch break I was ever likely to have.

Even then I could have backed out at that early stage, but the more I thought about it, the more intrigued I became at the thought of actually owning the *Britannic*. The fact that I was due to travel to Turkey to begin work on filming a Hallmark production of Homer's *Odyssey* left me with little time to waste, but within three weeks I had done my homework and set up Governcheck Limited, the company that would officially hold the legal title to the wreck. After that it was time for me to put my money where my mouth was. On the evening of 20 August 1996 I drove to JCB's Mayfair office at 3 Deanery Street, not wishing to trust the postal service due to an ongoing strike at the Royal Mail; as I watched the envelope containing my cheque drop through the letter box I knew there was no going back. Unbelievably, the *Britannic* was all mine!

The purchase of the legal title had actually been surprisingly uncomplicated, but now I had to stand back and, for the first time, ask myself what I was actually going to do with it. Amazing as it may seem, this question had

◀ The Department of Trade's original sale agreement, dated 20 July 1977.

scarcely occurred to me up to that point, although at that time there was no apparent pressure on me to get any structure in place. The *Britannic* had only been visited twice in the previous 20 years, and having personally seen the logistics involved in accessing the wreck, I knew that the odds were negligible that anyone would be planning to go back anytime soon.

How little I knew. The 1995 Ballard expedition, far from drawing a line under the mystery of the *Britannic*, had actually succeeded in bringing the existence of the wreck to the attention of the diving world. After *Titanic's Lost Sister* had been transmitted in the UK, suddenly the forgotten sister was anything but forgotten, and sure enough, the first contact came as early as the end of May 1997, from Jonathan Levingston, with a proposal to salvage the wreck by encasing it in liquid nitrogen until there was enough lift from the resulting berg to raise it to the surface. I was certainly intrigued enough by the proposal to call Mr Levingston to discuss his idea in more detail, remembering that something quite similar had once been proposed for use on the *Titanic*, although from an economic standpoint any such operation was clearly out of the question. More to the point, although my position at the time with the Greek Ephorate of Marine Antiquities was not yet established, I felt pretty confident that they would not be too thrilled at the prospect of 40,000 tons of corroding iron being unceremoniously dumped on a convenient beach so that the wreck could be opened to the public.

An inbuilt mistrust of the diving world was also holding me back from actively pursuing any exploration goals of my own. Two months later, however, the first enquiry from the world of technical diving arrived on my desk. The letter came from Kevin Gurr, then UK chairman of the International Association of Nitrox & Technical Divers (IANTD), who wanted to take a dive team to the *Britannic* in the autumn of 1997. When a similar application arrived from Nick Hope's Starfish Enterprise team, looking at a potential dive in the late summer of 1998, for the first time I began to suspect that I might have bitten off a little more than I could chew.

For those in the *Titanic* world who think that owning the *Britannic* is unbelievably glamorous – which I suppose it is – take my word for it when I say it is also something of a double-edged sword. Within a year of signing the legal papers I was beginning to realise that there was a lot more to managing this particular asset than I had originally thought, and with interest from archaeologists, scientists, historians, the war graves lobby, salvage experts and technical divers, each group with their own very different agendas, I suddenly found myself having to consider the legal options. A standard diving access agreement was drawn up by Philip Heartfield of Fishburn Boxer Solicitors, pretty much covering all the necessary legal niceties with regard to going inside the wreck or removing anything from the site, but at the same time all of this activity was suddenly bringing me to the attention of the Greek authorities. This was something that I had particularly wanted to avoid until I had a better idea of what *I* actually wanted to do with the wreck, and yet by the end of 1997 I was involved in detailed official correspondence with the Greek Ministers of Culture and Foreign Affairs, not to mention several face-to-face meetings with Captain Ioannis Fournarakis, at that time the maritime attaché at the Greek embassy in Holland Park, to ensure that everything was in order with the Ministry of Merchant Marine. I still remember the quizzical look on his face at our first meeting, no doubt wondering what kind of idiot would actually buy a shipwreck, to which I can only say *this* kind of idiot would buy a shipwreck. Even so, our meetings were always very friendly and he was happy to forward the required legal documentation to the ministry on my behalf.

In spite of this, my suspicion of the diving world still remained, so it seems strange that I was undertaking so much work on behalf of the 1997 and 1998 expeditions, particularly as I had no official involvement or financial interest in either trip. The reality, however, was that they presented me with an ideal opportunity to start formulating a dive plan for the future. I had nothing like the same access to the logistics or technology that Cousteau and Ballard enjoyed, but at the same time technical divers were practically queueing up to visit the *Britannic*. By harnessing this interest, I could at least start looking at the areas of the wreck where *I* wanted to go, so, burying my suspicions, I decided to cooperate and started work on my very first dive plan.

WORKING THINGS OUT

It is not easy to follow in the footsteps of luminaries such as Jacques Cousteau and Bob Ballard. Both had led groundbreaking expeditions to explore the *Britannic* utilising totally different exploration technologies, and the resulting media interest had left me with a proverbial mountain to climb if I was to come anywhere close to emulating their success. They had pretty much covered the exterior of the wreck, but practically nothing was known of the interior. The wreck of the *Britannic* thus remained full of mysteries, and if the 1997 and 1998 expeditions were to be of any value, my immediate task was to separate the fact from the fiction, while setting realistic and attainable goals.

So what exactly did we know? Between them, Cousteau and Ballard had answered many of the questions, but they had raised so many more. Cousteau's achievement in locating the wreck so far from its charted position was conspiracy theorists' gold, leading to speculation that the British had deliberately misplaced the wreck in order to conceal a secret cargo of illicit munitions. Combined with Bill Tantum's references to an internal explosion having blown through the ship, perhaps there was enough *prima facie* evidence to support that particular theory. Yet neither Cousteau nor Ballard reported finding any contraband in or around the wreck, so you would have thought that would have scotched the munitions theory once and for all, but even so the doubts persisted. Less easy to prove was the theory that the explosion had been caused by a mine or a torpedo, and the nagging question remained as to why the *Britannic*, which supposedly had been able to survive the same damage that had sunk the *Titanic*, succumbed to a single mine in barely a third of the time that it took for her sister to go down. Were the conspiracy theorists correct that the ship had been deliberately sabotaged in order to generate sympathy for the Allied cause in the USA, in the hope that America might eventually enter the war against Germany?

If the *Britannic* project was to be taken seriously I needed to avoid being drawn by the conspiracy theorists onto their chosen ground. In truth, by 1997 the issues of the misplaced wreck and the illegal munitions cargo were largely discredited – at least in my mind – and even if the charted position of the wreck was incorrect, the *Britannic*'s own log book, an open document that had been available at the National Archives since at least the late sixties, made it abundantly clear that the wreck lay three miles north-west of Port St Nikolo, which was pretty much where Cousteau eventually found it. Even the most inept of researchers could not have failed to notice this obvious detail had they actually bothered to look, although the issue of the alleged internal explosion would prove to be more problematic. At that stage, even if the case for the illicit munitions seemed unlikely, it was just not possible to completely rule out an internal blast of some description, meaning that for the time being Tantum's and Cousteau's theory concerning exploding coal dust still needed to be given some consideration.

Perhaps the most pressing objective, at least from my point of view, was to try to pick up where we had left off previously in the search for the mine that had supposedly sunk the ship. Our failure to locate the mine anchors in September 1995 still rankled, particularly as my experience on board the *NR-1* had convinced me that the strategy we had used was sound; in one night we had picked up so many sonar contacts at the bottom of the Kea Channel that had we not run out of time, I am still convinced that the most sensitive question, that of mine *vs.* torpedo, could have been resolved there and then. Even so, I could at least content myself with the knowledge that the evidence was still lying there, just waiting to be found.

All of these factors persuaded me that if the proposed expeditions were to be of any practical value, there needed to be a more planned approach to the exploration of the wreck. At first I imagined causing all sorts of ructions by going toe to toe with a group of hard-headed technical divers, telling them that it was my way or the highway. I could not have been more wrong. Far from ignoring my thoughts, both Kevin and Nick were extremely receptive to the notion of a properly coordinated search plan, as indeed was Jarrod Jablonski of Global Underwater Explorers, who also submitted an application for an expedition in 1999. Suddenly the possibility of co-ordinating three trips over three successive summers made me dare to believe that not only could I pick up where Cousteau and Ballard had left off, but there was even the possibility of solving the remaining mysteries.

All of this meant that I needed to be damn sure of keeping my focus on the smallest of details, and with this in mind I set about putting together what is probably still the most detailed and considered dive plan ever created for the exploration of any shipwreck by recreational divers. I always left the technical details regarding diving requirements to the individual team leaders – in fact, I have made it a point never to interfere in the logistical requirements of any expedition – but as far as the wreck itself was concerned, I was on firmer ground. Over the summer of 1997 every single historical and technical detail that I believed to be relevant was factored into the original plan, concentrating on the open watertight doors, the minefield and the coal bunkers. Ken Marschall also chimed in, asking for details of floor tiles, wall sconces and even any of the marble fireplaces that may have been on board. Everything was considered in the most minute detail, although none of us seriously believed that we would be able to tick off all of the targets on the list in one hit. I was playing a long-term game, confident that even if the first expedition hit a dead end, the next time we would at least know where not to go, and that is always a good thing. On the other hand, I also understood right from the start that I had to know when to step back. It was all very well me sitting in a nice comfortable office, setting goals that may or may not have been possible and telling the diver to get on with it, but I also knew that it was not my life on the line. With this in mind, I have always made it plain to every diver with whom I work that it will always be their decision whether to pursue any of the listed goals, and that if there was ever any concern about safety, it would be their call – and theirs alone – as to whether or not to continue.

The IANTD project would prove to be a learning curve not only for the divers, but also for yours truly. In 1976 Jacques Cousteau had used a three-man diving chamber to decompress, while in 1995 Bob Ballard had not used manned divers at all. By 1997 technical diving was still evolving, but work-up dives on shallower wrecks, including the *Lusitania*, had provided divers with invaluable preparation for depths of up to 119 metres on the *Britannic*, along with the even greater challenge of a minimum four-hour in-water decompression. By the end of October the IANTD group was ready. Any plans I may have had to join them on Kea were scuppered due to another filming commitment in a particularly wet and isolated part of Snowdonia, but if I thought that Kevin would be having a nicer time in Greece, I was sadly mistaken. The notion of taking an expedition to Kea in November had probably always been a bit ambitious, so I was not all that surprised to get a call to say that after nearly two weeks on the island the expedition had not only failed to make one dive, but the Greek permit had also expired. If it was to be allowed to continue, I also had to give my agreement to the Greek authorities, although fortunately we had already planned for this contingency. Being stuck in an isolated part of the Conwy Valley, a region where mobile phone reception was at that time practically non-existent, I had instead to send a hastily scribbled fax from an isolated pub near Betws-y-Coed, not at all sure it would suffice. Thankfully it did.

After 11 days on the island the team finally made it into the water, as the months of

preparation began to pay dividends. Diving at depths of up to 119 metres meant exposing not only the human body to almost 13 atmospheres of pressure, but also the associated equipment. Fortunately the technology for the divers' gas cylinders was already tried and tested, but issues with pressure also led to problems with the camera and lighting equipment, resulting in under-water photographer Dan Burton firing off an entire roll of film in only a few seconds because the pressure on the shutter-release button was so great that the motor drive could not be released. If that was not frustrating enough, power-supply problems on Kea also resulted in the base station of the Simrad side-scan sonar losing power, and with it some of the data regarding the debris to the north of the wreck. I was finally beginning to appreciate first-hand the issues with which Bob Ballard had to wrestle only two years earlier, and at times I even found myself wondering if it was a sign that the ghosts of the *Britannic*, perhaps frustrated at being disturbed after so many years of relative peace and quiet, were determined to make their presence felt.

At one point the floating decompression station was pulled by a strong surface current out

---

▲ The DERA sonar team aboard *Capetan Vasselis*. (*Britannic '97*)

of the agreed exclusion zone and straight into the path of a passing tanker, a source of excitement for the divers to say the least. Likewise, no one could have anticipated the moment when the Lavrio port police boarded the support vessel and, for a few minutes, Kevin was arrested on suspicion of having removed items from the wreck without permission. As it turned out, nothing of the sort had happened – indeed, my own agreement with the dive teams made it clear that nothing on the wreck should be touched or removed. Rather, it was a case of a simple misunderstanding, as the port police (and myself too, come to that) were unaware of the intention to lay a bronze plaque on the wreck in memory of Jacques Cousteau.

Perhaps most important of all was that everyone made it back safely. But thanks to Kevin and his team, I had quite literally put my first toe in the water of the *Britannic* exploration, and at long last I had my first decent photographic stills of the wreck. By the time Nick Hope's Starfish Enterprise team was ready to return the following September, many of the invaluable lessons learned on Kevin's trip had been incorporated into the revised dive plan, with diver propulsion vehicles (DPVs) in particular having proved to be the most efficient way to explore as large an area of the wreck as possible in the limited bottom time. Even so, I was determined to make sure

▲ The in-water divers' deco station. (*Britannic '97*)

▶ The 1998 decompression station at the surface, showing how close to the land the wreck lies. (Nick Hope, *Britannic* '98)

that the next team did not end up going over the same ground as the previous expedition, although at the same time I had to concede that as the individual teams were funding the expeditions themselves, they did at least have the right to take time out occasionally to explore the more eye-catching parts of the wreck that had already been seen.

There was, however, one key difference on the 1998 expedition which, although we didn't realise it at the time, would have a far-reaching impact not only on exploration of the *Britannic*, but also on technical diving itself. As per the previous year, the Starfish team members were all using open-circuit trimix technology, except for American diver John Chatterton, who would be using what is known as a closed-circuit rebreather. CCR technology effectively makes it possible to recycle air that has already been breathed by removing the exhaled carbon dioxide and passing it through a sodium hydroxide filter. Today rebreathers are commonplace in the world of technical diving – in fact, it is now largely considered to be the only credible option for any self-respecting technical diver – but in 1998 this piece of diving technology was still very much in its infancy. Compared with today's rebreathers, John's Aura 2000 was large, cumbersome and, it has to be said, unreliable. When it worked, however, the new technology brought with it considerable advantages – namely, reducing the number of diving cylinders and improving gas efficiency. From a technical diving perspective, the advantages were obvious, and from an owner's perspective the benefits of a diver using a piece of equipment that produced far fewer bubbles also meant that they could proceed further inside the wreck without impacting the anaerobic interior that had remained undisturbed for over 80 years. This was exactly the piece of equipment for which I had been waiting. Up to that point I had insisted that no divers should proceed any further into the hull than the promenades, which at that time remained largely open, but now, depending on the determination of the diver and the reliability of the new technology, the possibilities of going further into the wreck were tantalising.

In the end the diver was equal to the task, but sadly the rebreather was not. One of the goals that I had set in the original dive plan had been to possibly locate the remains of the firemen's tunnel. Having observed the twisted and jagged steel edges of the broken hull plates, I always felt this was possible, but given the huge scale of the structural damage in the area, I could not be certain that it would be safe to venture inside. I had always taken a 'we'll cross that bridge when we get to it' approach for myself, although no diver entering this part of the wreck could afford to be quite so cavalier. Even so, in September 1998 we crossed the bridge when John not only located the tunnel opening in the bulkhead, but managed to get inside it, even though he could only do so by removing his open-circuit bailout cylinders. Amazingly, on only the second expedition we were on the verge of ticking a massively important item off my list. However, all of a sudden the controller screen of the rebreather went dark. All that John could do was peer ahead into the darkened tunnel to see the gloomy outline of the first watertight door, which he said looked as if it was open, before turning around and beating a hasty retreat to his bailout cylinders in case his rebreather failed altogether. We never got the opportunity to have a second attempt at reaching Boiler Room 6 on the 1998 expedition, which, on the face of it, was hugely disappointing, but on the other hand John had confirmed that getting to the boiler room was indeed possible, and I knew that sooner or later we would be able to pick up where he had left off.

With additional data on the intact boiler room casings and the turbine engine room, as the old millennium drew to a close there was one last chance to gather additional information with Jarrod Jablonski's Global Underwater Explorers expedition in August 1999. The GUE expedition did not make any attempt to enter the firemen's tunnel, but instead concentrated on areas within the ship's focsle and in the forward cargo holds, where a closer examination of the intact aft bulkhead confirmed that Cousteau's speculation of an internal explosion in the reserve bunker had been mistaken. We even retrieved a small coal sample for analysis, although the tests ultimately revealed little, other than that the coal was bituminous and contained an average volatile matter content of about 15 per cent. After 83 years on the seabed there was

▶ John Chatterton checking the complicated innards of his closed-circuit rebreather, the technical diving technology that would change everything. (Nick Hope, *Britannic '98*)

1. The metal frame of the aft docking bridge. All the wooden decking in this area is long gone. (Rob Royle, *Britannic '98*)
2. The bath in what should have originally been the chief officer's cabin. (Jamie Powell, *Britannic '98*)
3. Some of the hard red algae, which can be observed in numerous places on the hull. (Jamie Powell, *Britannic '98*)
4. The portside running light. (Jamie Powell, *Britannic '98*)
5. A fallen bridge engine telegraph, once used to transmit manoeuvring commands to the engine room. (Jamie Powell, *Britannic '98*)
6. Interior view of the open portholes. (GUE 1999)

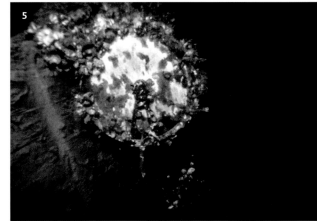

little point in conducting a methane analysis of the sample as the methane would have escaped years earlier through the pores in the coal. We also obtained the first detailed footage from inside the forward hold, confirming once and for all Cousteau's claim of 23 years earlier that the cargo holds were indeed empty, and not filled with an illegal cache of munitions. The Brits were finally off the hook!

HOLLYWOOD AND THE *BRITANNIC*

Looking back on everything that they achieved, it is perhaps sad that the '97, '98 and '99 expeditions have not received more of an acknowledgement in the annals of *Britannic* research. Perhaps this is because they were carried out at a time when the diving technology that was available limited their ability to achieve the goals that I set (and would later, more successfully, set again), but an important point that has never really been considered – at least, I don't think it has – is that these three expeditions constituted a pivotal and important learning curve, not only for the divers, but also for me as I continued to produce ever more detailed and ambitious dive plans. These three expeditions combined had collected so much invaluable data that for the first time I was actually beginning to think about taking a far more serious project to a broadcaster, in the hope that it would result in an ambitious and properly funded programme for the exploration of the *Titanic*'s forgotten sister.

Indeed, this already seemed to be happening, but not quite in the way that I had envisaged. In 1997 James Cameron had produced his hugely successful *Titanic* movie, so I was not particularly surprised when in February 1999 I received a phone call from a friend in the camera department to say that someone was about to produce a $2,500,000 TV movie based on the

Britannic. Not only that, but the production would be based at Bray Studios, barely five miles from my home! There is a belief in the film industry that the closer you live to a studio, the less likely you are to work there; sadly, this production bitterly proved the point, although as I was already committed to *The Tenth Kingdom* it probably made little difference in my case. In truth, it was probably just as well that I was working elsewhere, as I suspect that few directors would have been overly thrilled at the prospect of having an expert – let alone the actual wreck owner – on set analysing every little detail of a script that had more holes in it than the *Titanic*. Even so, with the production being based on my own doorstep, I decided to offer the art department the benefit of my experience, in the hope that I could at least help to make the visuals as historically accurate as possible.

As I walked into the dilapidated Portakabin at Bray that served as the production office, I was pleased to see Ivan Strasburg, a familiar face and also the film's director of photography, sitting there, flicking through a copy of Don Lynch and Ken Marschall's *Titanic: An Illustrated History*. He was quickly asking me questions about the lighting inside the ship, after which we strolled over to the art department to have a chat with Rob Harris, the production designer. Rob also could not have been more welcoming, and despite his limited budget, he was keen to get the set details as accurate as possible, discussing the bridge and boat deck sets that were nearing completion on Stage 1.

Perhaps the warning bells began to ring in my head when Brian Trenchard-Smith, the film's director, came onto the stage. Rob introduced me as 'the *Britannic*'s owner', and I will never forget Brian's first slightly cautious words to me as we shook hands, saying, 'Sorry about the artificial characters!' Straight away I knew that my instinct not to get too closely involved had been correct, although I did feel confident enough to mention to the production manager that the name of the *Britannic*'s captain was Bartlett, and not Captain Barrett as the script had it. I also remember being fobbed off with the explanation that they had to do that for legal reasons, although as Charles Bartlett had by then been dead for over 50 years, I was struggling to comprehend any legal reasoning behind the reluctance to make such a minor change. What I think they were really trying to say was thank you for your interest and please go away! I took the hint.

In the film industry there is a professional courtesy, more honoured in its breach than in its observance, whereby you do not go onto the set of another production unless you have been invited, even if you have friends working on the film. Having by then had the opportunity to read the script, I was also more convinced than ever that I should sit this one out, but when Rob called a few weeks later to ask if I could go into the studio to meet with Ray Corbitt, the American computer-generated imagery (CGI) specialist who had been tasked with recreating a digital version of the *Britannic*, I was happy to oblige. With over a hundred digital shots planned for the

▲ Overhead view of the boat deck set built on stage one at Bray Studios in Berkshire for the *Britannic* TV movie, a sadly less-than-faithful account of what really happened on the ship.

production, Ray also wanted to get his *Britannic* models looking as accurate as possible, particularly as the only visual reference he had up until that point was a CGI representation of the *Titanic* painted in the colours of a hospital ship. Unfortunately, by that stage the computer model was so far advanced that it was too late to go back and start from scratch, but I spent two hours going over the finer details of the Harland & Wolff rigging plans, by which time most of the changes had been photographed and noted down. At least I could content myself with the fact that it was as accurate as we could make it in the circumstances.

Despite the production's many weaknesses, I remember feeling particularly sad as I watched the sets being broken up at the end of filming, piled up and burned on the back lot, but later in the year I got a call from Ray thanking me for my help, and saying that they wanted to include my name in the CGI department credits. Of course I was delighted, but being aware of the huge

▲ The Marconi room set was built on a tight budget and therefore lacked technical accuracy, but it was an interesting portent to one of our major finds only three years later.

historical liberties taken in the screenplay, I asked him to make sure that I was listed as a technical consultant, and not as a historical consultant. To this day I do not know if it was a genuine mistake or if someone was having a laugh at my expense, but I still remember sitting in front of the television on a cold wintry afternoon in December 2000 to watch the film, fortified by a bottle of red wine to dull the pain, only to see myself listed at the end as the film's historical consultant!

For all of the problems with the film, psychologically I was still in a very good place. By the end of 1999 I was in a position that only a few short years earlier would have seemed all but inconceivable, not only being the owner of the wreck, but having helped to instigate and co-ordinate an exploratory programme that was now on the verge of answering so many of the questions that had surrounded the *Britannic* since the day she sank. As the new millennium dawned I was feeling so optimistic that, provided the Y2K bug did not result in the predicted computer meltdown that supposedly threatened the end of civilisation as we knew it, the possibilities seemed tantalising. In the end the much-feared millennium bug turned out to be a total non-event. As the lights stayed on while the bells of Big Ben chimed to welcome in the year 2000, I was already making plans for the future.

▲ The compact *Britannic* underwater sets being prepared for the movie's flooding sequences. Compared to the scale of James Cameron's 1997 *Titanic* movie, the difference in budgets is clear for all to see.

13

POLITICS, PRODUCERS & PARTNERS

Sometimes it takes the smallest of things to bring you back down to earth with a resounding bump. As far as the *Britannic* was concerned, for me that moment probably came during the IANTD technical diving conference, which was being held at the Coventry Hilton Hotel in February 1999.

Despite the fact that I was now working closely on the *Britannic* with the new breed of technical divers, for the most part I had chosen to keep my distance from the diving world, preferring instead to remain in my comfortable camera-department niche. Even so, the conference provided an interesting opportunity to finally meet some of the people who had helped me take my first faltering steps in the world of underwater exploration, and also to chat with Gregg Bemis, the owner of the wreck of the *Lusitania*. I took him to be something of a kindred spirit as we tried to fend off the divers from their worst excesses, and I think we both accepted that putting in place a framework for future access to the two wrecks was not necessarily a bad thing, provided that a critical element of control remained in place.

After the dinner was over I was saying my goodbyes to the various team members with whom I had been working for the last two years, when someone said to me, 'You're not at all what I expected.'

'Really. What were you expecting?'

'I'm not sure – just not you!'

It was an interesting putdown on which to ponder during the two-hour drive home, but the remark had contained a probing truth, because while I was not what that person had expected in a wreck owner, after two years I had also come to realise that owning the *Britannic* had turned out to be nothing like I had originally expected. I may have possessed the crucial piece of paper from the British government confirming my claim to its former legal title to the wreck, but it was becoming increasingly clear that my original intention of keeping everyone away from it simply was not going to play out. Then again, I was also becoming increasingly tempted to delve deeper and deeper into the wreck itself, when only two short years earlier I had been utterly determined to leave it alone.

Up until now, my involvement in *Britannic* research had mostly focused on the more exciting aspects of diving and filming, but the new millennium seemed to herald a very different approach. All of a sudden I was to become bogged down in aspects of maritime law and politics, as it finally began to dawn on me that the proverbial chickens were finally coming home to roost. I had a piece of paper that guaranteed my rights, but at the same time it was becoming increasingly clear that with those rights came responsibilities, and with the British government knee-deep in diplomatic discussions regarding the UNESCO Underwater Cultural Heritage protocol, it was inevitable that sooner or later I would become entangled in those deliberations too. I can still remember my first meeting at the Foreign Office in 1998, walking past the imposing statue of Robert Clive in King Charles Street and up George Gilbert Scott's elaborate marble staircase for the meeting to be held in the Map Room. The green-painted walls and orange curtains of this famous room (formerly the Colonial Office) seemed curiously dated, but the wooden case at the back of the room holding the old imperial maps could not fail to catch my eye. On the opposite wall hung full-length paintings of Wellington and Nelson, but while it is odd that I still vaguely recall thinking that the painting of Nelson needed a bit of a clean, my first visit to the Foreign Office had left an indelible impression on me. If I was going to hold my own in any talks regarding the *Britannic* and the UNESCO protocol, not to mention the matter of sovereign immunity for warships, as well as war-grave issues, I needed to become professional very quickly.

The following year it got even more complicated. The sinking of the MS *Estonia* in September 1994 had resulted in an international treaty being signed to protect the site, which had effectively become the final resting place of over 700 souls. With the Ministry of Defence perpetually concerned about war-grave issues in the UNESCO paperwork, the Department for the Environment, Transport and the Regions was now also pushing the Foreign Office for a similar treaty in relation to the *Titanic*, basing its argument on the justifiable principle that if a wreck protection treaty was good enough for the *Estonia* then it was also good enough for the *Titanic*. What had originally started out as a hobby for me was suddenly becoming a very serious business.

Away from the ongoing diplomatic discussions, I still needed to maintain a line of communication with the individual dive groups that were expressing an interest in the wreck. I was already committed to the GUE trip in August 1999, from which I would learn a great deal about the interior of the wreck, but the desire of the various dive groups to publicise their planned expeditions was beginning to trouble me as more and more *Britannic*-related enquiries landed on my desk. Discussions with one expedition proposed by the British Army Medical Services regiment came to a none-too-happy conclusion, while enquiries from unknown dive groups that lacked the technical experience of the previous groups left me feeling more than a little uneasy. I could still see the benefits of cooperating with what were still essentially recreational dive groups, and I was still willing to help any applications where I reasonably could, but only as long as they were up to the task of helping me to further my own work on the wreck. This may sound a bit selfish, but with the ongoing UNESCO and *Titanic* discussions, not to mention the mindset of the Greek Ministry of Culture, it was the only way that I could realistically juggle the very different requirements of British and Greek officialdom.

THE BREAKTHROUGH!

By the autumn of 2000 I was beginning to despair of ever finding the right person to take on the next meaningful expedition to the *Britannic*. To make matters worse, one of my contacts in the diving world informed me that someone called Carl Spencer was putting together an expedition to the *Britannic*, and that he was planning to make retrievals. The matter of someone putting together an expedition was not a cause for any particular concern – there was usually talk of a potential *Britannic* expedition going on somewhere – but the prospect of unauthorised retrievals from my wreck took things to a whole new level, particularly in view of the sensitive *Titanic* discussions in which I had become embroiled with the Department for Transport. The situation was made even worse by the fact that I was not around to actively pursue the matter, filming throughout the autumn in Yorkshire on a Gwyneth Paltrow film called *Possession*, after which I had scarcely a moment to catch my breath before having to fly out to Morocco to spend six weeks filming battle sequences on *The Four Feathers*. Figuring that the diving world, like the film industry, was a relatively small community, I hinted to one or two people that I was not amused, and it seemed to have the desired effect. Carl somehow got wind of the message that he and I were heading for a major confrontation, and we agreed to arrange a meeting as soon as I was back home.

Tuesday 5 December 2000 was an overcast and not particularly remarkable day in the run-up to Christmas, but I had little idea of the effect that day would have on the next eight years of my life. Carl had driven down from his home in the Midlands, and we ended up having lunch at the Waterman's Arms pub in Eton. Perhaps worried about my reaction to his previously covert activities, Carl had invited his diving buddy Richie Stevenson to accompany him for moral support, but he need not have worried. I had to make it clear that I had not been particularly happy to hear about his planned expedition second-hand, but at the same time there was something about his amiable demeanour that was more than a little disarming. By the time we were done Carl better understood my legal situation and, more importantly, he had a far greater understanding of the political and diplomatic discussions that were tying my hands.

As I left the meeting my thoughts were oddly conflicted. On the one hand I was still irritated by the thought that anyone should be making plans about my wreck behind my back, and yet I felt also that we actually had very much in common. Beyond the *Britannic*, Carl seemed to have a knack of choosing other projects that also interested me, top of his list for the coming spring being involvement in a venture to locate the wreckage of the famous *Bluebird K7*, which had claimed the life of Donald Campbell in January 1967 while he was attempting to break his own water speed record in the Lake District. Not only did they succeed in locating the wreck in March 2001, but a little over two months later Carl also found the remains of Campbell's body at the bottom of Lake Coniston, and acted as one of the pallbearers at the funeral later that year. Despite the inauspicious start to our relationship, it was Carl's undeniable enthusiasm for this fascinating project that persuaded me that he was a man with whom I could work.

The reality, however, was that even with the right team, we still had to go about obtaining the significant support and funding that only a broadcaster could bring to the project. Having worked in films and television all of my working life, the process of pitching a project and getting used to the occasional rejection really did not trouble me too much, as one by one possibilities with the BBC and several independent producers fell by the wayside. Anyone working in the camera department will recognise the all-too-familiar words of a line producer saying we want you to work on our film but don't have the money to pay the rate, and it would appear that while the *Britannic* was undeniably attractive to practically every producer with whom we spoke, their budgets simply could not stretch to the cost of a properly funded expedition without cutting corners. This could not work from our end because the one place where you absolutely cannot cut back on any budget is when you are filming 119 metres beneath the surface. We either did it right or we did not do it at all.

By the following summer we had made no headway whatsoever. In his frustration, Carl had even taken the step of reaching out to a submersible company to discuss the possibility of *Britannic* submersible dives, which would probably have been harmless enough had it not been for the fact that not long afterwards the company in question announced that two of its clients would be getting married in one of its submarines on the *Titanic*! The predictable outcry in the press was the last thing I needed, given the ongoing UNESCO discussions and, much closer to home, the *Titanic* wreck protection treaty, and by the time we sat down to discuss the progress made at that year's Birmingham Dive Show, the list of options looked pretty meagre. There was always interest, but never any commitment, and while it was easy enough for me to accept the situation and resign myself to a relatively quiet autumn, I could also sense Carl's frustration at the apparent lack of understanding by the television media industry. By the spring of 2002, further knockbacks from both the BBC and Channel 4 led to me feeling rather more gloomy and pessimistic as to the eventual outcome.

Strangely enough, however, the winter hiatus had worked well for me. Having become the vice-chairman of the Guild of British Camera Technicians, I had inherited a financial situation that required rather more attention than I had previously anticipated, awakening something inside me that I had never previously known existed. It had required a considerable amount of my time and effort to get the company back on the financial rails, and six months on I was feeling a lot stronger psychologically, and considerably more inclined to exert a bit more pressure on the producers with whom we would meet. It would not necessarily change the overall situation, but even if the answer was still no, I felt that it would be infinitely better to be told that after a couple of weeks, rather than allow the talks to drag on for several months and then still come to nothing.

The timing could not have worked better when one particularly warm spring afternoon Carl and I sat down to lunch with Peter Davey, a producer working for Carlton International in London. Not only was Peter's belief in the project plain for all to see, but he was also keen to set the ball rolling straight away. What we were discussing was certainly ambitious, but it was exactly the kind of project that could benefit from a co-production with two broadcasters. Along with Peter's interest came an enquiry from a new Greek company – Sea & Land Developing and Tourist Enterprises (SLDT) – which had been in discussions with a number of Greek government officials in the run-up to the 2004 Athens Olympics regarding the potential for *Britannic*-related tourism, and whose directors had been advised by the Greek Ministry of Merchant Marine to contact me if that project was to move forward. Suddenly the possibility of combining the media project with official Greek input seemed almost too good to be true. Within three weeks Peter confirmed that both National Geographic and Channel 5 were keen to support the project, as the final pieces of the puzzle finally began to slot into place. By the late summer I was at last ready to fly to the Greek island of Euboea to see about putting the first SLDT building blocks in place, and to start laying the groundwork at the Greek end for our *Britannic* expedition, which we had decided to schedule for the following September.

While I was happy enough operating in my own comfort zone, I also knew when to step back and let Carl work in his. Throughout the summer we discussed in great detail the previous targets that I had set for the earlier expeditions, and the new goals that I believed would need to be included if we were to keep the interest of National Geographic. By this time I was also a diver myself, if only qualified to 18 metres, but it was the first of several steps that I felt would be necessary for me to better understand the kind of people with whom I would now be working. The thought of actually diving down to the *Britannic* was never on my radar, and despite my new-found diving skills, I still realised that there was a world of difference between sitting in a comfortable office drawing lines on a set of deck plans and actually working in 400 feet of water. As a result, I always made it absolutely clear to Carl that whatever targets I might set, I was always prepared to be overruled by him or the individual divers if they felt that what I was asking was unreasonable or even downright dangerous. We both knew that I was setting the bar very high, and by the time I had finished marking up areas in the focsle, the superstructure, the turbine engine room and the elusive firemen's tunnel, Carl knew that he would need to select a team of seasoned and specialised divers.

▶ Marine microbiologist Lori Johnston on comms. (Leigh Bishop)

THE HOUSE OF CARDS

I remember the summer of 2002 being an incredibly exciting time as we began to make our preparations. Not only had Carl assembled a top-notch dive team, but my ambition to finally locate once and for all evidence of the elusive minefield was finally within reach. To undertake the sonar work, Carl had suggested Bill Smith, an engineer from Newcastle who not only had branched out into sonar work, but had been responsible for the project that had located Donald Campbell's *Bluebird* the previous year. Carl also suggested that we undertake the first round of scientific tests on the *Britannic* with Droycon Bioconcepts, the Canadian company that had been coordinating scientific work on the *Titanic* since 1996, leaving the broadcasters in no doubt that by incorporating a viable *Titanic* link we were giving them a truly unique project. However, as the summer moved into the autumn, my contacts at SLDT were becoming increasingly concerned that there was still no name to put on the permit application to the Ministry of Culture in Athens. The situation made no sense to me as National Geographic and Channel 5 had both committed to the project. However, the truth suddenly dawned that Carlton International had yet to sign the agreement as Carl was hoping to get a better deal with another broadcaster. Without intending to, Carl had placed me right in the middle of a situation that ran contrary to over 20 years of experience of working in the film industry, and its effect not only on my professional reputation but also on that of the *Britannic* was not something that I particularly wished to contemplate. I did not like this use of gamesmanship, but I also knew that nothing had been signed and that from the legal standpoint the broadcaster was still free to continue to negotiate.

Bearing in mind the much larger budget of an alternative option being proposed, I suppose I can understand why Carl had hesitated, although it didn't stop me from letting him know exactly how I felt about the situation. With Carlton's assurances that everything was in order, I could only advise my contacts in Athens that the application, as soon as the deal was signed in London, would probably be in the name of another broadcaster, but despite the lure of a possible tie-up with James Cameron's Earthship Productions, including the use of multi-million-dollar submersibles, there was still no commitment by the end of the year. We still had nine months to arrange the permit, which was easily enough time, but by the spring of 2003 we still didn't have the media green light. Even worse, my own questions to Carl were also going unanswered.

The crunch finally came in February 2003, when I received an email from Carl with the apprehensive subject line 'Comments likely to piss you off', asking me to agree to him being the sole contact with James Cameron's people. For the first time in our relationship I had to say no. Apart from being reluctant to allow anyone to make any unauthorised media deals on my wreck without my knowledge, I had already signed legal papers permitting the *Britannic* to be accessed only via SLDT for the two-year period that it would take to get the company established. My response was not what Carl had hoped for, but while our relationship would eventually survive

▲ The sonar team. L–R: Alain Douglas, Andonis (Greek skipper), Graeme Conagher and Bill Smith, proudly displaying their 410kHz GeoAcoustics towfish.

its first major crisis, it was at this point that he finally realised that the uncertainty could not be allowed to continue. I was definitely getting apprehensive, but with a meeting in London between Carlton and Earthship scheduled for April 2003, I knew that there was still enough time for the Greek paperwork to be processed, provided that there was immediate commitment to the project. Certainly the directors at SLDT seemed to believe this would be the case, but although the meeting went well, the final signoff on the media paperwork remained elusive. By this time I was having visions of over two years' worth of work going down the pan, and in truth I was not surprised when on 11 June we received the long-dreaded news that due to cost overruns on the planned *Titanic* dives that year, and the fact that James Cameron would no longer be available in September, Earthship had pulled out of the project with three months to go!

Carl had gambled and we had lost. As I called to give him the bad news I remember the stunned, almost embarrassed silence as he tried to find the words to explain how this particular house of cards had come crashing down. Utterly dejected, he then muttered, 'I just want to walk away from it.' I totally shared his feelings, but I also knew that after putting more than two years into the project, not to mention being fully aware of how it would look to my SLDT partners in Greece, I simply did not have the luxury of being able to just walk away. Resisting the urge to say I told you so, I asked him instead to keep his dive team on standby in case by some miracle we could salvage the unholy mess.

Peter, fortunately, still believed in the project, and on the evening of 11 June 2003 we set about putting together a *Britannic* expedition virtually from scratch, knowing that we had only three months to get everything in place. If I prayed that night for some sort of miracle, it never occurred to me that someone up there might actually have been listening, but within days Peter had reconnected with both National Geographic and Channel 5, the two principal backers of the project almost a year earlier, and both said that they were still interested. Unfortunately, in the intervening period a third of the British budget had been reallocated to other projects, but even cutting back as much as we dared, there was still a large shortfall, which amounted to the cost of the *Loyal Watcher*, the diving support vessel that Carl had chosen for the project. The *Watcher* needed to make the 4,000-mile round trip between Plymouth and Kea, and unless the money could be found to cover that expense, the figures simply did not add up. Suddenly I found myself having to either put my money where my mouth was and agree to cover the transit costs myself, or see two and a half years of work being flushed down the pan. What could I do? I agreed to cover the costs.

It would still take a ton of administrative work, made all the more pressing by the fact that because we were starting the application process so late in the year, it would be touch and go as to whether the permits would be delivered before the *Loyal Watcher* was scheduled to depart for Greece. While Carl was left to finalise the dive team's requirements, and my Greek colleagues did their best to see about getting the paperwork sorted, from this point onwards my only focus was on finalising my wish list as the owner for what would be the first *Britannic* wreck investigation to take on a seriously forensic approach.

Over the next few weeks I revisited every single archive and trawled through all the paperwork I had been studying for the previous 15 years, weighing up the evidence for and against the various theories surrounding the loss of the ship. Interestingly, eight years on from my first visit with Bob Ballard, my two primary goals still had not changed. I badly wanted to resolve the issue of whether it was a mine or a torpedo that had caused the initial explosion, and if we could penetrate the forward firemen's tunnel to obtain images of the forward watertight doors, then maybe – just maybe – it would have been worth my unplanned investment.

The mine *vs.* torpedo controversy would almost certainly be the most difficult to resolve. In his 1977 documentary, Jacques Cousteau had been filmed having dinner with several *Britannic* survivors; when he asked each of them whether they thought the *Britannic* had been sunk by a mine or a torpedo, all but one remained firmly convinced that their ship had been the victim of a German torpedo. In the face of such overwhelming evidence from people who had actually been there, the torpedo theory could not therefore be dismissed altogether. The reality, however, was that not one of Cousteau's survivors had seen the all-important torpedo itself, and almost immediately I began to consider the possibility of human psychology playing a role. The two witnesses who had reported seeing the torpedo tracks on the morning of 21 November 1916, Henry Etches and Thomas Walters, may well have been 100% sincere, but this did not necessarily make either of their testimonies true or accurate. The human brain can be susceptible to seeing what it thinks it sees, or even what it wants to see, and with other survivors reportedly seeing what they took to be a periscope, combined with the alleged sighting of a periscope when the *Burdigala* had been sunk in the same waters barely one week earlier, the psychological argument for human beings misinterpreting the evidence of their own eyes strongly suggested the possibility of a collective false memory.

The evidence for the mine, however, was more grounded in reason. In November 1916 the official investigation into the *Britannic*'s loss had concluded: 'The effects of the explosion might have been due to either a mine or a torpedo. The probability seems to be a mine.' No one could doubt for a moment that the *Britannic* had been sunk as a result of German military action – indeed, in a post-war interview Kapitänleutnant Gustav Siess freely acknowledged that it was one of the *U73*'s mines that had sunk the ship – but no matter how hard I tried to push the case for the mine, there was no getting around the official investigation's use of the word 'probability'. Like it or not, there would always be proponents of the torpedo theory, so to prove my case I had no option but to locate physical evidence of the mine barriers.

The limited sonar sweep of the area conducted by the *NR-1* in September 1995 had failed to identify any evidence of mines, but I reasoned that this had largely been due to the fact that we simply ran out of time. I tried to dismiss my mounting thoughts of the mine sinkers being dragged by fishing nets in the ensuing decades, which had also been an uncomfortable possibility back in 1995, and for no good reason I remained obstinately convinced that there would still be enough evidence at the bottom of the Kea Channel to prove the case for a mine once and for all. The supporting information at my disposal was still no greater than it had been in 1995 – namely, the mine barrier chart drawn by the U73's navigating officer on the morning of 28 October 1916 – and at times I even found myself wondering why I was staking so much on a single piece of paper, but by this time it was too late to be thinking along those lines. In the end all I could do was ask Carl to forward the information to Bill Smith, and to make sure that he had the ability to carry out sonar surveys in waters that were at least 400 feet deep. Like it or not, I was committed!

My second goal in 2003 lay inside the wreck, as I was confident that this was where I was more likely to succeed. However, it also carried with it more of an element of risk. I was thrilled when John Chatterton had been able to find his way into the firemen's tunnel in 1998, but five years on I was also beginning to appreciate just how hazardous the structure of the hull really was in this area of the wreck. I already knew from the 1995 ROV images that the damage was extensive, but it was only when reviewing the footage from the 1998 expedition, in which for the first time I could see fragile human divers swimming beneath hundreds of tons of damaged and twisted iron hull plates, that I began to appreciate the human implications of my wish list. It was precisely for this reason that I never interfered with Carl's choice of diver for the individual missions, confident that he would pick the right person for the task in hand. In the end, Carl's choice for the tunnel penetration was his long-time dive buddy Richie Stevenson, coincidentally the co-owner of the *Loyal Watcher* to whom I had recently had to advance the £10,000 fuel money to keep the expedition on track, so I was confident that if the target was feasible, Richie was the man to undertake the dive.

By the end of August we had done as much as was humanly possible. The dive and sonar teams were agreed, the dive plan was sorted, and the *Loyal Watcher* was outbound on her ten-day cruise to Kea. As I flew to Athens I felt as confident as anyone reasonably could that everything was in order, but even at that late stage the Greek gods seemed determined to make me suffer. The delay at the British end in selecting a broadcaster meant that the expedition paperwork had not been submitted to the Greek Ministry of Culture until the latter part of June, with the result that although everything had been processed, the final ministerial signature was not yet in place, as first a media charge had to be agreed by the Ministry. The loss of time might have been particularly costly had it not been for the fact that the infamous Meltemi wind was making conditions in the Kea Channel unsuitable for diving, but a rushed meeting at the Ephorate of Marine

Antiquities, along with the political support of Nikos Demenagas, then Mayor of Kea, meant that we had just enough time to meet with the Director of Antiquities to ensure that all was in place before everything closed down for the weekend.

Even then, just as I thought it was safe to go back into the water, the paperwork dropped one final bombshell, forbidding any sonar activities in the Kea Channel without the permission of the Hellenic Navy. At 5.00pm on a Friday afternoon the prospect of finding the appropriate official in the Ministry of National Defence was highly unlikely, and I had visions of the sonar team sitting around for another three days minimum before they could even begin work. With the possibility of the sonar work even being scrubbed altogether after so much planning and expenditure, I was beginning to wonder if I would ever find the *U73*'s elusive minefield, when Carl, as frustrated as we all were by this last-minute bureaucratic glitch, grabbed his mobile phone, muttering, 'Kostas may know someone!'

Kostas Nizamis was the director of the Greek Diving Center in Piraeus, and was handling the logistical side of the expedition, just as he had done in 1998. Given his years of experience working on salvage projects in Greek waters, there was a chance that he might know who to contact, but as I listened to Carl explaining the situation, all I could hear on the other end of the line was Kostas saying, 'Nai... nai... nai...' As Carl hung up all he could say was, 'He'll get back to me as soon as possible,' but I was not feeling particularly optimistic. It was at this point that the

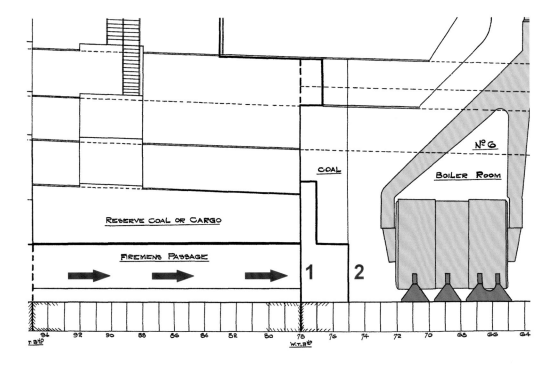

second miracle of the expedition kicked in. Within 20 minutes Kostas called back to say that he had spoken with his contact, and that permission for us to carry out sonar work in the Kea Channel had been agreed. In Greece, it really is a case of knowing the right person.

By yet another miracle we made it back to Lavrio just in time for the evening ferry to Kea, and for the first time on the trip I finally felt able to relax before beginning the first diving operations the following day. As the dive team carried out their final equipment checks, I spent that evening in the Britannic Bar, one of SLDT's more interesting contributions to the Kea economy, while Pavlos Loukas, the bar owner, plied me with the largest gin and tonics I have ever seen, and which were undoubtedly needed. For the dive team, however, not a drop of alcohol would pass their lips until the end of the expedition.

THE PLAN IS PERFECTED

For the first time, I had experienced the emotional rollercoaster of planning a *Britannic* expedition. It was nothing like I had expected, but despite the highs and lows, I was loving it. Getting the official permit sorted is rarely easy, but as soon as you have the all-important ministry paperwork the rest of the process is, in theory, relatively straightforward. Then again, even though I am the de facto UK owner of the wreck, owning the *Britannic* means that things are never straightforward, even for me. The reality is that my hands are still firmly tied by the Greek administrative system, and when it comes to accessing the *Britannic*, it is a complicated procedure at the best of times. The interesting thing, though, is that in spite of the undeniable frustration that accessing the wreck can sometimes create, on balance it does seem to work for me. The primary reason I had obtained the UK legal title to the wreck in the first place was to protect it, and the best way to protect any wreck is to properly control the access. Like any government department, the Ephorate of Marine Antiquities guards its domain with an iron fist, but although at 119 metres the *Britannic* is deep enough to keep her safe from the vast majority of recreational divers, she is still shallow enough for a determined team of more experienced technical divers. Fortunately every expedition is overseen by a representative of the Greek Ephorate, but while this creates unwelcome bureaucratic issues for the various expedition organisers, from an owner's perspective it is actually very reassuring to know that just by being there, the representative probably does more to help guard the site from the less scrupulous divers than any piece of legal paperwork can ever hope to achieve.

On the morning of Saturday 6 September our designated Ephorate representative, Vasilis

◀ The route to the forward boiler rooms and the open watertight doors.

▲ Gordon Bell hooking the shot line into the wreck.

Glezos, finally arrived on the island on the early ferry. Bureaucratic frustrations aside, the appearance of this powerfully built man, sporting a pair of dark sunglasses and riding a classic motorbike, was not at all what any of us had expected in a representative from the Ministry of Culture. His unconventional appearance quickly gained the approval of some of the dive team, and within half an hour of his arrival he had checked in to his hotel and come aboard the *Loyal Watcher* as we were finally cleared to depart for the wreck.

Finally we were back to the day-to-day aspects of wreck exploration, which was also my cue to step back. It was now up to Carl and his team to deliver everything that I hoped they could, although after the initial excitement of being on board the *Loyal Watcher*, the actual diving operations turned out to be pretty mundane, particularly as we had to wait while the divers completed their six-hour in-water decompression. On the other hand, there was more than enough excitement to be had watching Steve Wright, the *Loyal Watcher*'s skipper, manoeuvring his vessel to keep it between the divers on the floating decompression station and the numerous approaching vessels, which somehow appeared to be oblivious to the one-mile exclusion zone around the wreck for the duration of the exploration. Fortunately the *Loyal Watcher* had a reasonably high superstructure for a vessel of her size, and Steve was confident that the watch keeper on any of the approaching vessels would be able to see us in time to take avoiding action. As he said, 'In spite of our size we like to think that we can hold our own.' Even so, trust me when I say that playing chicken with the 112-ton *Loyal Watcher*, especially when there is a 20,000-ton leviathan bearing down on you, is not for the faint-hearted.

Despite all my preparation, there was also one more diving hazard I had completely failed to include in my supposedly meticulously crafted dive plan. I only became aware of it after a couple of days, while listening to the distinctive rattle of the *Loyal Watcher*'s engines carrying through

the water as I played back the video, but while the familiar noise seemed to provide a welcoming degree of reassurance to the divers as they went about off-gassing, their sudden startled reaction to a loud 'crack' in the distance could not go unnoticed. At first I didn't have a clue what had caused the noise, until someone told me that in fact it was the local Greek fishermen, some of whom had the playful habit of throwing a stick of dynamite into the water to stun the fish before catching them. Very fortunately they were far enough in the distance to cause no major hazard to the divers, but once I was aware of the problem I was no longer just watching out for the big ships, I was also on the lookout for the occasional caique with a dynamite-wielding Greek fisherman, in case it came too close!

For the next week there was nothing more that I could, or indeed should, do, other than assist in briefing the divers on their individual targets. Control of the actual filming remained in the capable hands of James Barker, the programme's director, and Mike Pitts, a professional under-water cameraman. However, as we sat in the lobby of the Karthea Hotel analysing the first day's footage, without having to say a word to each other we instinctively knew that we had a problem. To be fair, the technical divers required to film the wreck were not professional cameramen, so

▲ Director James Barker at *Loyal Watcher*'s helm as skipper Steve Wright keeps a watchful eye for any vessels straying into our alleged exclusion zone.

no one had been expecting miracles, but the images from the first day contained a mass of inconsequential shots of divers swimming around in the water. Even with a target almost 900 feet long, somehow we had managed to miss it almost completely, and with even more ambitious targets set for the following day, the underwater camera team members were gathered together for a crash course on the best way to get the images we needed. In effect it involved basic techniques of cuts and editing, such as keeping the movement slow and smooth, and pausing on objects of interest for at least five seconds to give the editors a chance. After we were done I expected that it would still be a day or two before the divers began to get the hang of it, but the one hour we spent that night in passing on our years of filming experience had been incredibly well spent. The following day's rushes were incomparably better, and after that I was confident that as long as the Meltemi held off, we would have everything that the broadcasters needed within a few days.

The camera lessons did not come a moment too soon, for on day two of the expedition, Carl decided that the time had come to send Richie Stevenson into the firemen's tunnel. I had already briefed Richie thoroughly on what to look for and where to go, so I recall actually saying very little to him on the morning of the penetration itself. Then again, that was possibly because

I also didn't want him to see just how nervous I was. As I watched him splash into the water I remember thinking to myself, 'Well, this is it,' bracing myself for the next six hours of unbelievable tension before he was scheduled to return to the surface.

The afternoon seemed to take an eternity to pass. I don't recall the exact time, but as Richie finally broke the surface and clambered aboard the *Loyal Watcher*, I could see in his face how tired and cold he was. Although I was desperate to find out if he had the answer to the question that I had been asking for over ten years, I instinctively knew that now was not the time to rush in and ask. Perhaps sensing my apprehension, Richie gave me the thumbs-up to signal that he'd been successful, so I just stayed in the background and waited to hear his comments recorded on camera for posterity. Perhaps it was just as well that I did, as Richie's piece to camera when asked about the watertight door by Geraint Ffoulkes-Jones, our designated dive marshal that day, clearly showed just how drained he was after his experience. Somehow Richie managed to find the words to put everything in a technical diver's unique perspective, as he replied, 'Well

◀ Every diver was carefully briefed on where to go and what to look for. (Antonello Paone)

▲ Leigh Bishop keeping his cool before entering the water.

▲ Carl Spencer makes his first dive.

▲ The first open watertight door. (Rich Stevenson)

▲ Closer view of the second watertight door. (Rich Stevenson)

I'm just concentrating on making sure the camera doesn't shake and I'm making sure that my rebreather is still firing and I'm just making sure that I know where I am – and I don't give a fuck what kind of door it is!'

That night, as I sat in the lobby of the Karthea Hotel going over the video of Richie's dive, I reflected on the essential truth in his response. I was mesmerised by every moment as the camera moved along the dark tunnel with the twisted metal walkway and handrails everywhere, to the point at which he finally arrived at the vestibule leading into Boiler Room 6. For me it was a landmark moment in over ten years of research, yet when planning the dive, I had been sitting in a nice comfortable office, drawing lines on a massive rolled out Harland & Wolff deck plan. For Richie, and for other divers like him, however, my wish list was a very different matter, as they were the ones risking life and limb to answer the questions that had led us to that point. Richie knew that the call was always his as to whether to turn back in the event that it was too dangerous to proceed any further, and no one would have held it against him if he had done just that, but to this day I am glad that he managed to pull it off.

As for the images, it was impossible to miss the two unmistakable openings where two closed watertight doors should have been, confirming that the 1916 British report had been correct in

▲ The Marconi multiple tuner.

1 & 2. The firemen's staircase 'tween decks. (Leigh Bishop)

3. An encrusted bridge engine telegraph, the glass face still intact and covered in red algae. (Antonello Paone)

4. Part of the chandelier frame in the main entrance.

5. Inside the officers' ward.

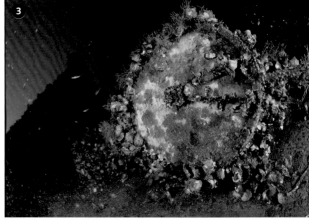

1. Richie Stevenson beside the port propeller that accounted for all thirty fatalities on 21 November 1916. (Leigh Bishop)
2. Edoardo Pavia beneath the aft shade deck. (Antonello Paone)
3. A medical chest near the second-class library.

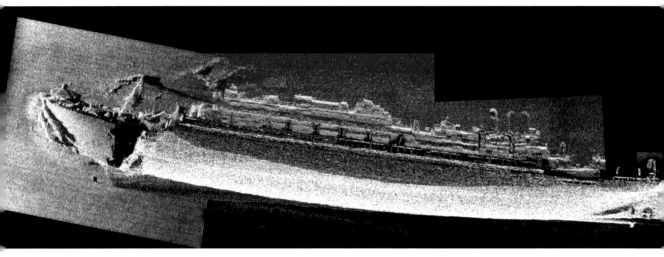

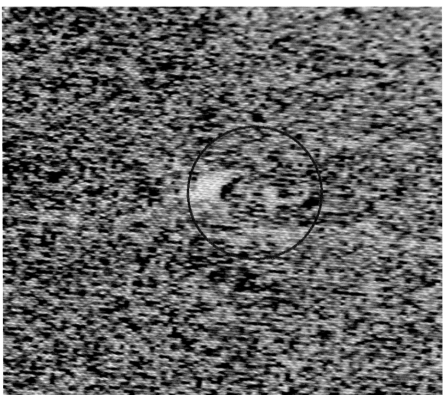

▲ Composite sonar of wreck. (Bill Smith)

▲ Sonar image of cracked eggshell, later confirmed to be a mine. (Bill Smith)

stating that the doors in this part of the ship had failed to close. That had not come as any great surprise, as the footage was confirming exactly what I had expected to see, but what came next was something that no one could have possibly imagined in their wildest dreams. Still sitting comfortably in their wells, in spite of the wreck having lain on its side for 87 years, four Scotch marine boilers, each weighing over 100 tons, remained firmly fixed in position, with some of the equipment looking as if it had been submerged for only weeks rather than almost a century. At one stage Richie tantalisingly pointed the camera between two of the boilers, peering into the gloom and perhaps thinking about the possibility of going further inside the ship. However, he wisely decided to stick to the plan, turned around and began to retrace his route, like Theseus escaping from the Labyrinth after slaying the Minotaur, following the thread that he had laid behind him.

As I sat and watched the footage several times over, all of a sudden I was now thinking about getting to the next watertight door between Boiler Rooms 6 and 5. Even though we had accomplished everything that I had wanted to achieve, already I wanted more, but that would have to be for the future. Even so, to this day I clearly recall the 2003 images of the firemen's tunnel and the forward stokehold as being the most exciting piece of *Britannic* wreck footage that I have ever analysed – and probably that I ever will.

DOTS IN THE SEA

After that, for me the rest of the expedition seemed to be an anticlimax, as I left Carl's dive team to their own devices in obtaining the all-important images that the broadcasters needed. The discovery of the ship's Marconi multiple tuner was an additional thrill, as was the fact that we were able to take an initial look inside what appeared to be a reasonably intact turbine engine room, but from this point on my attention was focused, oddly enough, on what was going on away from the wreck.

I had managed to stay out of the way of our intrepid sonar team for practically the entire week. After a preliminary discussion during which I went over the historical information with Bill Smith once we were on Kea, I quickly realised that there was no point wasting time giving advice to a man who clearly knew his business, so I simply left him and his support team, Graeme Connacher and Alain Douglas, to get on with it. Like any second unit, Bill and his team were actually more than happy to be off on their own with nothing to worry about but their own shot list. In the morning, Andonis, the skipper of the *Stella*, the Greek fishing vessel we had hired for the sonar operations, would take his boat out of Port St Nikolo himself in order to comply with the Greek regulations, but once he realised that Bill could handle the vessel, he was more than happy to hand over control once out in the Kea Channel. After several hours trawling up and down the search area, it would then be Bill, Graeme and Alain's turn to sit back and relax for a couple of hours while Andonis shot his nets, before returning to Port St Nikolo to sell his catch to the local bistros for their evening menus. All things considered, I think I would have much preferred being with Bill's sonar team than on the *Loyal Watcher*.

In spite of the detailed information available in the historical record, it is interesting that we did not find the minefield quite where we expected it to be. The line drawn by the *U73*'s navigating officer, Oberleutnant zur See Martin Niemöller, was certainly a good one, but some of Bill's sonar contacts had been a little further out in the channel than we had expected them to be. The data, however, was everything that I could have hoped for. At first the images seemed to be little more to me than vague dots, but to Bill's more expert eye, the acoustic shadows thrown up by the anomalies on the seabed could be discerned easily. More import-antly, the sonar contacts appeared to be evenly spaced and in a relatively straight line. God, as we all know, does not build in straight lines, and I instinctively knew that at last we had the first tangible evidence that there was a minefield pretty much where the Germans had claimed it to be 87 years earlier. Surely the mine *vs.* torpedo issue could now be resolved once and for all?

Given everything we achieved on the 2003 expedition, it is sad to recall that the trip ended under a bit of a cloud. Unfortunately, the media fee payable to the Greek Ministry of Culture for a commercial project had been delayed in the transfer process from the UK, resulting in the permit being suspended until the agreed payment had been received. The last two days of the expedition were scheduled for the weekend, but the delay meant that the money could not possibly be received before the following Monday, by which time our permit would have expired anyway, effectively meaning that the expedition would come to an end two days earlier than planned. The frustration at losing the last two days was slightly offset by the fact that the Meltemi wind would have made diving impossible on the Sunday anyway, but in spite of the last-minute disappointment I was already thrilled with the results. It had cost me a small fortune, but we had delivered everything that the National Geographic and Channel 5 programmes could have hoped for, and certainly everything that I had wanted to achieve.

The post production analysis turned out to be almost as fascinating as the expedition, reveal-ing all sorts of small discoveries that had gone completely unnoticed during the initial viewing, and I can still remember how National Geographic and Channel 5, whose initial treatments for their respective programmes were completely different from each other, slowly began to con-verge as the editing process continued. We had started out with the intention of producing two very different programmes, but by the time the editing was completed, the two seemed remark-ably similar. The race to transmit first was won by National Geographic, which aired *Titanic's Doomed Sister* as part of its *Mysteries of the Deep* series, on 12 March 2004; Channel 5's *The*

Curse of the Titanic Sisters followed suit 12 days later, but six weeks earlier than originally scheduled due to the fact that the National Geographic programme had already been transmitted.

For myself, the process had left me a lot more experienced and a great deal wiser, if not necessarily wealthier, but at least I could now confidently say that finally we were beginning to solve the last mysteries of the *Britannic*.

▲ The 2003 team.

14

THE PROJECT WIDENS

The ambitious scope of the 2003 project left me feeling that I needed time to let things settle down for a bit afterwards, but at the same time I was eager to maintain my underwater contacts, so I was doubly pleased when the phone rang one cold January afternoon in 2004 and I heard Kirk Wolfinger's voice asking if I would help to coordinate three UK episodes of the *Deep Sea Detectives* series he was producing for the History Channel. The programmes covered the Loch Ness Monster (a personal favourite), a U-boat mystery in the Moray Firth and the wrecks of the German High Seas Fleet in Scapa Flow – a project I had actually pitched the previous year. Without either of us knowing it at the time, this relationship would culminate the following year in what was probably one of the most ambitious and financially risky projects Kirk would ever undertake: on 10 August 2005, we boarded the Russian research vessel *Akademik Mstislav Keldysh* from St John's in Newfoundland. Our destination – the *Titanic*!

Truth be told, I have generally tried to steer clear of *Titanic*-related projects, if only because as a rule they bring with them considerable political grief and, more often than not, personal abuse from some of the more extreme elements in the *Titanic* world. Even so, the 'ribbons of steel' that had apparently been observed on the seabed in August 2000 were enticing enough to give us hope that we were going to find something amazing, so how could I possibly say no? In the end the ribbons did not turn out to be quite what we had hoped for, but by the time the expedition was completed we had located and mapped both pieces of the *Titanic*'s double bottom and, more importantly, for the first time analysed the nature of the ship's break-up. The resulting shallow-break theory put forward in the programme by marine architect Roger Long would completely revise how we looked upon the *Titanic*'s last minutes afloat, and, more importantly, Roger's analysis would go on to focus on potential issues in the design of the Olympic-class expansion joints. When he became aware of the modified joint arrangements in the *Britannic*'s superstructure, the reasoning behind the post-*Titanic* superstructure design suddenly became worthy of further investigation.

When we studied the compression and tension features in the two sections of the *Titanic*'s double bottom, the steel indicated tension breaks at the tank top and compression in the hull plating, consistent with a slower and more progressive break, followed by the grinding together of the separated hull sections by the tenuously connected hull portions. The cracks in the double bottom were very clean, while the upper works of the bow section had been forced down and outwards, both of which were at odds with the high-angle-break theory. Instead, they suggested that the break-up began at a shallow angle, with the initial crack, possibly due to an expansion joint notch effect, appearing to have begun in the region of the strength deck just below or near the aft expansion joint.

Expansion joints are intended to help reduce stresses in a vessel's superstructure. Ships can be designed with similar strength and flexibility without the need for expansion joints by using heavier steel in the superstructure, but the joints basically allow the assembly to be constructed as buildings on a raft instead of on a ship's hull, and making the superstructure irrelevant to overall hull strength and stiffness issues had the added advantage of being easier and less expensive to build. The drawback, however, is that the expansion joints could introduce structural discontinuities, resulting in high degrees of stress where the side bulkheads are attached adjacent to the expansion joint in the strength deck. In other words, as the *Titanic* slowly sank by the head, the aft bulwark expansion joint would have been acting as a point of stress concentration.

◀ Outside the old Howard Hughes hangar in Playa Vista, this film miniature used for James Cameron's 1997 *Titanic* perfectly illustrates the belief in the high-angle break. (Ken Marschall)

From my point of view, this was also an angle of investigation that I had long wanted to pursue more closely. The Board of Trade's own surveys in the early 1930s had highlighted a number of structural issues regarding the liners *Majestic, Leviathan* and *Olympic*. If stress and fatigue could have been such a factor in a sister ship, then might it have been an equally significant factor in the extreme bending experienced by the *Titanic* while flooding? One Board of Trade memo from the 1930s was particularly revealing:

> A significant fact that is apparent in all the cases of failure of topside structure in these large vessels is that the failure occurs in close proximity to expansion joints immediately above. Owing to the stiffness of the erections any flexure in the structure tends to concentrate in the strength deck below, at the position of the expansion joints, and it appears to me that in order to distribute the flexing over as large an area as possible, the number of expansion joints should be increased.

Bearing in mind that by the time of this memo the *Britannic* had lain at the bottom of the Kea Channel for almost 15 years, it seems unlikely that the Board of Trade would have retained any detailed knowledge of the modifications to the ship's superstructure. Nevertheless, by 1913 Harland & Wolff had already done exactly what was being suggested in the Board of Trade's own internal paperwork almost 20 years later, installing an additional expansion joint in the *Britannic*'s superstructure. The thicker hull plating in parts of the *Britannic*'s superstructure also raises the question of whether it was significant that the ship's modified joints had been relocated away from the area where, in the *Titanic*, such a high concentration of stress would have occurred during the sinking process.

During the post-expedition conference at Woods Hole in December 2005, Roger was surprised to see a plan of the original Olympic-class expansion joints showing the joint extending into the B-deck bulwarks. To him this was irrelevant to the purpose of the superstructure joints, and in fact potentially compromised the integrity of the hull girder. The cracks that developed in the *Olympic, Majestic* and *Leviathan* in later years clearly demonstrated that these larger vessels operated at a pretty high stress level in normal service, but while Roger was not suggesting that the *Titanic* broke in half because of this design feature, perhaps the question concerning the break-up was not so much why she broke so early as how she held together as long as she did under the enormous hogging stresses of the flooding.

Even the most cursory glance at the forward expansion joint on the *Titanic* clearly showed that it had been opened up, almost certainly due to the impact of the bow section on the seabed, while the aft joint had all but disappeared in the tangle of debris that had once been the mid-ship section. But had the joints in the *Britannic* fared any better? We had certainly looked at the expansion joints prior to 2006, in an effort to detect any potential opening during the sinking process, but the exterior of the wreck is so heavily encrusted with saddle oysters that it is often difficult to see anything at all. If we were going to study the *Britannic*'s expansion joints more closely, what better way to do it than by carrying out an internal inspection of the joint along the A and B deck promenades? Fortunately the ratings for the History Channel's *Titanic's Final Moments: Missing Pieces* documentary were so good that the broadcaster not only agreed to the follow-up programme, *Titanic's Achilles Heel*, but as part of the investigation a smaller one-hour programme would also be filmed at the same time, during which John Chatterton and Richie Kohler, the co-hosts of the *Deep Sea Detectives* series, would take a closer look at the *Britannic*'s superstructure. Sure enough, in September 2006 I once again found myself headed back to the Kea Channel.

ACHIEVEMENT AND ANTICLIMAX

The 2006 expedition should have easily been able to follow up on the huge success of the 2003 exploration, yet coming within about 20 feet of my ultimate goal but not achieving it remains one of the great frustrations in my experience of *Britannic* research. From a professional stand-point, I found the prospect of using the Woods Hole cameras on the wreck undeniably attractive, and after the success of the 2003 expedition I was confident that, three years on, we would be able to pick up right where we had left off. Yet in the end, everything that could go wrong seem-ingly did. The problems came thick and fast, with a mysterious stomach bug on the island playing havoc with most of the dive team, while a combination of assorted equipment and logistical issues conspired against us. When Parks Stephenson, one of our historical consultants, was mugged by a taxi driver in Athens, the vibes I began to feel were even less encouraging, but I became a little more optimistic once we were finally in the water.

Straight away the task of locating and filming the internal expansion joint, our main reason for being there, fell to American divers Richie Kohler and Mike Barnette, but even that proved to be a little more complicated than expected. As I watched the two divers moving slowly along the B-deck promenade, looking for a clearer view of any potential opening in the joint, the lower light levels in the dimly lit promenade did nothing to help, while the build-up of 90 years of marine life on the now-horizontal promenade deckhouse walls made their task doubly tricky. Even so, Richie and Mike did locate the joint, and very quickly determined that there was not the slightest indication of even the smallest of openings. Whatever might have happened to the *Titanic*'s expansion joints, there was no indication whatsoever of any similar structural issues having occurred when the *Britannic* sank. Of course, it was too early to say whether this was down to the modified expansion joint arrangement, as the stresses that built up in the *Britannic* as she listed increasingly to starboard were very different to those experienced in the *Titanic*, but it clearly indicated that this area of the hull had stood up well to the external and internal forces exerted on the sinking ship. Did this prove that Harland & Wolff had learned their lesson?

Equally intriguing was an observation made by two other members of the team. American divers Mike Pizzio and Mike Fowler had been tasked with examining the external joints more closely, and their observations revealed that beneath the 90-year-old biomass, at the base of the joint in the B-deck bulwark there was a bulb-shaped opening, similar to the base of a glass thermometer, which was not apparent on any of the expansion-joint drawings for either of the first two Olympic-class vessels.

On the face of it, the 2006 History Channel expedition did therefore succeed in obtaining the information we had sought for the *Titanic* project – namely, that Harland & Wolff had made modifications to the *Britannic*'s expansion joints – but for John Chatterton and myself there was also one important piece of unfinished business. In 1998 John's attempt to reach the watertight

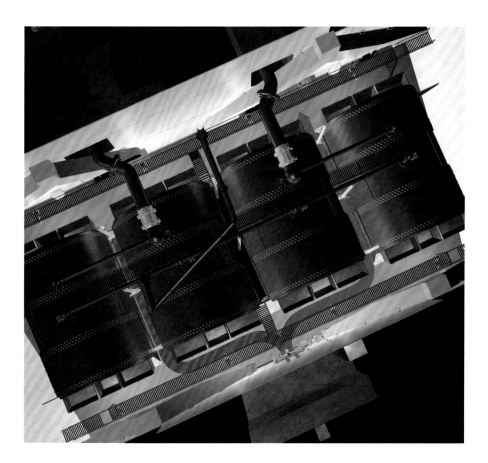

doors leading to Boiler Room 6 had been frustrated by a malfunctioning rebreather, but since viewing Richie Stevenson's 2003 footage I had been fixated on the notion of squeezing past the boilers in order to make it to the next watertight door. According to the 1916 Admiralty report, this door was partially closed, and I wanted to know why. So, it appeared, did John and Richie. This was a chapter of the investigation that we all wanted to close, and 6 September 2006 was the day we chose to do it.

No matter how structurally sound the boiler room seemed to be, I was always nervous about the idea of penetrating it, even if John and Richie remained professionally calm and detached.

◀ Launching Bumblebee, the largest of the Woods Hole underwater cameras used on the 2006 expedition.

▲ The divers' planned route to the third open watertight door. (Parks Stephenson)

As experienced wreck divers, they had doubtless been in far tighter spots than the dark void into which they were about to venture, but even so, we went over the *Britannic*'s layouts in the closest detail so that there would be no surprises.

Everything about John and Richie's 2006 boiler-room footage was instantly recognisable to me, closely resembling what I had seen only three years earlier: the pipes along the roof with the lagging still perfectly preserved; the raised floor of the firemen's tunnel to the right; two rusting shafts with rusticles; the low-hanging pieces of the broken ceiling to the left. Then there was the missing section of raised walkway to the right and a mysterious circular access hole in the now-vertical floor, after which John and Richie arrived at the first watertight door where the jagged rusticles still hung like fangs in the top of the open frame. Moments later, they passed through the vestibule and were into the forward stokehold, exactly where Richie Stevenson had been three years earlier. But while I felt far less tense during the 2006 penetration than I had in 2003, from here on was a whole new, dangerous world turned on its side. Detailed images of the boilers, the diamond-patterned metal floor, the overhead walkways, the engine room telegraphs and the pristine stoking indicators left me more convinced than ever that structurally the *Britannic*'s interior was in an unbelievable condition. After completing a thorough video

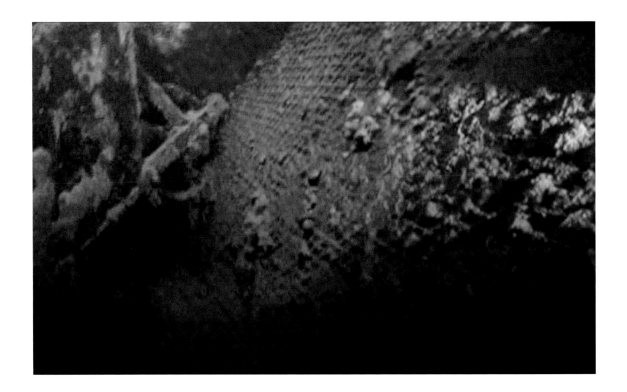

examination, John dropped down a few feet and squeezed himself into the narrow 20-foot passage running between boilers C & D, beneath the 102-ton boiler that hung only inches above. We were now just moments from reaching the third and final open door when, as the end of the passage loomed out of the darkness, the way was blocked by a trimmer's wheelbarrow, wedged tightly in the space between the two boilers. No matter how hard John tried to shift it, the wheelbarrow remained resolutely in place, refusing to budge. There was perhaps the briefest glimpse of the next coal bunker before the image disappeared in a massive cloud of swirling yellow rust, but even as it started to clear, it was obvious that the wheelbarrow remained stubbornly wedged in place. Barely 20 feet from our goal, John had no option but to reverse back out of the passage and return to the surface, where we could plan an alternative route for another day.

Despite the initial disappointment, the outlook for getting an image of the third open watertight door still looked good, even if it meant following a more circuitous route between boilers A and B. Sadly, however, our hopes for the remainder of the expedition were about to be dashed. In the original application, permission had been specifically requested to go inside the wreck, and as the UK owner of the wreck, my company had agreed to this request. For some reason, however, the necessary permission to go inside had been withheld by the Greek Ministry of Culture, even though there had been no issues about going inside the wreck on any of the previous trips. Somehow, this small but crucial detail had gone unnoticed in the run-up to the 2006

◀ The damned wheelbarrow! (Lone Wolf Media)

▲ The 2006 team with the support vessel *Apollon*. (Leigh Bishop)

expedition, which, unintentionally, had breached one of the terms contained in the permit. An already difficult situation was made even more complicated when on another occasion the support vessel *Apollon* drifted away from the wreck in the current, and as a result, one of the hanging Woods Hole cameras inadvertently obtained images of the seabed away from the wreck. Even though they revealed nothing more than a relatively featureless sandy desert, taking such images was also specifically forbidden in the permit.

If it hadn't been for the language issues, I still like to think that it would have been possible to keep everything on track. However, a few days into the expedition we had unexpectedly lost our representative from the Greek Diving Center due to a family bereavement, and with no one on hand to act as a conduit between the expedition and the Ephorate, it proved impossible to resolve the situation. The lesson I took home with me was that in future I would insist on proper liaison at all times, and make absolutely sure that the designated Ephorate representative was fully aware of what was going on. That, however, was for the future. For now, given all the problems we had faced up to that point, the undeniable subliminal message I was receiving was that it was time to go home.

In the end it was all resolved amicably enough: the misunderstandings were clarified, the impounded footage was returned and an invitation was extended to the company by the Ministry of Culture to return to the wreck in the future. Unfortunately, though, with the programme now

in the final editorial stages, there was little practical chance of any return to the Kea Channel before the transmission date, so the condition of the watertight door between Boiler Rooms 6 and 5 would have to remain a mystery. However, the fact that we had come within 20 feet of answering the question remains my greatest frustration, and I remain convinced that had we dived the following day, we would have obtained the image of the final open watertight door. On a more positive note, I suppose that we had at least learned from John and Richie's dive that we would need to plan an alternative route. Although it was not the result for which any of us had hoped, at least we already had our strategy ready for next time.

SCIENCE AND THE *BRITANNIC*

Britannic: Titanic's Doomed Sister aired in the spring of 2007. For the most part I was reasonably happy with the end result, but the frustrations of the expedition had left me determined to make sure that things would be different the next time I returned to the wreck. Feeling that it would be best to let the dust settle, I had no plans to return in the short term, but inevitably the offer of a collaboration with the Hellenic Centre for Marine Research (HCMR) proved simply too good to resist. As well as wanting to maintain as much momentum on the *Britannic* as possible, for some time I had also been keen to encourage as much official Greek involvement as possible, and the HCMR/Elkethe is a Greek governmental research organisation. The preliminary discussion with Professor Vangelis Papathanassiou was very fruitful, and throughout the winter of 2007/08 we began to plan what would become the first proper investigation of the marine life on the wreck. For the time being, my watertight-door aspirations would just have to wait.

The collaboration with Elkethe brought with it a number of considerable advantages, as the RV *Aegaeo* was a purpose-built scientific vessel, designed for both submersible and ROV operations. The submersible came in the form of the Comex-built *Thetis*, which was capable of retaining constant communication with its surface support vessel, and came equipped with a sonar echo sounder, high-resolution underwater cameras and a powerful bank of lights ideal for colour photography. The 5½-tonne *Thetis* could dive as deep as 600 metres, placing the *Britannic* comfortably within her rated depth range, and to complete the starting line-up was the Deep Sea Systems Max Rover, a 750kg ROV complete with its own positioning system, lights and camera.

Inevitably, any properly planned *Britannic* expedition creates publicity, and 2008 was no exception. At the Greek end, Stamos Barsim's Olyvon production company was already making

◁ Aboard the RV *Aegaeo*, with the pick of the HCMR's underwater technology.

a series with Elkethe, for which the 2008 *Britannic* operations would take up one episode – similar to the arrangement with Cousteau in 1976. To keep the British end up, Mike McKimm from BBC Northern Ireland, in the process becoming the first Belfast journalist to visit the wrecks of both the *Titanic* and the *Britannic*, would also be along for the ride. At a more official level, Panagiotis Kamennos, then Greek Alternate Minister of Merchant Marine, Aegean and Island Policy, spoke at the pre-expedition press conference to provide official support and to wish the expedition well. If everything went according to plan, within a week we would have completed our work, and the official structure would be in place for the long-term project of which I had been dreaming for the previous ten years.

The one thing that does not change, however, is the capacity of the Greek weather and technical issues to frustrate things. The northern Meltemi wind can be particularly strong between May and September, and with speeds of anything up to 40 knots, it can wreak its own particular brand of havoc in the Kea Channel. It generally blows at its strongest in the afternoon, and quite often it might drop in the evening, lulling you into a false hope of being able to dive the next day, only for the wind to pick up again the following morning. You quickly come to accept that the weather is the one thing you absolutely cannot control, but at least the *Aegaeo*

▲ *Thetis*'s seabed sampler.

▶ Countless sponges cover the higher parts of the wreck.

could anchor in the relatively sheltered waters of Legrena Bay, overlooked by the spectacular Temple of Poseidon at Cape Sounio, where we could make any technical adjustments before the ops began.

As I think back on all of my *Britannic* experiences, in spite of its inauspicious start, the 2008 expedition still remains my most enjoyable cruise. Although there was some media involvement, for the first time I had practically nothing to do in the way of script consultation, briefing divers or worrying about regurgitating the historical aspects of the *Britannic*'s story for the cameras. All I had to do was sit in the observer's seat of the *Thetis* and enjoy the view, although my first dive had to be aborted when problems with the in-water comms meant that we had to return to the surface after barely ten minutes on the wreck. Fortunately we were close to the southern tip of Attica, so the replacement parts were on board the following morning, and with the communications restored, we were able to pick up where we left off.

With the radio repairs completed, the following morning would be when I gained my first proper and unimpeded view of the *Britannic*. And what a view it was! As I stared at the wreck through the 90mm acrylic sphere, amused at how the concave lens in the crystal-clear waters made the 900-foot hull look like a large model, I strangely recall thinking for the first time, 'My God, is that really mine?' Owning the legal title to the *Britannic* is an unusual claim to fame by any stretch of the imagination, but for the first time I was beginning to appreciate first-hand exactly why divers, scientists and maritime historians have such a fascination for the wreck. I have kept a relatively detailed journal on all of my *Britannic* expeditions – as Oscar Wilde once said, one should always have something sensational to read – but this would be the first time that I experienced the luxury of being able to write down my own detailed thoughts of what it is like to visit the *Britannic*:

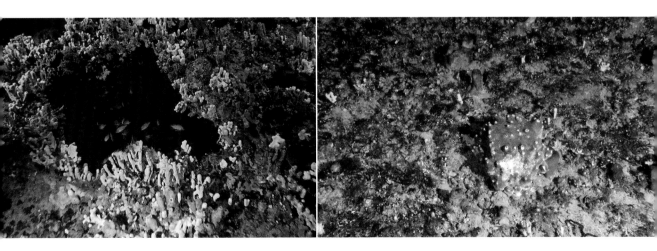

Thetis Submersible Dive #2

Date: 19th September 2008

Support Vessel: RV *Aegaeo* (Elkethe)

Thetis Pilot: Kostas Katsaros (Elkethe)

Observer: Simon Mills (JAFO)

Duration: 129 Minutes

Maximum Dive Depth: 108 Metres

As *Thetis* descends to the wreck of the *Britannic* the light slowly decreases with depth. Just as noticeable is the gradual change in the external colour temperature, as the colours with the longer wavelength in the visible colour spectrum decrease. The first to go is red, quickly followed by orange, yellow and green, as each colour is filtered from the increasingly deep water. At 108 metres we can clearly see the desert-like bottom of the Kea Channel; a

▲ An electrical distribution box. (Rudi Asseer)

▲ One of the crew showers in the focsle. (Rudi Asseer)

flat, muddy and featureless landscape, with only the occasional rock interrupting the monotony of sand.

As we move forward something begins to emerge from Cousteau's 'Stygian gloom'; what at first appears as a huge shadow gradually reveals itself to be the *Britannic*, sister-ship of the *Titanic*. Sister-ships perhaps, but there is a world of difference between the two wrecks. The *Titanic* rests 3,800 metres down in the cold, pitch-black waters of the North Atlantic, twisted and broken into two main sections some six-hundred metres apart; the *Britannic*, on the other hand, lies only 119 metres down at the bottom of the spectacularly clear and warm waters of the Kea Channel, and even after more than ninety years on the seabed she is spectacularly intact.

Moments later the submarine lights are switched on, as the *Britannic* suddenly becomes an oasis of unbelievable colour and life. To all intents and purposes the wreck has become an artificial reef, comprising a complex and unique ecosystem. Unlike the *Titanic*, on the *Britannic* there is hardly a rusticle in sight – at least, not on the exterior. The coralligenous substrate on the wreck has instead become home to all of the main Aegean benthic organisms, including filter feeders such as sponges, bivalves, bryozoans and tunicates; the higher parts of the hull support white colonies of Filograna tube worms, with the upper sides of the wreck dominated

▲ A discarded mug in the debris. (Rudi Asseer)

▲ The large berm that has developed beneath the shade deck.

by a huge variety of sponges, particularly around the deck railings and the level of the promenade deck. Further down the sponges are not so big, as the coralline hard and soft red algae, and an incalculable number of saddle oysters, cover the wreck from top to bottom. Large lobsters can be seen sitting in the open portholes on the higher port side of the wreck, also an occasional moray eel holed up in one of the ventilators, while numerous schools of fish (predominantly anthias) are everywhere.

The *Britannic* lies on her starboard side, seemingly sleeping, at an approximate angle of eighty degrees. Much of the hull is supported by the seabed, except for where it drops away closer to the upper works of the ship, in some places creating a substantial overhang beneath the superstructure.

We start our tour from the bow, where the metal plates of the ship's prow are corrugated as the foc'sle was pushed into the seabed. As we move back over the wreck, across the buckled base of the still-attached foremast (the lookout's cage is still attached

▲ Professor Vangelis Papathanassiou guiding the Elkethe Underwater Activities team.

but the wooden floor is gone), about forty metres from the bow a huge chasm suddenly opens up beneath the forward well deck, where the hull broke as a direct consequence of the weight concentrated in this area while the stern of the ship was still above the surface. For so long mistaken for an internal explosion, the reality is that a huge chasm, maybe sixty-feet across, opened up as the almost detached bow dropped down to the seabed – a bit like cracking open an egg! Even so, in spite of the apparent devastation both of the two-and-a-half-ton Stothert & Pitt cargo cranes still remain fixed resolutely in position.

The forward starboard gantry davits are twisted but still remain attached, while higher up the engine telegraphs and ship's wheel pedestal on the bridge have fallen from their mountings, remaining attached to the hull only by their chains; the wheelhouse telemotor remains fixed, with a few red floor tiles still attached around the base. The port running light is undamaged and as we move further aft it is clear that although the boat deck bulwarks have rotted away, practically every davit remains firmly attached, obscured only by thick layers of saddle oysters. All of the pine decking is long gone, even though from a distance the ridges of caulking give the appearance of it still being there, while nearly all of the teak woodwork and handrails display a reasonable degree of preservation. All four funnels lie just to the north of the wreck, largely intact although in the process of gradual collapse under their own weight, while the massive open funnel casings show no evidence whatsoever of any internal structural collapse. Remembering that the 100-ton boilers in Boiler Room No. 6 were still seated firmly in their cradles only five years ago, this comes as no surprise; if anything it confirms that Harland & Wolff really knew how to build a ship!

Two huge and very old fishing nets hang lifelessly from the two aft girder davits, so thickly encrusted that in places it is difficult to see their latticework structure, and as we drop down below the *Britannic*'s perfectly preserved stern the massive twenty-three-foot diameter port propeller, the cause of all the casualties of the sinking, is unmissable. In fact all three propellers still remain attached, the lower starboard propeller, with one blade partially buried in the seabed, partially obscured by another old fishing net hanging from the 102-ton rudder, still turned slightly to port. Even then *Thetis* manages to slide beneath the rudder for a unique view of the four-bladed central propeller.

After two hours our time was up. Kostas turned the switch and the *Thetis* gently began the short journey to the surface; in spite of the slightly rough conditions the recovery goes without a hitch and ten minutes later we are once again safely secured on the fantail of the RV *Aegaeo*.

THE FINAL GOAL

My *Thetis* dive remains my most memorable aspect of exploring the wreck, but the other high point of the 2008 expedition was being able to pick up where Bill Smith had left off five years earlier. In September 2003, Bill had pinpointed the location of what looked to be the *U73*'s mine barriers, but we had not been able to get that all-important photographic image of an actual mine. Without photographic evidence, a number of diehard torpedo conspiracy theorists were still determined not to believe that we had found the minefield, so I discussed the old problem with Vangelis Papathanassiou and he was more than happy to help.

As we headed west, with the 750-kilo Max Rover seemingly dragging the 778-ton *Aegaeo* in its wake, an intense sense of nervousness came over me. I had been looking for the visual evidence of the minefield since Bob Ballard first visited the wreck 13 years earlier, but although I was confident that Bill had located it in 2003, all of a sudden the doubts came flooding in. I remembered Bill telling me that the line of mines pretty well tallied with the 1916 chart, except that the barrier was a little further out into the channel than indicated, but other than that, we really were flying blind. What if the mine barrier was not where we had so confidently said it was after all? What would National Geographic and Channel 5 say, bearing in mind that we had so definitely concluded in their 2004 programmes that we had found it?

As I sat in the *Aegaeo*'s lab gazing at the featureless seabed while Max crawled along the seabed at a sedate two knots, I wondered why we should succeed in locating the barrier where the US Navy had failed in 1995. Part of the *NR-1*'s problem had been that the sophisticated sonar had picked up so many contacts – most of them probably being rocks – that it was impossible to know where to look in such a short period of time. As we skimmed along the seabed in an area where we already knew there was probably a minefield, Max's video camera pointed in one direction only, and I recall a succession of encouraging objects coming into view, only to be disappointed when each target turned out to be nothing of interest. One particular anticlimax came when a metallic object turned out to be nothing more than an old diver's cylinder lying on the seabed – almost certainly the one lost on Kevin Gurr's 1997 expedition; I even remember making a mental note to have a word with him about littering the Kea Channel the next time I saw him. The Greek scientists, on the other hand, suddenly became very excited as a couple of ancient amphorae came into view, making absolutely sure that the positions were carefully logged before moving on. We were finding all sorts of stuff on the seabed, but nothing remotely resembling a First World War minefield, and I began to wonder if I was destined to spend the rest of the voyage – if not my life – chasing ghosts on the seabed. Were oil barrels, rocks and amphorae all that the Kea Channel had to offer?

The minutes turned into hours. I could sense that everyone was losing interest in the muddy gravel landscape that is the bottom of the Kea Channel, and bearing in mind that Vangelis had already extended the trip by 24 hours due to the time that we had lost because of the high winds, I was seriously beginning to wonder how much longer they could afford to humour my ridiculous obsession. Suddenly, something dark appeared on the monitor, just off to the right. As the pilot turned Max towards the new target, I began to sense that there was something different about the mysterious object. It had clearly been on the seabed for decades, being covered in the same sort of biomass that has virtually encased the *Britannic*; whatever it was, I had absolutely no

▲ The mine!

doubt that it was man-made. As Max manoeuvred around the object, the powerful mechanical arm was extended to grab hold of what appeared to be an electrical cable in an attempt to flip the object over to inspect the cleaner underside. Unfortunately the object was too heavy and the cable came away in the mechanical grip, but by then it hardly mattered. The shape and size of the metal fragment, combined with a machined hole in part of its base, left me in absolutely no doubt. After 13 years of planning, in a little over four hours we had located and photographed a fragment of a detonated German mine casing, almost exactly where Gustav Siess claimed to have laid it 92 years earlier. At last there could be no doubt whatsoever. We finally had unequivocal evidence confirming that the *Britannic* had steamed into a minefield, just as the Germans had claimed in 1916.

I had wanted to spend the last couple of days of the 2008 expedition on Kea, relishing my triumph and quietly enjoying the successful culmination of 13 years of searching, but right on cue the Meltemi returned with a vengeance, this time with such force that practically every yacht in the area had run for cover. The captain of the *Aegaeo* was understandably reluctant to take his ship into the crowded waters of Port St Nikolo, but by that time it hardly mattered. For me, one of the great riddles of the loss of the *Britannic* had been solved once and for all, courtesy of Bill Smith in 2003 and Vangelis Papathanassiou in 2008, and as the expedition returned to Piraeus on the evening of 22 September 2008 I felt more optimistic about the future of *Britannic* exploration than ever. We had completed a totally successful expedition in partnership with a Greek governmental organisation, and the possibilities of further collaborative work, particularly involving going inside the wreck, seemed not only like the next logical step but also highly probable.

Once again, however, the Greek gods had other ideas. As the *Aegaeo* returned to Piraeus it quickly became clear that while we had been working in our own little cocoon at sea, in the space of a week the entire world outside had changed beyond imagination. No sooner had we departed from Piraeus at the start of our cruise than Lehman Brothers Bank had filed for bankruptcy in America at the start of a process that would see the global markets plummet and bank after bank bailed out by their governments to avoid a worldwide financial meltdown. With talk of an economic downturn to rival the Great Depression of the 1930s, suddenly the entire world stood on the brink of a financial precipice, and with the already embattled Greek economy set to disappear completely down a black hole, whatever thoughts, dreams, ambitions or desires I may have had for the *Britannic*, by the autumn of 2008 it was clear that the international crisis would dominate any future plans for years to come.

For the foreseeable future, Simon Mills and the HMHS *Britannic* would not be particularly high on anyone's agenda. Having started the project only weeks before so full of optimism, I had no choice but to accept that Project Britannic was dead in the water.

A SEQUENCE OF UNFORTUNATE EVENTS...

As the autumn days grew increasingly short the news from my friends in Greece became equally despondent, as their country continued to teeter on the brink of financial collapse. Barely a month earlier I had been on top of the world after finding my mine fragment, yet now there seemed to be no prospect of any movement for the foreseeable future.

One particularly gloomy Sunday afternoon in October seemed to match my mood perfectly, but when the phone rang I decided to try and sound as upbeat as I could, even if I didn't necessarily feel it. Almost immediately I was greeted by an animated and enthusiastic voice at the other end of the line saying, 'Simon, it's Robert!'

'Robert?'

'Robert Ballard.'

Suddenly I sat bolt upright in my seat. 'Bob? Hi. Long time no hear, how are you?'

Hearing from Bob was absolutely the last thing I had been expecting. Although we had exchanged letters and emails in the 13 years since the 1995 expedition, I don't think we had actually spoken in all that time, so if Bob Ballard was calling me, then it had to be something important.

It was. Never one to waste time, Bob quickly explained that he and National Geographic were looking for a project on which they could collaborate, and one of the ideas in development was a possible return to the *Britannic*. If I was up for it, he would include it in their meeting agenda at the end of the month. There was no question as to whether I was 'up for it', and whether I would be happy to include the *Britannic* in the party! Two weeks later it was official: National Geographic had committed to a live broadcast from the *Britannic* in November 2009 using Bob's new research vessel, the EV *Nautilus*, and the ROVs *Hercules* and *Argus*. At this stage, none of the planned activities involved very much input from me, but then Bob said that they also wanted to arrange an earlier expedition with technical divers to obtain some pre-recorded high-definition footage from inside the wreck. This was something with which I was happy to help.

▶ Setting up the Woods Hole control centre aboard the *Commandant Fourcault*, more commonly referred to as 'video village'. (Leigh Bishop)

▶ One of the divers being lowered into the Kea Channel. (Leigh Bishop)

Thinking back to the success of the 2003 expedition, I immediately thought of Carl Spencer, and we agreed to meet at the International Convention Centre, where he was in the process of setting up the 2008 Eurotek Advanced Diving Conference. He had initially sounded very interested when we spoke on the phone, so after driving all the way to Birmingham, I was surprised when he suddenly told me that personal commitments, along with the fact that he was planning a follow-up expedition to locate the missing *X5* submarine in Norway, meant that he would not be available. That was easy enough to accept and I was happy to wish him well, although as I drove home I recalled feeling more than a little annoyed that he could not have given me the news on the phone and saved me a 200-mile round trip. Fortunately I had other contacts with whom I had worked previously on other underwater projects, and as it would turn out John Thornton, a technical diver from Orkney, was happy to step in.

With everything seemingly in place, as Christmas approached I began to liaise with Dana Kemp at National Geographic in Washington, DC on the development of the project, but all the while it was not difficult to see that the schedule was slipping. The global financial crisis had hit Greece particularly hard, and to further complicate matters, the violent rioting in Athens that autumn had become so serious that the US State Department had warned American nationals to avoid visiting Greece unless absolutely necessary. As a result, Maryanne Culpepper, National Geographic's executive vice-president of editorial and new business development, had to delay her fact-finding visit to Athens. The delay hadn't ever really worried me unduly, and I always remained confident that the project would go ahead, but it would not be until January 2009 that she was finally able to make the trip to Athens.

Everyone seemed confident that the permit would be granted, but with only three months left to complete the application and get the logistics sorted, the possibility remained that there might not be enough time to get everything together in time for April. The suggestion to delay the expedition until May made a great deal of sense, but on the other hand it also created issues for John, as his diving charter business in Orkney began to get busy at about the same time. The matter seemed to resolve itself when Kirk Wolfinger called to say that National Geographic had asked him to take on the filming of the pre-recorded segments – something that pleased me no end, given our previous track record – and that Carl Spencer had agreed to assume the role of dive team leader in place of John. I never found out what had come of Carl's planned *X5* expedition that year, or why he changed his mind, but I remember calling him that same night to welcome him back into the fold – if a little later than originally intended – and to tell him that the formation of the dive team would be his call entirely. Even then it would not be until early March that we would find the time to meet and discuss my proposed dive plan in detail, although I always suspected that he knew exactly what I was thinking even before we sat down in the Panavision viewing theatre to go over the details. Just as I had been in 2003, I was confident that he would find the right person for the job.

In the coming weeks the plans changed considerably, as the project expanded far beyond its original scope. Originally I had been thinking in terms of a similar operation to that of 2003, which had been so successful, but before long specialised underwater cameras from Woods Hole were being included in the budget – about which I heartily approved – while the 489 GRT *Commandant Fourcault*, an impressive Belgian diving support vessel, had become a key factor in an expedition the scope of which seemed to grow by the day. All of this came at a cost, and as the project developed in some areas, inevitably there had to be cutbacks in others. None of these changes impacted in any way on the safety aspects, nor would any of us have allowed them to do so, but the additional expenditure on the diving side of the project meant that other aspects of the production, including the actors' recreations, had to go. Never having been a particular fan of recreations, I wasn't unduly bothered by this, and if it meant being able to have a fully equipped vessel manned by a crack team of technical divers using state-of-the-art

▲ Evan Kovacs and Bill Lange checking out Bumblebee II, an upgraded version of the earlier underwater camera used in 2006. (Leigh Bishop)

cameras back on my wreck, well, what possible problem could I have had with that?

By the end of April, when everything seemed to be coming together nicely, the first complications began to arise. Just as the *Commandant Fourcault* was about to depart from Antwerp, news arrived from Athens that although the permit had been granted, permission to go inside the wreck had been refused. Governcheck Ltd, the company in whose name I held the legal title to the wreck, had given the necessary permission, but whether we could go inside the *Britannic* depended on obtaining the agreement of both Governcheck and the Greek Ministry of Culture. The cost of delaying the *Fourcault* in Antwerp was unthinkable, so even before the appeal to the Central Archaeological Council the ship was en route to Haslar to take on the British diving equipment. No one wanted to contemplate having to turn the ship around in the event that

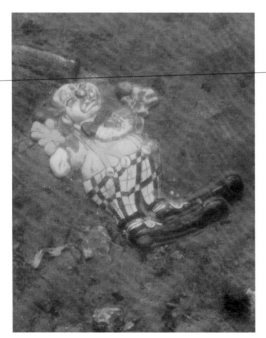 

official permission to go inside the wreck was withheld, but on Tuesday 28 April the Central Archaeological Council met in Athens to decide the expedition's fate. Memories of the problems from 2006 came flooding back, but by the time the meeting was concluded, the council had accepted that we were only planning to photograph the *Britannic* using 'wreck-friendly' equipment; in the end, permission was granted not only to film inside the wreck, but also to anchor over the site in order for Woods Hole to carry out nocturnal ROV operations.

By 17 May I was finally on my way to Athens, confident that within two weeks National Geographic would have the makings of a live broadcast of which they could be proud. Of course, it is never quite that straightforward when diving on the *Britannic*, and as ever, Aeolus, the Greek god of the winds, seemed determined to remind us that he still had some say in the matter. We had planned to commence diving operations on Wednesday 20 May, but right on cue the Meltemi decided to make its presence known. The wind blew, and we were scattered; for three days all I could do was stand in the St Trias churchyard and stare at the white horses out in the Kea Channel, while the *Commandant Fourcault* rode at anchor in Port St Nikolo.

▲ The Auguste clown that would come to haunt me in the following days.

▲ Carl Spencer logs the day's activities on 22 May 2009.

After what seemed an eternity, the gods finally seemed to take pity on me, with Saturday 23 May dawning gloriously sunny and tranquil. Having already had breakfast at the Karthea Hotel, I strolled aimlessly along the Port St Nikolo waterfront, waiting for the RIB that would shortly be taking us out to the *Commandant Fourcault*. In spite of the now customary Meltemi mayhem, I was feeling reasonably optimistic about our schedule for the next few days, the forecast being for low winds for the coming week, so I knew that not only would we be able to get everything that National Geographic needed, but we would also be able to concentrate on one or two other areas where I wanted to go, starting, it hardly need be said, with the watertight door. Everything seemed good with the world, when all of a sudden I froze dead in my tracks, startled by the vision of what appeared to be a face staring up at me from the harbour bottom. Lying on the seabed, with a casually discarded bottle above its head, lay a pre-pressed plastic Auguste clown. For a few seconds the sad look on the clown's face, contrasting with the bright red hair, green eyebrows and baggy yellow and black chequered trousers, had totally thrown me, but even after I had recovered from the initial surprise, for reasons that to this day I still do not understand I suddenly felt an overwhelming sense of apprehension as I gazed at the motionless figure lying in the water. Muttering to myself that I was just being an idiot, I quickly picked up my pace and headed for the landing stage, putting the image out of my head. I had little idea at the time just how much it would come back to haunt me in the coming days.

Although we were at last in the water, our first day was not entirely straightforward. The wind was no longer blowing, but the Kea Channel was still in the process of settling down, and Carl was the nominated dive marshal for the day, having to deal with the added complication of the down line, which had been laid the previous day, having dragged in the strong current during the night. By the time everything was sorted, most of the first day's dive team had been in the water for something like eight hours, but with Jarrod Jablonski and Casey McKinlay having already found their way to the bottom of the forward staircase, the chances of being able to enter the *Britannic*'s Turkish bath within the next couple of days were looking good. Leigh Bishop and his trusty stills camera had done more sterling work inside the focsle, so much so that I was even beginning to have visions of the main targets being imaged within a couple of days. None of us, however, had bargained on the tragic events to come.

THE END OF THE DREAM?

Sunday 24 May could not have started on a more promising note. As the RIB approached the *Commandant Fourcault*, the surface in the Kea Channel was glassy smooth. In the distance the outline of the island of Makronisos could just about be made out in the morning haze, but, crucially, there was not a breath of wind. Once aboard, I took a quick look at the day's order of

battle, noting that Richie Stevenson and Richie Kohler were slated to film the watertight door between Boiler Rooms 6 and 5, the stills photographers were given free rein to obtain as many pictures as they could take, while Evan Kovacs would handle the in-water filming for the production. The targets were a little different to the sequence of operations that we had discussed the previous day, and I recall feeling rather annoyed that the alterations had been made without keeping me in the loop, but it was only a relatively minor change in emphasis and hardly worth mentioning at that time. Instead I simply made a mental note to have a quiet chat later with Carl about keeping me better informed.

As for Carl, he was about to return to the *Britannic* for the first time in almost three years. His primary task that morning would be to retrieve the Droycon science platform that he himself had placed on the wreck in September 2003, before positioning a new experiment in its place and then moving inside the forward main staircase to the Marconi room to relocate the multiple tuner, whose retrieval there and then, if National Geographic could get permission, I was even willing to consider. My job that morning – every morning, really – was simply to provide any information if the divers had any last-minute queries, and then to stay quietly in the background

▲ Jarrod Jablonski emerges exhausted after an eight-hour in-water decompression. (Leigh Bishop)

▶ The *Commandant Fourcault* anchored in the Kea Channel on 24 May 2009. In spite of the glassy smooth surface, there was still a very strong current running below.

until everyone was in the water. The last to disappear beneath the surface that day was Carl, at 12.56pm, after which I knew that I could look forward to kicking my heels for the next six hours while we waited for everyone to return to the surface.

With the open decks of the *Fourcault* suddenly quiet, this was the time, as was normal in any diving day, when there was absolutely nothing for me to do as I paced around the deck, pondering on the two Richies' watertight-door footage that I would hopefully be analysing in a few short hours. I recall practically nothing of the first hour, except that at about 2.00pm I found myself strolling aimlessly into the saloon, where the Woods Hole technicians had installed their video village. As I moved closer to the console I remember Kirk looking up with a concerned expression on his face and saying, 'Evan has just sent up his emergency SMB!' Nobody knew exactly what was wrong, other than that there appeared to be a gas problem of some description. The change in atmosphere on the *Fourcault* was suddenly very noticeable, and I quietly moved away as the pre-prepared safety procedures kicked in.

While everything at the surface still appeared to be calm, 40 metres below it was a very different story. After Carl had retrieved the old scientific experiment and replaced it with the new one, he had entered the officers' deckhouse as planned in order to relocate the Marconi

1. The forward portside 50-cwt Stothert & Pitt cargo crane, still fixed firmly in position. (Leigh Bishop)
2. The open watertight door between boiler rooms 6 and 5. What should have been a major triumph for the expedition was sadly overshadowed by the tragic events less than an hour later. (Evan Kovacs)
3. An intact staircase covered in debris. (Leigh Bishop)
4. Part of the windlass apparatus. (Leigh Bishop)
5. Cargo hatch 1, inside the focsle at the level of the shelter deck. Behind the iron railings lies the ship's forward windlass gear. Note the almost pristine condition of the wooden floor. (Leigh Bishop)

tuner. Having filmed him disappear inside, Evan had returned to the floating decompression station, where he would begin his slow return to the surface. By the time he had ascended about 15 metres above the wreck, he looked down to see Carl, just above the port bridge cab. Something was wrong. Carl not only looked very uncomfortable in the water, but the sight of so many bubbles immediately above him suggested that for some reason he was no longer on his rebreather, and had instead switched to his open-circuit bailout cylinders. More concerning was the fact that Carl was coming up fast – too fast – and he would only be stopped from going further when Evan descended to hand him his second-stage regulator from his own bailout.

With the crisis seemingly over, they began to ascend the shot line together, at which point Evan released his yellow surface marker buoy to alert the support divers that they had a gas emergency. Dropping down the line to assist, Leigh Bishop then handed Evan his own trimix bailout, while Carl continued to breathe from Evan's cylinder. The arrangement continued to work until they reached a depth of about 50 metres, when Carl appeared to fumble as he tried to attach Leigh's cylinder; Evan quickly managed to clip it in for him, but even at this stage Carl, although breathing heavily, still seemed to be alert enough to note the gas mix and plug it into his dive computer.

As Evan and Carl continued to ascend at a more controlled rate, at a depth of about 40 metres they eventually arrived at an innocuous-looking yellow gas cylinder, attached to the floating decompression station. No one would have thought anything of it as he switched over to this cylinder, before attempting to tie his reel onto the shot line to help him stay connected in the strong current, but moments later, as he fumbled to clip on to the yellow cylinder, Carl suddenly seized the shot line and began to convulse. As Carl's regulator fell from his mouth Evan made an instinctive grab for it as he tried to replace it, while at the same time purging it. But being unable to replace it in Carl's mouth or to inflate his buoyancy vest, there was no choice other than to signal the support divers to take Carl to the surface. It would be the last time that Evan would see him alive.

Up top on the *Fourcault*, few of us had any notion of the drama unfolding barely 40 metres below. I knew there was a problem of some description, but it was only when I saw Pim de Rhoodes, the owner and captain of the *Commandant Fourcault*, running aft towards the onboard decompression chamber to commence the emergency pre-check sequence that I realised that whatever was happening down below was very serious. After what seemed like an eternity, although in reality it was probably only a couple of minutes, I heard the powerful engines of the RIB support boat speeding towards the *Fourcault*. On the one hand I knew that I needed to stay out of the way, but I also needed to know what was happening. As I moved over to the starboard side, keeping my distance from the medical team who were standing by further aft, I finally caught my first glimpse of two divers being winched out of the water; I could see no faces, but

there could be no mistaking the fact that one of the divers on the platform was giving mouth-to-mouth to the other motionless figure, who at that time I firmly believed was Evan.

The ensuing minutes were fraught with commotion intermingled with the unbelievable anxiety of not knowing what was happening. I remember hearing someone shouting for a knife to cut away the injured diver's drysuit, while Dr Petar Denoble and his two-man medical team stood by to administer CPR and oxygen. With all the activity going on, I still could not see the injured man, but from an occasional glimpse through the crowd formed by the medical team, the support divers and the television production personnel, I could just make out the motionless body lying on the deck. It was only at this stage that I began to realise that it was not Evan – the build was wrong. A few moments later a larger break appeared in the crowd, just large enough for me to get my first glimpse. For the first time I realised that it was Carl Spencer, our dive team leader and my fellow *Britannic* friend and colleague of over eight years and three *Britannic* expeditions.

As the turmoil continued about me I heard Peter Nicolaides, a Greek diver on Carl's team and also a veteran of Cousteau's 1976 expedition, calling ashore to alert the emergency services,

▲ The Droycon steel platform shortly before retrieval after 69 months on the wreck. (Leigh Bishop)

along with vague details of a conversation between Pim and Petar about using the *Fourcault's* Bell Jet Ranger helicopter to fly Carl to the Naval Hospital in Athens. It certainly made sense from a time point of view, but Petar was more concerned about the lack of space in which to carry out the necessary emergency procedures and felt that it would be better to wait until the Greek Super Puma helicopter arrived. Unable to contribute anything meaningful to the life-saving activities myself, all I could do was suggest that perhaps we should at least move the *Fourcault's* helicopter so that the upper deck would be clear when the emergency services arrived. As I watched Pim take off and head towards the Kea helipad I could only imagine what must have been going through his head, knowing that in all probability his friend was already dead and that there was nothing more he could do.

It took 40 minutes for the Greek helicopter to arrive. During that time Petar and his team did everything and more to keep even the faintest vestige of hope alive, but there comes a time when you have to accept the inevitable. Moments after the Greek winchman had been lowered onto the *Fourcault* I sensed a noticeable drop in tempo; the crowd around Carl's motionless body began to disperse, and at that horrible moment I instinctively knew that it was over. At 3.50pm, as Carl's shrouded body was winched from the ship, I remember standing just aft of the bridge, alone with my thoughts as I watched the helicopter disappear towards Athens over the nearby island of Makronisos. It would be another three hours before the last of the divers had completed their decompression and returned safely to the surface, during which time none of them had been aware of what had happened, the stunned silence that greeted them on their return to the ship being their first hint of the tragedy.

The atmosphere on board the *Commandant Fourcault* as the ship returned that evening to Port St Nikolo was something that I cannot even begin to describe, but as we dropped anchor that night across from the village of Vourkari, I knew that it was only the beginning of the ordeal still to come. Until this point I had never lost a friend in a diving accident, although I did have friends and colleagues who had been killed in filming accidents, so I had a good idea of the legal maelstrom that would follow. That night, as I looked across the harbour from my hotel balcony towards the twinkling lights of the distant *Commandant Fourcault*, I knew that no one on board would be getting very much sleep. It was no easier for me, alone on shore; every time I closed my eyes, all I could see was the face of the Auguste clown that had given me such a start only the previous day, seemingly laughing back at me. I actually recall being almost grateful when the phone in my hotel room suddenly rang at 1.45am and I was asked to go immediately to the

▶ With Kirk Wolfinger, watching Tom Wadsworth flying his ROV from the comfort of the *Fourcault's* saloon. (Leigh Bishop)

Kea port police station to assist in cataloguing Carl's dive equipment before the appointed representative of the Attica coroner arrived on the morning ferry to take it back to the mainland. As if it was not bad enough having to reassemble Carl's shredded drysuit on the port police office floor, I remember being strangely fixated on the issue of one of the boots being missing. In the overall scheme of things it was utterly irrelevant, but in spite of everything that was going on around me then, I still recall this trivial detail. It must have been close to 4.00am before I finally got back to my hotel, but the combined visions of the Auguste clown and the missing boot pretty much guaranteed that I would get no more sleep that night.

THE MAN IN THE MIDDLE

In March 1917 Henry Stewart Anderson, the senior medical officer on the *Britannic*, had written to Anne Cropper, the widow of Lieutenant John Cropper, in response to her written request for details of her husband's death on the day that the *Britannic* sank. In his carefully considered reply, Anderson had observed how most of the survivors of the sinking found that certain impressions of what happened that day stood out vividly, while much still remained blurred or indistinct to the point that sometimes it was difficult to be quite sure of any particular incident.

Over the following days I came to understand exactly what he meant, so much so that I had to make sure that I jotted down detailed notes of everything that happened in case I needed them later. The reality, though, is that I came to dread each day of my isolation on the island of Kea. I was very much on my own, at times seeming to be a part of neither the dive team nor the production company, to the point where I felt like an outsider on my own wreck. In spite of this, I still found myself caught right in the middle of the legal discourse between the Greek authorities and the filmmakers, even though it was increasingly apparent to me that I was not being told everything by either side. However, nothing could have prepared anyone for what unfolded after the main witnesses had been interviewed on the day after the accident, when I learned, almost unbelievably, that Carl himself had somehow marked the cylinder from which he was breathing when he began to convulse as 'air', when in fact it contained a Nitrox 50 gas mix. Breathing this gas mix at a depth of 40 metres would very quickly have subjected any diver to a condition known as central nervous system toxicity, whereby the partial pressure of oxygen rises to a potentially lethal level in the human body. Quite how Carl – of all people – could have incorrectly marked up a cylinder of Nitrox 50, which then found its way to a depth of 40 metres on the decompression station, is as incomprehensible to me today as it was then, and it was a mistake that was to prove fatal.

The ensuing days were curiously reminiscent of the movie *Groundhog Day*, as I awoke each morning to find myself acting as a virtual information conduit between the various parties, essential to the communication process and yet seemingly trusted by nobody. The dive team wanted to continue with the project, if only to finish it for Carl's sake, but while I was prepared to assist where I could, as the legal discussions continued between the Ephorate and the National Geographic representatives, I became increasingly convinced that this would not be practical. The incident had caused such a stir at the Ministry of Culture that all diving in the area had been suspended, including a totally separate expedition to the wreck of the *Burdigala*, which lay a little over a mile from the *Britannic*. Even if we could get around this suspension, with the DAN medical team always having been scheduled to fly home after the first week, National Geographic would only countenance the idea of continuing if a specialised diving doctor was present. For a moment I began to think that it might actually happen, but the slightest doubt about the remaining medical facilities was enough for Steve Reverand, then vice president of specials at National Geographic, who had flown in from Washington, DC a few days earlier, to officially call a halt to the expedition. It was a decision that disappointed many on the team, but one of the reasons the *Commandant Fourcault* had been selected by National Geographic in the first place was the apparent safety offered by its decompression chamber, and without an adequate number of medically trained personnel to operate it safely, the implications for continuing were clear for all to see. For myself, I felt torn down the middle. On the one hand, I was prepared to continue with the expedition if circumstances had allowed it, but on the other, I appreciated the concerns from National Geographic's point of view. Even so, as the meeting broke up, while I do remember a sense of disappointment, I also recall an overwhelming sense of relief that it was over. On balance I remain glad that Steve took the decision to call it a day as far as the manned dives were concerned, although permission was ultimately obtained from the Ephorate for the Woods Hole ROVs to return to the wreck.

In spite of the tragedy, Steve had indicated that National Geographic still wanted to pick up on the project later in the year, but as I left Kea the following afternoon I think we both knew in our hearts that it would not happen. The ensuing weeks seemed to drag out interminably, as the legal fallout from the accident resulted in a virtual shutdown of dialogue. Even though I was not subject to a non-disclosure agreement on the expedition (amazingly, no one had ever asked me to sign one), I totally understood the need to remain silent while the Attica coroner's office continued with its investigation in Athens. Although I was not involved in the National Geographic project even in a nominal production capacity, as the owner of the UK government's former legal title to the wreck I was well aware that anything I might have said in public could have serious legal repercussions for any number of people. Even so, I could not help feeling that anything I had to say would not have been nearly as contentious as some of the rubbish I had been reading online. Several weeks later I forwarded my own legal statements to Greece, all the while unable to shake the feeling that parties on both sides would treat anything I might contribute with extreme caution.

It was probably one of the toughest times of my life, if not *the* toughest, but no matter what my feelings were, I knew that I had to remain as detached from it all as possible. The last thing I wanted was to find myself coming to regret one poorly judged public comment in the event of my ever being called as a potential legal witness. The situation seemed to drag on forever, until, on 10 February 2011, almost 21 months after the accident, the South Staffordshire coroner finally held the mandatory inquest into Carl's death. It would still be some time before I was able to obtain the official record of the hearing, but Andrew Haigh, the coroner, was able to take evidence from a meticulously prepared report written in the days immediately after the incident by Leigh Bishop, Carl's closest friend, and was finally in a position to address openly the issues that had for so long remained buried.

Even today I look at the catalogue of events leading up to Carl's death with a sense of melancholy and dismay, uncertain as to how any diver with so much experience could have allowed it to happen. Much that was revealed at the inquest had been understood before we left Kea, with issues around Carl's lack of preparation, lack of dive fitness and unfamiliarity with new equipment all being acknowledged factors. As I listened to the catalogue of events that occurred on the day that Carl died, a perfect storm of factors appeared to lend an almost tragic inevitability to what happened that day. The incredible fact that Carl had not dived in the 11 months preceding his fatal dive to the *Britannic* had already become reasonably common knowledge, while his new drysuit and other unfamiliar equipment and his failure to carry out a comprehensive pre-dive buoyancy or weight check while on Kea convincingly explained why he may have appeared to be over-weighted and uncomfortable in the water.

It was at this point that diving physiology began to take over. Given the stress that would have been caused by the combination of Carl's lack of dive preparedness, physiological factors and the heavy workload, I particularly recall Kevin Gurr speculating that Carl's apparent heavy breathing, headache and fumbling actions could suggest that he was experiencing a condition known as carbon dioxide retention, whereby working hard or in stressed conditions forces a diver's breathing pattern to change, to the point where the body retains carbon dioxide. The condition is not necessarily fatal in itself, but if the person suffering from it is not properly ventilated, it can impair judgement, potentially leaving even the most experienced of divers confused. Carl's constant switching between his rebreather and his open-circuit bailout cylinder suggests that he himself may have suspected that he had a CO_2 problem, and Kevin also noted that when he was seen leaving the wreck he actually swam straight past two emergency bailout cylinders before then missing all of his deep safety stops. It was only Evan and Leigh descending to meet him and hand over their own emergency bailout cylinders that had stopped Carl in his tracks.

I don't think that even Carl would argue with the claim that up until this point it had certainly not been one of his finest dives. Nevertheless, even at this late stage everything was still retrievable, and with the assistance of the expedition's support divers there is no reason to doubt that he would have been able to complete a revised in-water decompression and return safely to the surface. It was only when Carl began to breathe from the crucial and incorrectly marked Nitrox 50 cylinder that he suddenly began to convulse, at which point the support divers had no choice but to take him to the surface. Even allowing for all of his earlier problems on the dive, ultimately it was the resulting oxygen toxicity 'hit' that would prove fatal; in spite of everything that the DAN medical team tried in order to retrieve the situation, the reality is that Carl almost certainly drowned before reaching the surface.

Ten years on, the closing words of the coroner's inquisition still ring painfully true, acknowledging that Carl was a very experienced and competent diver and expressing his regret that '... from a sequence of unfortunate events, it should lead to his death'. As I reflect on these words I still think back on that series of events, not just on the day of the accident, but also in the run-up to the expedition itself. My profession as a camera technician has from time to time placed me in potentially hazardous situations; indeed, I have known several friends and colleagues killed alongside cameras or in aerial accidents while filming. However, while it is possible for me to accept this occupational hazard, Carl was, and indeed still is, the only friend I have ever lost in a diving accident, and even though I had no involvement in what happened, I will never be able to escape the thought that he died on my wreck. This made things not only very different but also very personal, and in spite of the coroner's verdict of accidental death, I continued to live through my own personal hell with feelings of guilt about what happened. I would go on to spend several years endeavouring to get a very considerable degree of personal anger out of my system, and from time to time I still ask myself if I could have done anything that would have made a difference, but after years of analysing Carl's actions I finally came to realise that none of what happened that day was my fault, or indeed anyone else's. A more detached person would almost certainly have come to the same conclusion in a fraction of the time.

The reality, though, is that ten years on it makes little difference. The *Britannic* project could never be the same again.

PICKING UP THE PIECES

By the spring of 2010 the *Britannic* was still an open wound, especially as Carl's death remained an open case as far as the Attica coroner's office was concerned. On the other hand, the legal fallout in America had been largely resolved – at least it had for me – though the nine months following the accident had amounted to one of the most complicated and unhappy periods of my life. I no longer knew if I wanted to continue along the path on which I had first started 14 years earlier, as I suddenly began to think the unthinkable, wondering if perhaps the time had come for me to dispose of my legal title to the *Britannic*. I remember even making a number of unofficial enquiries, but I never really followed up on them with any great alacrity, which perhaps suggests that my heart was not quite in it.

Whatever my plans for the future, there was, however, one lingering issue that needed to be sorted. On 2 June 2010 I found myself in the office of Mrs Anastasia Strati, an expert on maritime law at the Ministry of Foreign Affairs in Greece, to clarify legal issues relating to the *Britannic* after a 2007 law had placed any wrecks over 50 years old in the jurisdiction of the Ministry of Culture. We were both quite amused to realise that the UK government's legal paperwork

actually put me in a unique position in Greek law. The documentation confirmed my rights to the UK government's former legal title beyond question, in effect giving me rights that the Greek government could not obstruct, but at the same time the wreck does unquestionably lie within Greek territorial waters, so I was still obliged to follow the established Greek administrative system via the Ephorate of Marine Antiquities. As we left the ministry I felt totally at ease with everything we had discussed, while the caveats outlined by Mrs Strati also seemed to be a cause of no great concern. In fact, for the most part, the Ephorate and I both wanted pretty much the same thing.

The most interesting notion to come from the meeting was that my legal paperwork, although valid, was more than a little dated. It is one thing to possess that all-important piece of paper, but the document was by then more than 30 years old, so was it any surprise that it sometimes caused confusion in the Greek corridors of power? Figuring that I would see about getting something a little more up-to-date once I regained my appetite for *Britannic* exploration, I kicked the matter into the long grass, until the spring of 2011, when an enquiry from Paul Allen, co-founder of Microsoft and owner of the MY *Octopus*, to take his private submersible to the wreck began to nudge me back into the real world. I had never dealt with the issue of private submersibles or multi-billionaires before, so the application was breaking new ground for me, and while I asked friend and fellow *Britannic* researcher Michail Michailakis to take care of the application process in Athens, I realised that the time had come for me to sort out the legal paperwork at the British end. From previous experience I expected it to be quite straightforward, but unfortunately the Department of Business, Innovation and Skills – the successor to the Department of Trade, which originally sold on the government's legal title to the wreck – thought otherwise.

It all started well enough. Although the DBIS information line had proved unable to answer any of my questions, I eventually found myself speaking with Rod Siddall, head of records research in the ministry's records management service. After examining a copy of the original document, he seemed to be persuaded in favour of my request, his only real concern being that the requested authentication letter should be signed by the correct ministry official. It all sounded simple enough, except that finding someone willing to sign it was a whole other matter. It wasn't that the DBIS had any doubts about the legitimacy of the paperwork at that time; rather, the problem was that its own records had been destroyed after the 30-year storage period had expired, so with no records against which to cross-check, no one from the ministry was willing to sign on the dotted line.

◀ Titanic Quarter. The old Harland & Wolff slipways in Belfast are now scheduled sites.

A simple request – or so I thought – was suddenly turning into a legal minefield. I could almost understand why the paperwork was causing a few issues at the Greek end – after all, what chance did the Greeks have when even the British government department that had issued the paperwork in the first place was having difficulties confirming its legality? Suddenly I found myself having to tell the DBIS in no uncertain terms that the *Britannic* project represented 15 years of work and investment, and that if they were unable to guarantee their own paperwork, there was the serious possibility that the matter would be escalated. Rod was equally taken aback by the situation, but between us we managed to avoid this eventuality by agreeing that I should take all of the original documentation to the DBIS offices in Wandsworth, where he and a legal colleague would take a closer look. It is always amazing what a friendly chat and a cup of tea can achieve, and after cross-checking an old departmental directory from the 1970s it quickly became apparent that everything was in order. The necessary letter to confirm the paperwork's authenticity was agreed, but mindful of the 30-year rule, before leaving I also made absolutely sure that a new *Britannic* file had been created, so that there was once again an official record at the ministry.

Dealing with bureaucratic organisations is never straightforward, particularly when you are trying to preserve your rights at the same time as you are trying to understand their official position. Very often they each have completely different outlooks, so I was having to juggle the interests of archaeologists, scientists, the media, the war graves lobby, the various British and Greek authorities and technical divers. At times I felt like General Custer, surrounded at Little Big Horn with arrows coming at me from all directions, yet at the same time the ludicrous

▲ Preparing the Triton 3300/3 submersible for launching.

▶ For a vessel of 24 metres in length, the *U-Boat Navigator* supports a remarkable array of underwater technology.

situation with the DBIS had quite possibly been just what I had needed to snap myself out of my state of self-pity. For the first time in almost three years I began to look at the *Britannic* with a degree of enthusiasm once again, having finally taken the first step into re-entering the world of underwater exploration.

There was still a way to go, and I remember staying very deliberately in the background throughout the spring of 2012, as the centenary of the *Titanic*'s sinking came and went. Throughout it all I went out of my way to avoid the hysteria, and I made as few public comments as possible, but as the summer turned to autumn, an old acquaintance threw one more unexpected spanner in the works. Paul Louden-Brown, the man who 16 years earlier had first alerted me to the fact that the *Britannic* was actually owned by a private individual, called from Belfast to say that the *Titanic* centenary had gone down so well that Titanic Belfast were looking to develop other exhibits, to the point that they were interested in the public display of *Britannic* artefacts. Was I interested?

On the face of it, the proposal was an extremely attractive one, but for some unknown reason I hesitated. Despite everything that had happened, though, I wasn't daft enough to discount the possibility altogether. Ten days later, I flew to Belfast to meet with John Doherty at Titanic Belfast, for whom Paul was acting as a historical consultant. Over a post-tour coffee we agreed that all things were possible, but in spite of my improved relations with the Ephorate I also knew that even though I owned the *Britannic*, there was little chance of my being able to remove any artefacts from Greek territorial waters without the agreement of the Greek Ministry of Culture. The most

1. The *Triton 3300/3* lighting the way to assist the divers entering the breach.
2. As if photographed from my own private TIE fighter, my favourite shot of the wreck taken in 2014. (U-Boat Malta)
3. The partially open roof of the chartroom, immediately aft of the wheelhouse. (U-Boat Malta)
4. The *Perseo* ROV illuminates the 16-ton focsle anchor, still lying securely in its well. (U-Boat Malta)
5. The *Triton 3300/1* submersible illuminates the anchor chain capstans on the focsle. (U-Boat Malta)
6. The 23-foot-diameter port propeller. (U-Boat Malta)

helpful way to obtain that cooperation would be to take things to the diplomatic level. As it happened, Titanic Belfast came under the aegis of the Department of Enterprise, Trade and Investment (DETI), and with John and Paul both prepared to ask the minister, Arlene Foster, to send an appropriate official letter through the established diplomatic channels, how could I possibly say no?

Nothing ever happens overnight, particularly in diplomatic circles, but the process still took longer than I had expected. First the proposal had to be approved by the Foreign & Commonwealth Office in London, meaning that it would take four months before the ministerial letter was actually on its way to Athens, after which it would be another four months before we would receive an official response. When it came, however, it was everything that we could have hoped for, expressing not only the particular interest of the Greek Minister of Tourism, Mrs Olga Kefalogianni, but also confirming that the project had already been discussed during a meeting with the UK chargé d'affaires in Athens. There was still much to cover concerning getting the project up and running, but the critical point was that the Greek government was open to discussing how it might help in its implementation.

In the meantime I was making sure that I kept things moving in the background. At about the same time as I received the Titanic Belfast proposal, I had begun to liaise with U-Group, a Russian-Maltese underwater research organisation with a subsidiary company, U-Boat Malta Ltd, based in the Mediterranean. With ambitions of their own to film a project on the *Britannic*, in early 2014 I began to consider the possibility of combining their underwater resources with the diplomatic backing for the artefact-retrieval project. If they could somehow be brought together, the result could be a hitherto unimaginable project. After the tragic events of May 2009 I remained understandably cautious, but I was also becoming increasingly aware that U-Boat Malta's *C Explorer* submersible could provide a whole new way of exploring the wreck, as it was able to operate safely at depths of up to 300 metres for anything up to eight hours.

Divers would still be necessary for any internal work, but as far as the exterior was concerned, I loved the idea of using submersibles.

THE MALTESE CONNECTION

By July 2014 I was in Valletta for the first meeting, which I hoped would result in a combined way forward for both projects. Indeed, my first encounter with Anastasia Budykho seemed to go so well that within a couple of hours we had covered most of the initial ground, but perhaps the most interesting aspect of the meeting came when Anastasia asked if I had ever considered selling my title to the wreck. Had she asked me that question a year or two earlier, I might have jumped at the opportunity, but on this occasion, while not categorically saying no, I hesitated to discuss the idea in too much detail, and I was inwardly relieved when no figure ever came up in the discussions. More than anything, this seemed to confirm in my own mind that I was once again beginning to see the *Britannic* as part of my future, and by the time I had looked over the *U-Boat Navigator*, taking a closer look at the vessel's submersible, ROV, wet bell, double-lock decompression chamber, sonar and gas mixing stations, I realised that for a vessel of 24 metres the *Navigator* packed in an awful lot of underwater technology. With Malta also being barely 500 miles from the Kea Channel, the logistical aspects alone suddenly looked so much simpler. As I returned to London everything appeared to be on track. U-Boat Malta was happy to provide me with copies of any resulting wreck images for my work, and we continued to make preparations for the planned underwater operations on the assumption that we would be starting work during the autumn, by which time the Meltemi wind would be past its summer peak – hopefully.

I have lost count of the number of times I have made the crossing from Lavrio to Kea, but on Monday 8 September 2014 I once again found myself aboard the ferry *Macedon* for the late-afternoon crossing to the island. Arriving back at Korissia for the first time in five years, after checking in to the Karthea Hotel, my customary staging post when on the island, I quickly found

the *U-Boat Navigator* and we set about planning the following day's activities. Running true to form, the Kea Channel currents seemed deceptively calm that night, but when I woke in the morning to the eerily familiar sound of the wind howling down the Karthea's corridors, I instinctively knew that any chance of an early launch was not on the cards. If nothing else, the delay allowed me to take a call from Christos Psaltis, a political officer at our embassy, who confirmed that they were getting up to speed on the project; however, they had not made enough progress at the time to justify a meeting with Andrew Staunton, then British deputy ambassador who was handling the discussions on behalf of the DETI. On the one hand it was a bit frustrating, but on the other, it was enough for me to know that we had at least established a direct line of communication.

For the next two days the Meltemi continued to blow, making it impossible to safely launch the submersible. At one stage I became so fixated on an almost threadbare Liverpool FC flag attached to a pole on the house right next to my balcony that the words 'You'll never walk alone' began to seriously annoy me, but as it turned out, the delay resulted in an unforeseen opportunity that would potentially transform my relationship with the Ephorate of Marine Antiquities.

I have always tried to maintain friendly communications with the officials who are sent out by the Ephorate to oversee any activities on the *Britannic*. It's true that its constant vigilance can sometimes be a bit frustrating, but at the same time it has also been very reassuring from an owner's point of view to know that the Ministry of Culture takes its stewardship of the wreck so seriously. Up to this point I had usually found myself speaking with the Ephorate through intermediaries or lawyers, and although on the surface the discussions generally seemed friendly enough, at times I could not shake the feeling that somewhere along the line something was being lost in translation. I always had a pretty good idea as to where the Ephorate stood on most matters, but for some time I had not been entirely convinced that it really knew where *I* was coming from. That was to change when, quite unexpectedly, I found myself speaking with Aikaterini 'Katy' Tagonidou, an official representative who, although just as friendly as the previous guardians, spoke good English. For the first time I was speaking with the Ephorate directly rather than through intermediaries, and for the first time I think we finally began to understand each other.

After three days on the island the tattered Liverpool FC flag had begun to settle down. If it hadn't, I think I was probably in the frame of mind to climb out onto the roof and tear it down, but the sight of a white-hulled Costa liner with a buff, black-topped funnel passing over the wreck that morning somehow also felt like a good omen. Sure enough, a few hours later, the

◀ Port St Nikolo.

C Explorer was finally in the water, and shortly before midday I was once again alongside the *Britannic*'s huge 23-foot-diameter propellers. It had been six years since I had last been down to the wreck, but I was pleased to see that the old girl was looking as good as ever. For the next three hours Dmitry Tomashov, the submersible pilot, expertly guided his tiny craft over and around the *Britannic*, more often than not using the current rather than the submersible's motors to drift over the wreck. By the time we were done, all of the key areas of interest had been pinpointed and discussed with Evgeny Tomashov, the project director, but more importantly from my point of view, Dmitry had used the on-board sonar to measure the depth of all four of the funnel casings; with readings of between 17 and 20 metres, he had quickly confirmed that after almost one hundred years on the seabed, the wreck's internal structure had still not collapsed in any of these locations.

The next day would also be my last on the island for that particular trip. I wasn't expecting to make a second dive myself, but Evgeny asked if I would go down again in order to advise the Russian presenter of the programme. Experience has taught me that no *Britannic* expedition is ever complete without a technical glitch of some description, and on this occasion it would happen on my second dive when, after barely ten minutes of filming the propellers, the camera monitor suddenly went black. With the cameras stowed in external housings, there was no choice but to return to the surface to fix the problem, but there was still just enough time for me to make one last visit, and for the next two hours I helped guide the submersible and film the key areas on the wreck. For the first time ever I was the one controlling the filming on my wreck, and I loved every minute of it! Not only that, but as we delved deeper into a hitherto unexplored area of the stern we located yet another engine telegraph, so deeply covered in biomass that it had been missed on previous occasions. Before the U-Boat expedition I had felt that I already knew my wreck really well, but after September 2014 I had more additional information on the exterior than I had previously thought possible. As I left the island on the Friday evening ferry, I felt thoroughly optimistic. The previous time I had left the island, back in 2009, the clouds of Carl's accident hung very heavily over everyone and everything, but five years on, it seemed as if finally I had put it behind me.

THE BREAKTHROUGH

With diplomatic communications up and running and U-Boat Malta set to continue filming the following year and also willing to consider cooperating in the conservation project, everything was as structured as I could make it, but the most productive aspect of the 2014 dive came early in the new year when, at Katy Tagonidou's suggestion, I was invited by Dr Ageliki Simosi, then Greek Director of Marine Antiquities, to give a presentation on the *Britannic* at the Ephorate's fortieth-anniversary conference on marine archaeology. Speaking to an audience of seasoned marine archaeologists is intimidating at the best of times, but even more so when the venue is the Parthenon Museum and the subject is a wreck that is by no means from the classic Greek period. However, at long last the *Britannic* seemed to finally be getting the attention that she had for so long been denied. More interestingly, several of the speakers were suggesting that the Ephorate should consider cooperating with media-sponsored projects – something we had already been doing for 15 years – and when at the end of the day Dr Simosi asked for a private meeting, I was happy to oblige. Truth be known, I had actually arranged to stay over in Athens for two or three days after the conference in the hope that this would happen, and the gamble had paid off. Over a warm spring weekend I strolled around Athens, going over in my head exactly how I would handle the discussion, making absolutely sure that I did not say the wrong thing. Perhaps inevitably, I found myself sitting in the empty Panathenaic Stadium, where over 30 years earlier, in December 1983, I had filmed for several weeks on my first-ever foreign location, when we had packed the stadium with thousands of Greek extras in a recreation of the first modern Olympics of 1896 for a Columbia Pictures' television mini-series. That particular March afternoon three decades on it was almost as if I had gone full circle, only now the stadium was practically deserted and totally silent, giving me plenty of time to revisit a few old ghosts and, at the same time, plan what I knew would be a crucial meeting.

Not daring to be late, I arrived at the Ephorate exactly on time, to be immediately ushered into Dr Simosi's office by Katy. I was not at all sure what to expect. For as long as I could remember, the Ephorate had generally dealt with *Britannic* ownership issues with a degree of caution; in fact, it was always the elephant in the room, the subject neither party really wanted to bring up for fear of complicating things. This time, though, I could sense from the atmosphere as I sat down that it was going to be different. Unlike the considered position the Ephorate had always adopted in the past, Dr Simosi's first question to me was direct and to the point: how could I help the Ephorate to develop *Britannic*'s tourism aspects? I almost had to pinch myself! This was exactly what I had been hoping to achieve for ten years, and I quickly felt confident enough to move on to the subject of the proposed Belfast conservation project.

We probably achieved more in our discussion that morning than we had in the previous 12 years, and when I mentioned the good response I had received from the Greek minister, we immediately agreed that the best thing to do would be to re-establish positive diplomatic communications, at which point we could discuss things further. Our 40-minute chat was also pivotal in sorting some form of structured access to the *Britannic*, as we agreed that no recreational divers should be allowed to go inside the wreck. However, mindful of the planned conservation project, we also discussed the possibility of allowing internal scientific or archaeological work to be carried out on the wreck, provided that the project followed the existing administrative

235

process. But that was all for the future; by the time I left the office to make a mad rush to the airport, I realised that in the space of three days I had achieved everything that I had set out to do and more. The way I felt at that moment, I could probably have flown home without help from the plane.

Picking up where Arlene Foster had left off, DETI's new minister, Jonathan Bell, was happy to confirm the department's ongoing support for the *Britannic* project, and by the first week of June diplomatic communication was again established with Athens. Once again we could plan for the resumption of activities in the spring of 2016, which coincidentally would also mark the centenary year of the *Britannic*'s sinking, but while the stars seemed to be lining up perfectly, once again events beyond my control were about to play their hand. With Greece still tottering on the precipice of financial catastrophe I had never been expecting things to move particularly quickly, but as it stumbled from one political crisis to another, the lack of a response from Greece to the DETI letter, while frustrating, reflected the situation I knew the country was facing. The ongoing financial bailout talks seemed interminable, and with two elections and one referendum taking place within a period of eight months, 30 months after my meeting with John and Paul in Belfast I was seriously beginning to wonder if we would ever be able to move forward. Then, just when we were least expecting it, a response to Minister Bell's letter suddenly arrived from the Greek Ministry of Culture, confirming that not only were they interested in the proposed *Britannic* project, but that they were also open to the possibility of a fruitful and close co-operation. Had we finally pulled off the impossible?

If only it had been that simple. That Greek ministerial letter was dated 7 September 2015, but only three days later the focus of political upheaval switched from Athens to Belfast, as the fallout from the murder of a former member of the Provisional IRA led to accusations that the IRA was in breach of the ceasefire agreement. As the DUP ministers walked out of the Stormont Assembly en masse, I instinctively knew that the game was up as far as any planned retrievals for 2016 were concerned, and I had little doubt that with the entire Northern Ireland Peace Process on the brink of collapse, the reality was that for the time being the *Britannic* project was not a priority for anyone except me.

As the political crisis deepened, so did my sense of despair. When I first obtained the legal title to the *Britannic* it had never for a moment occurred to me that an international financial crisis, along with issues relating to sectarian violence, politics and diplomacy, would cast such a huge shadow over what I thought would be a relatively straightforward marine conservation project. All I could do for the time being was try to keep things moving as much as possible, in the hope that the political situation would stabilise. With little prospect of any retrievals being made in 2015, I had already decided not to fly out for the planned U-Boat Malta operations that year, which were largely a repeat of the previous year's activities, only this time utilising

additional light sources, but I continued to hold out hope that maybe – just maybe – we might still be able to pull a rabbit out of the hat for 2016. Things did indeed begin to look more promising six weeks later, when the Stormont Executive was once again up and running, while the publication of the Fresh Start agreement and implementation plan seemed to augur well for the future, but I still knew that it would take a miracle to have everything ready in time for the summer of 2016.

As I watched with growing despair the prospect of any retrievals during the *Britannic*'s centenary year going up in smoke, I could at least console myself with the fact that U-Boat Malta had one last summer of activities planned in Greek waters. Even so, as I watched their cameras going into the water one last time, I knew with an overwhelming sense of disappointment that had it not been for the political crisis in Northern Ireland we might very well have been doing so much more. I could at least console myself with the thought that the BBC was on hand to cover the expedition for the national news, and also to produce a documentary that would be transmitted closer to the centenary.

On a more encouraging note, at the beginning of October 2016 the Municipality of Kea organised its first conference to commemorate the centenary of the sinking of both the *Burdigala*

▲ Yiannis Evangelou, Mayor of the Municipality of Kea, with myself at the '100 Years Kea Shipwrecks' conference. (Günter Bäbler)

and the *Britannic* in the Kea Channel. I relished the fact that for the first time, instead of giving a presentation to a relatively narrow focus group, I would be speaking to a varied audience comprising archaeologists, marine biologists, explorers, technical divers and historians, such disparate groups that I had worked so hard over the years to bring together. I have always understood that the *Britannic* will probably never have the significance of the classic period for the Greek archaeological community, so I wasn't prepared for the moment when I heard Dr Simosi for the first time refer to me in her keynote speech as the UK owner of the *Britannic*. With that, I began to finally realise how far we had come in the 21 years since I had first set eyes on the wreck.

Seven weeks later we had to do it all over again. This time it was Titanic Belfast organising their own commemoration of the centenary, exactly one hundred years to the day that the *Britannic* was sunk. The weather could not have been more different to that we had enjoyed during the Kea conference. While Greece had been warm and sunny, the freezing, misty conditions on the old Slipway No. 2 at Belfast, the very spot from where the *Britannic* had been launched, provided a stark contrast. Even so, it seemed oddly appropriate. As I listened to the individual speakers I reflected on how far not only the *Britannic* had come, but also the old Harland & Wolff site itself. Twelve years earlier, when I had first visited the site, I was struck by

▲ Memorial wreath laid in the Kea Channel to commemorate the centenary of the loss of SS *Burdigala* and HMHS *Britannic*, both sunk by a *U73* mine within a week of each other.

a scene of total desolation and industrial decay, but on 21 November 2016 all I could see was a rejuvenated slipway dominated by a state-of-the-art *Titanic* visitors' centre, while in the distance I could just make out the muffled sound of the whistle of the preserved passenger tender SS *Nomadic*, struggling to be heard through the heavy fog shrouding the Hamilton Dock. The White Star Line's Olympic-class liners have clearly left their mark on Belfast.

The centenary, however, is by no means the end of the story. In many ways perhaps it is just the beginning. On the surface little seems to have happened on the *Britannic* for the last two years, yet behind the scenes the foundation stones for the long-planned conservation project have been very much laid: communications with the Ephorate of Marine Antiquities seem to be stronger than ever, while the direct involvement of the National Museum of the Royal Navy leaves me with the definite belief that something positive can still come from the plans that I first set in motion over 20 years ago.

As I mull over the chain of events that have led me to this point, I can reflect on the many highs and lows of underwater exploration, the successes and failures, as well as the frustrations, the triumphs and the tragedies. Rather than dwell on the opportunities that have been lost, I prefer to view the centenary as a positive milestone, and to think of the opportunities that could still lie ahead. For me, the challenges now undoubtedly lie inside the *Britannic*. I made it intact to the first centenary (barely), and although I won't be around to see the next, having now been observing the wreck for over 20 years I have little doubt that she will make it.

APPENDIX:
THE WRECK OF THE *BRITANNIC* TODAY

KEA AND PORT ST NIKOLO

Since 21 November 1916 the *Britannic* has been located approximately three miles north-west of Korissia, on the island of Kea in the western Cyclades. Getting to the island is very easy, with several daily sailings from the port of Lavrio, the 16-kilometre crossing taking about one hour.

With an overall size of 131 square kilometres, rising at its highest point (Profitis Ilias) to 568 metres, Kea's permanent population stands at 2,470. This number can easily triple in the high season as the island is located close to the Attica mainland, so it has become a popular weekend destination for Athenians, many of whom have second homes there. This gives the island a more traditionally Greek feel.

Kea's history dates back to the late Neolithic era and early Bronze Age, so the *Britannic* is still a relative newcomer to the island's story. Even so, the recent centenary commemoration highlighting the sinking of the French troopship *Burdigala* and that of the *Britannic* has generated a far greater awareness of the marine history lying off the island's north-western coastline. The *Britannic* is now classified as a protected monument, with access carefully controlled through

The entrance to Port St Nikolo.

Aerial view of Korissia, where the *Britannic* survivors came ashore. (Leigh Bishop)

The harbour road between Korissia and Gialiskari, haunted, according to local lore, by the spectral figure of a nurse who died on the *Britannic*.

approved visits only. Permits for recreational divers are restricted to the exterior, while permission to penetrate the wreck is not normally given without the joint agreement of the Greek Ephorate of Marine Antiquities and Governcheck Ltd, the UK-based company that currently holds the UK government's formei legal title.

THE EFFECT OF THE WRECK ON THE BENTHIC ENVIRONMENT

In September 2007 Professor George Papatheodorou, working on behalf of the Laboratory of Marine Geology and Physical Oceanography and the Marine Biology Research Group of the Department of Geology and Biology at the University of Patras, carried out a marine biological mapping of coralline algae in the Cyclades Islands. As the area is considered a very important

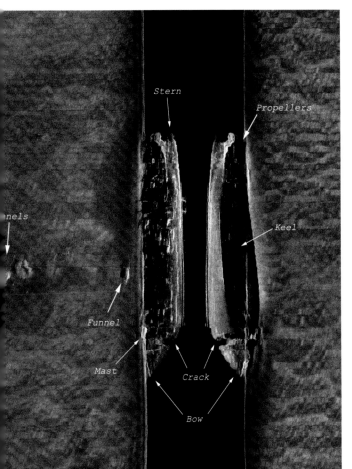

local fishing ground, the survey included a study of the coralline algae in the Kea Channel, their formation morphology, distribution, development conditions and relation to fisheries.

Coralline algae are one of the most important constructors of biogenic habitats. In the Mediterranean Sea the dominant coralline algae species form crusts, which to a side-scan sonar can appear very similar to hard rock bodies on the seafloor. Sonographs showed that the coralline algae form clusters of small circular reefs, with diameters or major axes in the range of five to ten metres, while the sub-bottom profiles revealed that the coralline algae are developed on both hard and sandy substrate, rising to a height of between 0.5 and 2.5 metres.

The 2007 sonar survey would serve as an invaluable curtain-raiser for a follow-up marine biological wreck survey by the Hellenic

◁ 2007 side-scan sonar. (Professor George Papatheodorou, University of Patras)

Centre for Marine Research in September 2008, when for the first time the intention was to focus on the fauna and flora on and around the *Britannic*, while at the same time studying their biological effects on the wreck.

Artificial substrates, including shipwrecks, serve as useful models for the study of patterns of ecological succession, as well as for studying the response of the various organisms that live on the surface of the wreck to environmental variations. As with any marine environment, exposed surfaces quickly develop a layer of attached organisms. Known as biofouling, the process typically begins with the adsorption of inorganic material on hard surfaces, followed by the settlement of bacteria and algae. Over time a complex and diverse fauna and flora community will develop, but while natural reefs display less marked variations, shipwrecks have become oases of biodiversity and productivity. The survey therefore not only helped to increase our understanding and knowledge of organisms present on the *Britannic*, it also helped determine the potential for shipwrecks or man-made structures to function as artificial reefs.

I clearly recall from my 1995 dive in the *NR-1* that the bottom of the Kea Channel consisted predominantly of flat, muddy sand, with the occasional rock coming into view to break the monotony. To the more trained eye of the Elkethe marine biologists, however, discontinuous areas of a coralline algae known as 'maerl' are also present. The largest species found to be living in this apparent desert are some burrowing anemones and the occasional Sabellidae polychaetes – a marine worm distinguished by its feathery gills – but generally speaking there is little to recommend the bottom of the Kea Channel to any passing marine biologist. That is, until you arrive at the *Britannic*.

The *Britannic* has to all intents and purposes become an artificial reef supporting a complex habitat and ecosystem. She is completely covered in settled fauna and flora, with interesting variations between the uppermost portions of the structure and the seabed. All of the main benthic organisms growing on the coralligenous substrate are filter feeders, consisting largely of sponges, bivalves, bryozoans and tunicates. On the higher parts of the superstructure, white colonies of the serpulid polychaete worm Filograna were observed, with some sponges, while the upper edges of the wreck are dominated by a large variety of sponges, mainly Agelas oroides and Aplysina sp., with some Haliclona mediterranea and Ircinia sp. around the portside railings at the level of the boat deck. A little lower down, the biofouling consists of smaller sponges and coralline hard and soft red algae (Lithothamnion, Lithophyllum and Peyssonnelia types), with some green algae and saddle oysters (Anomia ephippium).

The underside of the wreck, where the light level is lower, is dominated by the same saddle oysters and smaller biofouling organisms, while at the level of the seabed the biofouling consists only of flat red coralline algae, with a clear sediment space where the wreck meets the seabed. A low berm has formed adjacent to the hull, consisting predominantly of saddle oysters and

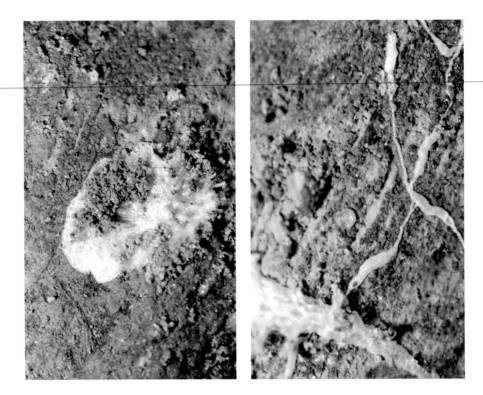

maerl, probably resulting from fall-off from the wreck, with some spatial Spongia- and Ircinia-type sponges.

All three of the areas described contain substantially different habitats. The composition of the benthic communities on what is essentially an artificial substrate, ranging in depth from 85 to 114 metres, is very different to that of the natural hard bottom communities, while the physical nature of any surface, including its roughness, its thermal capacity, its organic composition and even its colour, has been shown to affect the settlement of a variety of microscopic marine organisms. As the material used in the *Britannic* is primarily iron, the differences in the various biofouling communities is therefore thought to be due to a number of environmental gradients, such as light, depth and even the surface orientation of the individual habitats.

One thing, however, is undeniable. The *Britannic* now supports healthy colonies of lobsters and moray eels, and a substantial number of fish species, predominantly anthias. There is now more life on the wreck than there ever was when the ship was in service.

▲ Microscopic images of the inside of a *Britannic* rusticle. (Droycon Bioconcepts)

THE EFFECT OF THE BENTHIC ENVIRONMENT ON THE WRECK

Rusticles are one of the prominent natural features that have been analysed on the *Titanic*, and they are slowly but surely devouring the wreck. As the iron in the *Titanic*'s hull oxidises, tiny bacterial microbes feeding off the iron have combined to form the stalactite-like formations that will one day weaken the hull to the point where it will collapse. In 1996 the first rusticle samples were retrieved from the *Titanic* for analysis, and two years later four steel test platforms were placed on the wreck. These long-term experiments were designed to be placed in specific areas on the wreck in order to determine the effects of rusticle development on a range of steel coupons (small samples that had been subjected to varying types of damage, including heat, stress and gouging); when they were retrieved, the loss of iron from each steel coupon over a period of at least five years could then be measured.

Reasoning that if this kind of investigation was good enough for the *Titanic* then it would surely be equally valuable on the *Britannic*, the 2003 expedition took similar steps to analyse the environmental effect of the Aegean benthic colonies on the wreck. The first step was to deploy a biological activity reaction test platform, the primary test used to analyse the types and aggressiveness of bacteria found on the wreck. The platform itself was deployed inside the first portside window at the level of the B deck, where it was left for 72 hours, during which time individual test vials were exposed to the ambient nutrient flow, gases, currents and light. An early indication of the aggressive bacterial environment came in the form of strips of ordinary colour slide film that had been incorporated in each of the three test vials. During the film's immersion, the bacterial environment resulted in the removal of over 90% of the film emulsion, indicating a highly aggressive bacterial environment.

Ever since the *Britannic* sank in 1916 the iron surface of the wreck has been colonised by iron-rich bioconcretions. These formations resemble closely the hanging mineral deposits found in limestone caves, known in the geological world as stalactites, which, viewed under a microscope, actually reveal many similarities to the rusticles observed on both the *Titanic* and the *Britannic*. Closer examination of the rusticles shows them to be complex structures with a porous matrix incorporating water channels, reservoirs and ducts connecting to the exterior. A number of rusticles were sampled, and a number of microbial variations concentrated within the rusticle were identified using specially designed biological activity reaction tests. These included sulphate-reducing bacteria (SRB), iron-related bacteria (IRB), heterotrophic aerobic bacteria (HAB) and slime-forming bacteria (SLYM), each demonstrating its own unique qualities.

The samples collected on the *Britannic* indicated a highly aggressive SRB population, while the IRB are commonly found in the presence of oxygen and so are easier to detect. The HAB are able to degrade organics as their source of energy and carbon, which makes them ideal in determining the dominant types of flora, as well as any aerobic or anaerobic activity within the

⬆ The recovered steel platform, showing how the metal has corroded.

⬆ A different type of corrosion, where the bacteria have literally tunnelled through the modern steel sample.

samples, while the SLYM are able to produce profuse amounts of slime, which literally coats and binds the cells together. Together, these different bacteria make it possible for the rusticles to exist.

Perhaps the most valuable information gathered involved microscopic examination of the rusticles, which revealed that their structure was somewhat different to the rusticles previously observed on the *Titanic*. The intricate channels, reservoirs and crystalline structures remained as before, but the *Britannic*'s rusticles displayed a much more compact and tightly woven matrix due to the conditions found in the shallower, nutrient-rich and more oxygenated waters of the Aegean, enabling a much wider group of organisms to compete for nutrients, gases and habitat. The *Britannic*'s rusticles are not the dominant organisms on the wreck, unlike those on the *Titanic*, and have instead adapted to their environment, becoming more defensive in structure. Nevertheless, there is still a variety of biologically active areas where rusticles have become the domin-

ant flora, particularly inside the wreck, most likely due to variations in light, nutrients and oxygen concentration.

The next stage was to deploy a steel test platform similar to that which had been used to such great effect on the *Titanic*. These platforms incorporate metal strips from a variety of modern steel types found in maritime vessels, and are used to determine the long-term effect of rusticle and concretion activities. The platform was positioned at a depth of 95 metres on the port side of the promenade deckhouse, just aft of the fourth window of the forward main entrance, and within days rusticles were already beginning to infest the steel samples. The platform, however, needed to remain undisturbed for at least five years before any meaningful data could be derived.

To ascertain the effects of the steel on rusticle activity, three grades of steel were employed in metal strips, which had been either hammered, twisted, burned in bunker oil or tempered in order to compare them with a control sample. When the platform was eventually recovered, each of the strips would be subjected to a sequence of scientific activities that would allow the total dry weight and iron content of the rusticles to be measured, in order to determine how much of the iron had been extracted from the steel. Not surprisingly, the first stage of the analysis was to compare the steel strips left on the *Titanic* with those of the *Britannic* to determine the most notable variations, with the most noticeable difference being a far more intense growth of organic matter on the underside of the metal platform left on the *Britannic*; this matter was not only very irregular in form but also included a number of shells in the biomass.

After the biomass had been removed from each of the strips, a gravimetric determination measured how much steel had been lost to the biomass during the 69 months on the wreck. There was clear evidence that the steel had been attacked by a number of corrosive forces, with one strip in particular showing a distinctive pitting form of corrosion at one end, while on another the corrosion had actually turned into a full perforation of the steel strip itself, having burrowed through nine millimetres of steel. Bearing in mind the length of time in the water, the rate of perforation equated to a rate of 0.13 millimetres per month. Some of the strips had also lost significant amounts of steel due to lateral corrosion, and there was evidence of lateral pitting on the edges of several of the metal strips. This pitting was even more unusual in that it occurred only within the central two millimetres of the steel strip, while approximately two-thirds of the mid-section had been perforated with cavities that penetrated into the steel. In sum, the perforation of the steel, the lateral dishing of the steel's surface and the lateral line of perforations along the narrow side of the metal strips all resulted from what is known as microbiologically influenced corrosion (MIC).

Gravimetric evaluations of the amount of iron lost from the steel samples through MIC found that over the 69 months of exposure the metal strips had collectively lost 662 grams, equating to 29% of the total steel originally contained within the platform. With some reasonably hard data at our disposal, we could finally begin to compare the rates of corrosion on the *Titanic* and the *Britannic*, with an interesting comparison arising from the findings concerning the weight of biomass recovered from the metal strips and the amount of steel lost through MIC. The analysis clearly indicated that the annual corrosion rate for the unprotected steel strips was almost three times faster in the *Britannic* experiment than it had been shown to be in the data obtained from the three platforms recovered from the *Titanic*. This may be due to the larger number of life forms, of an infinitely more diverse nature, attaching themselves to the hull steels at the much shallower depths at which the *Britannic* lies, but inevitably with such a high rate of corrosion the question arises as to how much longer the *Britannic* will continue to exist as a recognisable structure. If the *Titanic* really is doomed to collapse within 20 years, then, based on the measured rate of corrosion, the outlook for the *Britannic* could be equally grim.

On the face of it, it seems like a relatively simple equation, but things are rarely that straight-forward. The saving grace for the *Britannic* was that she sank more quickly than the *Titanic*, without generating such high levels of stress. The *Titanic*, on the other hand, not only broke apart at the surface but then sank at a relatively high speed before hitting the ocean floor. This created varying differential stresses in the iron, whereas the *Britannic*'s relatively soft landing resulted in far less overall stress. While we may therefore be able to speculate on a possible time frame leading to the ultimate collapse of the *Titanic*, the nature of the deterioration in the *Britannic* suggests that while the hull plates are gradually being riddled with corrosion, the wreck may remain substantially intact for years to come, before one day being subject to a sudden collapse when the steel weakens to the point that it can no longer support the weight.

Fortunately the more recent sonar analyses inside the four funnel casings by U-Boat Malta show no evidence whatsoever of any internal structural collapse, so the prospects for the *Britannic*'s continued existence as a recognisable entity, at least for the foreseeable future, look encouraging. Thanks largely to the filming carried out between 2014 and 2016 by U-Boat Malta, Synergy Group/360 Productions and Evan Kovacs, at long last the wreck of the *Britannic* can also be properly analysed in the detail it deserves.

THE FOCSLE

As well as the stern, the *Britannic*'s focsle remains one of the most photogenic areas of the wreck. All of the capstans, manufactured by Napier Bros. of Glasgow, remain firmly in place, as do the 16-ton focsle anchor, the anchor crane and the chains. Interestingly, the focsle is also one of the few areas where any wood on the exterior of the wreck remains in reasonably good condition. The pine decking further aft has disappeared completely, but considerable elements of the teak deck planking in the working areas of the outer hull are still recognisable.

The 16-ton anchor, still secure in its well on the focsle.

▲ The anchor chains and capstans, with much of the teak decking still well preserved.

1. The *Britannic*'s corrugated bow, crumpled as it was driven deeper into the seabed.
2. All of the focsle machinery is still attached.
3. The heavily encrusted lookout's cage. The lookout's phone and bell are gone.
4. The weather cover above hold no. 1. It is almost completely intact.
5. The crumpled base of the foremast, but still attached to the focsle.

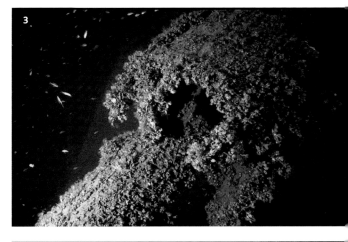

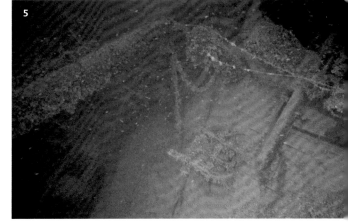

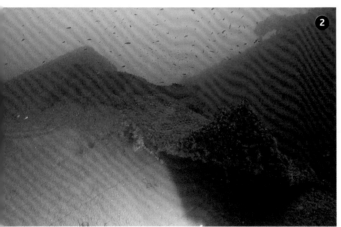

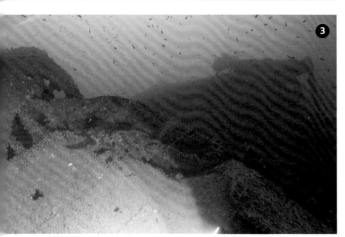

THE HULL BREACH

It is impossible to state categorically the initial scale of the damage caused by the mine's explosion. The only contemporary evidence to hand relates to the experience of the hospital ship *Braemar Castle*, which on 23 November 1916 also fell foul of one of the *U73*'s mines in the Mykoni Channel, with the resulting damage reportedly extending about 40 feet along the hull and being up to eight feet wide. The nature of the initial damage can probably be gauged by the recollections of Kapitän zur See Christoph von Egidy, who commanded the German battle cruiser SMS *Seydlitz* at the Battle of Jutland:

> Where the rivets had gone completely, the holes could be stopped with wooden pegs. Where they only leaked, which they did in great numbers – more than enough for our needs – they became a distinct menace because there was no way to plug them effectively.

As well as the force of the explosion, its location is also an important factor. Any explosion follows the line of least resistance, with the shock waves generally dissipated equally in all directions, but for the captain of any ship the worst possible scenario is an under-bottom explosion, where over half of the mine's explosive force is directed into the hull. From the available evidence it is clear that the explosion certainly occurred very low down in the *Britannic*, with the firemen's passage at the level of the tank top being so severely damaged

1. Sonar scan from 2007 emphasising the break in the hull beneath the forward well deck. (Dr George Papatheodorou, University of Patras)
2. An intriguing fold in the fractured hull plates.
3. A distinct crack is visible in the broken plates at the level of C and decks.
4. The jumbled debris filling the space between the two sections of the hull. The focsle winches are just visible to the right.
5+6. Two recognisable vents in the chaotic jumble of debris.
7. Divers swim into the break, with a section of the double bottom clearly visible to the right.
8. Aft of the break, another twisted hull plate beneath the undamaged forward superstructure.

in the initial blast that Captain Bartlett's own report referred to 'probably the whole of the fore part of the ship's bottom being destroyed'. This might also account for Captain Heard's observation that nobody had reported seeing a column of water thrown up by the explosion.

The answer to the mystery of why there is such huge damage in the area of the *Britannic*'s hull beneath the forward well deck almost certainly lies in the manner in which she sank. Some of the survivors related in news reports that during the last moments *Britannic*'s stern rose high into the air, almost to the point where it became perpendicular to the water. Straight away this conjures up visions of a *Titanic* movie-style departure from the surface, with the ship diving 'perpendicularly into the depths', as related by Rev. John Fleming in his book. However, the simple fact is that the ship could not possibly have sunk in this manner. The *Britannic*'s overall length was just short of 883 feet, which would have made it impossible for the ship to plunge perpendicularly into waters that are barely 400 feet deep.

Unlike the *Titanic*, the *Britannic*'s bow touched the seabed before the stern disappeared from view; as a result, the stresses that tore the *Titanic* apart before she sank were concentrated at an entirely different point on the *Britannic*. Once the *Britannic*'s bow had touched the seabed, practically the entire weight of the vessel would have been concentrated in the forward part of the ship, an area already severely weakened by the effects of the explosion. The stresses exerted would have been massive, and they were exerted in such a way that the steel plates would fracture and buckle in an entirely random manner. In the world of marine forensics this is known as 'chaotic fracture', and this phenomenon alone easily explains the crucial fact that a number of the hull plates are bent outwards.

In spite of this heavy damage the hull still remains largely intact, even if only by virtue of a number of deck plates at the level of the shelter deck. The two 50cwt Stothert and Pitt cargo cranes still remain comfortably in situ, which might even suggest that the overall structural integrity of the surviving deck in this area is much greater than might be expected. The fact that the *Britannic* has also been lying on her starboard side for one hundred years makes this all the more remarkable.

THE FIREMEN'S TUNNEL

For so long, the most crucial area of investigation into why the *Britannic* sank has been the watertight doors in the forward part of the ship and their failure to close. There is no doubt that had these doors closed, the *Britannic* would have survived her encounter with the *U73*'s mine, but instead they remained open, and 55 minutes later the *Britannic* was gone. It would be another 87 years before the first ghostly images of the open doors would be seen, but an analysis of what appears to have happened has always been possible by studying the loss of three other hospital ships, where the evidence seems to suggest that the causes of the *Britannic*'s demise were by no means unique.

When the hospital ship *Asturias* was torpedoed in the English Channel on 20 March 1917, the damage inflicted by a single torpedo was extensive, with the ship's stern tube being split, the hull plating in the blast area shattered, and the starboard propeller and sternpost completely blown away. Fortunately the port propeller remained functional and the captain managed to beach his ship near Salcombe Bay, but even before the *Asturias* had been refloated a survey of the damage showed that the internal stepped bulkheads had proved to be a particular weakness, along with problems caused by ventilating shafts and piping passing through the watertight bulkheads. Crucially, although the watertight doors in the aft shaft tunnel had been closed, some

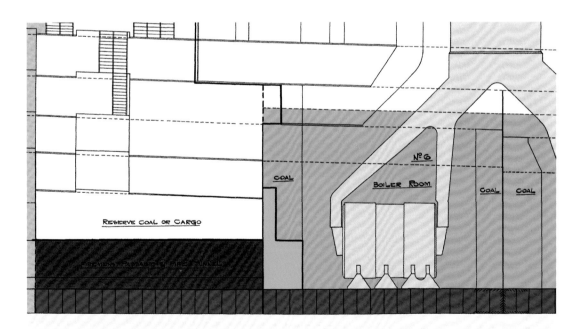

⚠ Plan of the tunnel and forward boiler rooms.

of the bulkheads and framework had been so distorted by the explosion that they had been unable to close completely.

Likewise, when the *Dover Castle* was torpedoed in the Mediterranean on 26 May 1917, the ship's second engineer, LJ Henderson, would later testify that one of the engine room's watertight doors would not move, while the report into the torpedoing of the HMAT *Warilda* on 3 August 1918 is equally revealing, the key testimony in this case being given by Lance Corporal J Schofield, who reported that the watertight door in F ward, located immediately above the location of the explosion, had been so warped by the concussion that he could not close it properly.

The 1916 report into the sinking of the *Britannic* contained the tantalising suggestion that the watertight door between Boiler Rooms 6 and 5 may have been partially closed, presenting us with the opportunity to analyse a potential weakness in the design not only of the Olympic-class liners, but of early-20th-century ships as a whole. It all looked straightforward enough on one of the *Britannic*'s general arrangement plans, and in terms of distance it is only a small matter of about 170 feet, but in the end it took 12 years of meticulous planning and cooperation with the right dive teams to safely complete this particular journey and verify the truth of that report.

▲ The broken hull at bulkhead C, leading into the tunnel.

1. The firemen's raised walkway.
2+3. The first two open watertight doors at the vestibule leading to Boiler Room 6.
4. CGI render of an Olympic-class boiler room. (Parks Stephenson)

1. One of the 159 boiler furnaces.
2. A sediment-covered Evershed & Vignoles boiler room telegraph receiver, with a stoking indicator beneath an overhead walkway.
3. One of the Stone's ash expellers in the tank top.
4. Clearer view of an intact Kilroy stoking indicator.

5. Pump machinery in the ash expeller recess.

6. Frozen in time for 100 years, an abandoned fireman's shovel in a furnace indicates just how quickly the forward boiler rooms were evacuated.

7. The claustrophobic space between boilers A and B, leading to stokehold 10.

8. The mechanism for the watertight door between Boiler Rooms 6 and 5.

9. The bevel gear to which the handle to close the watertight doors would have been attached. There is no trace of the handle itself.

MAIN HULL SECTION

All of the deckhouses, with the exception of the wooden captain's bridge and the aft mortuary, are completely in situ and show little sign of collapsing even now, although isolated patches of deterioration, particularly in the portside children's playroom, are visible. Even on the bridge there are identifiable remains of what once existed. At least three of the bridge engine telegraphs (manufactured by JW Ray Ltd of Liverpool) still hang in their original position, though they have all fallen from their mountings, while the wheelhouse telemotor (built by Brown Bros., Edinburgh) still remains firmly attached. The bridge wheel pedestal is still in position, although it too has fallen from its mounting and hangs at the angle of the deck.

Further aft, nearly all of the davits and associated deck machinery remain attached and in their original position. The only noticeable signs of corrosion in this area seem to be in parts of the solid bulkhead, which runs along the entire length of the boat deck, although the thicker steel plates of the main hull show no visible signs of deterioration. A number of openings are easily accessible to allow further investigation of the ship's interior, as even now we have only just scratched the surface.

▲ The torn remains of funnel no. 3 above the hull casing.

1. Detail of the ladder on the forward set of girder davits.
2. The starboard bulwark rotted away, with the forward superstructure rising clear of the seabed.
3. A well-preserved teak handrail, with the remains of the bridge compass binnacle covered in biomass.
4. Two bridge engine telegraphs.
5. The fallen pedestal for the ship's wheel.

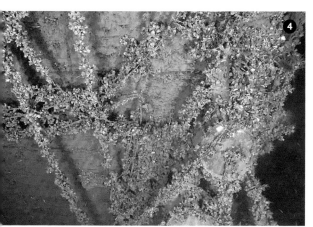

1. Netting obscures the aft wheelhouse, where a fallen fuse box can just be seen.
2. Ridges of caulking above the chartroom giving the impression of the pine decking still being in place.
3. The deck railings above the officers' deckhouses are heavily encrusted with saddle oysters and sponges.
4. Looking down on the boat, promenade and B decks.
5. The port running lamp, having seemingly been moved at some stage by a diver.

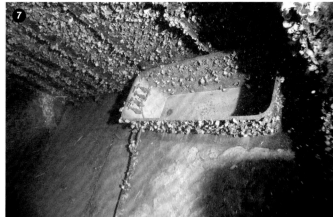

6. Forward officers' deckhouses, with the forward bulkhead rotted away. The bath actually occupies the area originally intended as the chief officer's cabin.

7. Another view of the bath. The four taps were for hot and cold running fresh and salt water.

8. Lift winding cable drum.

9. The almost completely intact weather cover above the forward main staircase.

10. An exposed Sirocco ventilator fan drum.

1. The four legs of the compass platform still firmly fixed
   to the deck above the first-class lounge.
2. Looking up at the portside Welin davits.
3. The detached mainmast lying on the seabed.
4. Funnel casing no. 1.
5. Corrosion in the thin steel of the forward weather bulkhead.
6+7. Funnel no. 1 lying on the seabed.
8. Exhaust steam pipe.
9. Inside the casing for the fourth funnel. The large fallen pipe
   served as the exhaust flue for the galleys.

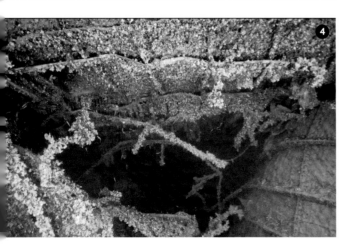

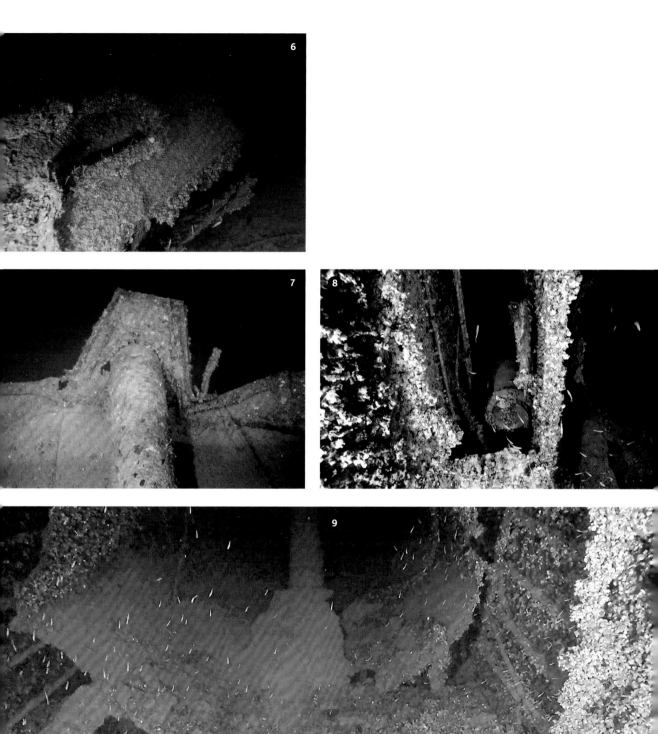

THE STERN

From the photographic standpoint the stern remains perhaps the most dramatic part of the wreck. With the entire stern frame, all three propellers and the rudder still completely intact, the resulting images of this area can only be described as awe-inspiring.

▲ The wreck's completely intact counter. (U-Boat Malta)

1. Closer detail of the aft shade deck and docking bridge.
2. The port propeller, responsible for all thirty casualties of the sinking.
3. The encrusted stern and propellers, with the 102-ton rudder still turned slightly to port.
4. The centre propeller for the turbine engine, cast from 22 tons of solid manganese bronze.
5. The less accessible starboard propeller, with the tip of one blade partly buried in the seabed.

BIBLIOGRAPHY AND SOURCES

Anderson, Roy. *White Star* (T. Stephenson & Sons, 1964)

Ballard, Robert D. & Archbold, Rick. *Lost Liners* (Madison Press, 1998)

Beaumont, John CH. *The British Mercantile Marine during the War* (Gay & Hancock, 1919)

Beaumont, John CH. *Ships and People* (Geoffrey Bles, 1926)

Bellou, N, Smith, C & Papathanassiou E. *Britannic Shipwreck Survey – Report of Field Operations*: 17th-22nd September 2008 (Hellenic Centre for Marine Research, Greece)

Chirnside, Mark. *Olympic Titanic Britannic: An Illustrated History of the Olympic Class Ships* (History Press, 2012)

Cullimore, Roy & Johnston, Lori. *Microbiological Evaluation of the Potential At-Site Corrosion of the Steels Used in the Construction of HMHS Britannic* (Droycon Bioconcepts, 27 August 2009)

Douse, Boswell. *Maritime Engineering Science: Assessment of the Stability of the Sister Ship of RMS Titanic (Britannic)* (University of Southampton, 23 September 2017)

Fleming, John A. *The Last Voyage of His Majesty's Hospital Ship Britannic* (Wordsmith Publications, 1998)

Garzke, W, Mills, S, Dulin, RO, Bemis, FG, Ridder, D, Foecke, T & Brown, DK. *The Saga of HMHS Britannic: A Preliminary Marine Forensic Analysis.* (SNAME Symposium Proceedings, September 1998)

Gibbons, RH, & Prendergast, Maurice. *The German Submarine War: 1914-1918.* (Constable & Co., 1931)

Hackett C & Bedford, JG. *The Sinking of the S.S. Titanic: Investigated by Modern Techniques* (Royal Institution of Naval Architects, 1996)

Jessop, Violet. *Titanic Survivor* (Sheridan House, 1997)

Johnston, Lori. *Final Report of September 2003 Expedition – Scientific Examination of the HMHS Britannic* (Droycon Bioconcepts, 23 December 2003)

Kohler, Richie & Hudson, Charlie. *The Mystery of the Last Olympian: Titanic's Tragic Sister Britannic* (Best Publishing Company, 2014)

Louden-Brown, Paul. *The White Star Line* (Titanic Historical Society, 2001)

Mills, Simon. *HMHS Britannic: The Last Titan* (Shipping Books Press, 1992)

Mills, Simon. *HMHS Britannic 2003 Expedition Report: Kea Channel, 1st–12th September 2003* (Governcheck Ltd, 21 June 2005)

Mills, Simon. *Hostage to Fortune: The Dramatic Story of the Last Olympian, HMHS Britannic* (Wordsmith Publications, 2002)

Mills, Simon. *Preliminary Findings of Expedition to the Wreck of HMHS Britannic, Kea Channel* (Governcheck Ltd, 2000)

Mills, Simon. *The Unseen Britannic* (History Press, 2014)

Moss, Michael & Hume, John R. *Shipbuilders to the World: 125 Years of Harland & Wolff, Belfast 1861–1986* (Blackstaff Press, 1986)

Mullins, CR. *Report for Marine Forensics Panel: Coal Analysis of Sample 137490* (Minton, Treharne & Davies Ltd, 2000)

Oldham, Wilton J. *The Ismay Line* (*Journal of Commerce*, 1961)

Plumridge, John H. *Hospital Ships and Ambulance Trains* (Seeley, Service & Co., 1975)

Stettler, JW & Thomas, BS. *Flooding and Structural Forensic Analysis of the Sinking of the RMS Titanic* (2012 International Marine Forensics Symposium, National Harbor, MD, April 2012)

Thomas, Lowell. *Raiders of the Deep* (Heinemann, 1929)

Engineering Magazine (27 February 1914)

The Shipbuilder Magazine (February 1914)

The Titanic Commutator (journal of the Titanic Historical Society)

Hospital Ship Britannic website: http://hmhsbritannic.weebly.com

Public Record Office of Northern Ireland (PRONI)

Shipwrecks of the Greek Seas: Dive into their history. Aikaterini Laskaridis Foundation, 2015.

UK National Archives

DOCUMENTARIES

The Cousteau Odyssey: Calypso's Search for the Britannic (The Cousteau Society, for KCET, 1977)

Titanic's Lost Sister (Varied Directions, for NOVA, 1996)

Doomed Sisters of the Titanic (MPH Entertainment, for the History Channel, 1999)

Inside the Britannic (Brentwood Communications, for Discovery Channel, 2002)

Titanic's Doomed Sister (Carlton International, for National Geographic, 2004)

The Curse of the Titanic Sisters (Carlton International, for Channel 5, 2004)

Britannic: Titanic's Doomed Sister (Lone Wolf Documentary Group, for the History Channel, 2007)

In the Shadow of the Titanic (BBC Newsline, 2008)

Titanic's Tragic Twin: The Britannic Disaster (360 Production, for the BBC, 2014)

INDEX

271

ACKNOWLEDGEMENTS

Sadly the available space simply doesn't allow me to list every single member of the individual dive teams who over the years have helped to make this book possible. Nor would any of this have been feasible without the collective assistance of individual broadcasters such as the BBC, Carlton International, Channel 5 Television, Discovery, the History Channel, National Geographic and Nova-WGBH. It is no exaggeration to say that without their crucial support, so much of what we know today would still be unknown.

Inevitably I have to name names, and for their direct assistance and contributions to this book I would particularly like to acknowledge the help and support of Dr Robert D Ballard, William Barney, Nikoletta Bellou (Hellenic Centre for Marine Research), Leigh Bishop, Dan Burton, Mark Chirnside, Jenny Clark, Cyril and Lionel Codus, Dr Roy Cullimore (Droycon Bioconcepts), Yiannis Evangelou and the Municipality of Kea, Alasdair Fairbairn, Kevin Gurr, Nick Hope, John Hynes, Lori Johnston, Karen Kamuda (Titanic Historical Society), Evan Kovacs (Woods Hole Oceanographic Institution), Anton Logvynenko, Paul Louden-Brown, Ken Marschall, Tom McCluskie, David McVeigh (Harland & Wolff), Margaret Meehan, Michail Michailakis, Jonathan Mitchell, Antonello Paone, Dr Vagelis Papathanassiou (Hellenic Centre for Marine Research), Dr George Papatheodorou (University of Patras), Jamie Powell, Rachael Robinson (Massachusetts Institute of Technology), Rob Royle, Eric Sauder, Vern Shrock, Captain Peter Starling (Army Medical Services Museum), Parks Stephenson, U-Boat Malta, Stephen Weir (National Museums of Northern Ireland) and Kirk Wolfinger (Lone Wolf Media).